Ultimate Flutter for Cross-Platform App Development

Build Seamless Cross-Platform Flutter UIs with Dart, Dynamic Widgets, Unified Codebases, and Expert Testing Techniques

Temidayo Adefioye

www.orangeava.com

First published: February 2024

Published by: Orange Education Pvt Ltd, AVA™

Address: 9, Daryaganj, Delhi, 110002

ISBN: 978-81-96994-70-9

www.orangeava.com

Dedicated To

My beloved Parents:

Clement Olusegun Adefioye
Esther Olubanke Adefioye

About the Author

Temidayo Adefioye is a seasoned software engineer with a passion for innovation and a proven track record of excellence in the field. As the author of *The Technical Business Equilibrium*, he shares his wealth of knowledge to guide professionals through the dynamic intersection of technology and business.

With a strong foundation in software development, Temidayo has consistently demonstrated his expertise in creating reliable and cutting-edge mobile applications. His commitment to staying at the forefront of industry trends has led him to collaborate with renowned companies such as Pluralsight, LinkedIn Learning, and Meta. Temidayo's freelance work showcases his ability to navigate complex technical landscapes and deliver solutions that meet the highest standards.

Temidayo Adefioye is not only an author but also the visionary founder of SwitchCon, a platform that embodies his dedication to fostering collaboration and innovation within the tech community. His leadership extends to the educational sphere, where he currently owns two courses on LinkedIn Learning, providing valuable insights to aspiring and seasoned professionals alike.

Beyond his achievements in software engineering, Temidayo has made significant contributions as a technical consultant for top organizations. His strategic guidance has influenced the development and success of projects, earning him a reputation as a trusted advisor in the industry.

Driven by a mission to empower software engineers, Temidayo is actively involved in mentoring and guiding professionals to achieve their career goals. His commitment to knowledge-sharing is evident in his courses, writings, and speaking engagements, where he distills complex concepts into accessible insights.

As a forward-thinking individual, Temidayo Adefioye continues to play a pivotal role in shaping the future of technology. His multifaceted approach, blending technical proficiency with a business-oriented mindset, positions him as a thought leader and influencer in the software engineering landscape.

About the Technical Reviewer

Jonathan John is a distinguished software developer with a career spanning over 7 years and a specialized focus on Flutter development for more than 4 years. With a professional portfolio that includes a two-year stint as an esteemed Flutter Trainer, Jonathan has cultivated a deep-rooted expertise that transcends various sectors such as technical education, health tech, and financial services. His proficiency in creating sophisticated Android and iOS applications underscores his skillful command of the Dart programming language and a profound understanding of user-driven design. A GATE-qualified talent with a foundational degree in Electronics from the University of Jammu, Jonathan's academic accomplishments have been further augmented by his studies in Artificial Intelligence at London South Bank University. His comprehensive education has been instrumental in integrating advanced technological methods into groundbreaking development projects.

Throughout his notable career, Jonathan's roles have highlighted his fervent embrace of core software engineering principles, driving forward development teams with a commitment to Agile and MVVM frameworks. His experience is marked by leadership positions at BoostMySites, where he diligently served as a Flutter Trainer for two years, and at ESPA Learn, where his involvement spanned research, development, and technical consultancy across diverse technical environments. Jonathan is currently at the forefront of mobile app development, pioneering the use of machine learning techniques to create applications that are not only functionally superior but also analytically intelligent. His approach to innovation encapsulates designing applications that enhance digital interactions and push the envelope in adaptive user experiences. His devotion to high-quality software craftsmanship is closely tied to his passion for mentorship, as evidenced by his significant contributions to developing the next generation of developers through structured training programs. Jonathan's broad array of experiences, enriched by his GATE qualification and multifaceted industry exposure, has made him a leading figure in the realm of tech. As Jonathan propels his career forward, he continues to influence the software development industry both as a prolific creator of robust mobile applications and as a visionary leader who navigates the complexities of an ever-evolving technological landscape. His commitment to delivering elite solutions that align with user expectations and entrepreneurial standards makes Jonathan John not just an innovator but a paragon of technological progress and an inspirational figure in the field of software engineering.

Acknowledgements

I extend my heartfelt gratitude to my dad, whose belief in my potential ignited my journey in technology. His encouragement and support during the early stages of my career laid the foundation for my pursuit of software development. Additionally, I want to express my deepest appreciation to my late mom, Esther. Her enduring belief in my abilities continues to inspire me every day, and her contribution remains an integral part of my journey.

To my friends and team, your immense support has made this journey both fulfilling and enjoyable. Thank you for standing by me, offering insights, and being an integral part of this incredible adventure.

This book is a reflection of the collective efforts, encouragement, and belief from those around me. To everyone who has been a part of this journey, thank you for being an integral and cherished part of my story.

Preface

In 2018, I found myself at a crossroads in my career. A friend approached me with an exciting opportunity to join his company as a mobile developer. It was a chance for me to transition from my role as a backend developer and delve into the world of mobile app development once again. You see, my tech journey actually began as a mobile developer back in my university days.

After a series of interviews, I landed the job, but to my surprise, I was the sole developer on the team. My very first task was to propose a cross-platform technology that could enable us to build an app for both Android and iOS platforms. At the time, React Native seemed to be the go-to framework. It was popular, well-documented, and had a thriving community. So, I made the recommendation, and we started working on projects using React Native.

However, I soon experienced a significant challenge. The design aspect of React Native proved to be a stumbling block for me. My app's UI fell short of my product designers' expectations, and their dissatisfaction became a recurring issue. Determined to find a solution, I delved back into research mode in 2020. It was during this exploration that I stumbled upon Flutter, a revolutionary cross-platform framework that promised speed, stunning aesthetics, and exceptional performance.

Eager to improve my app's design and overall user experience, I embarked on a journey to master Flutter. The progress was remarkable, and even my designers took notice. One of them, impressed by the transformation, expressed an interest in learning Flutter and asked me to share some resources. At first, I thought it was a jest, but he proved me wrong by immersing himself in learning Flutter at his own pace. He leveraged his design skills on Figma and seamlessly translated them into Flutter code. It was a testament to the power and potential of Flutter in creating beautiful and responsive user interfaces.

If you, like me, are seeking to elevate your app's experience and unlock the true potential of cross-platform development, you have made the right decision in picking up this book.

As technology continues to evolve, Flutter has emerged as a powerful framework for building beautiful and natively compiled applications from a single codebase. This book serves as your comprehensive guide to learning Flutter, from the basics to advanced UI designs, cross-platform development, and effective testing strategies.

Section 1: Getting Started with Flutter

In the initial chapters, we'll embark on a journey to learn the basics of Flutter. **Chapter 1** reveals Flutter's environment and key principles, laying the groundwork for your subsequent exploration. **Chapter 2** delves into Dart programming, the language that powers Flutter, while **Chapter 3** focuses on Flutter widgets and UI elements, laying the groundwork for creating appealing user interfaces.

Section 2: Building Modern UI Designs

Here, we dive into the art of crafting modern UIs. **Chapter 4** guides you through styling, theming, and creating interactive UI designs. **Chapter 5** explores working with images, media, and incorporating engaging effects. In **Chapter 6**, we tackle typography, slivers, and advanced UI techniques, unlocking the full potential of Flutter's expressive capabilities.

Section 3: Creating Cross-Platform UIs

As we move forward, we transition into the realm of cross-platform development. **Chapter 7** teaches you how to build adaptive UIs for various platforms, including an exploration of different Flutter architectures. **Chapter 8** addresses navigation and routing, while **Chapter 9** demonstrates how to leverage device features and APIs for a seamless user experience.

Section 4: Testing and Debugging Flutter UIs

In the final stretch, we turn our attention to testing and debugging Flutter UIs. **Chapter 10** covers unit testing for UI components, ensuring the robustness and reliability of your applications. The book concludes in **Chapter 11** with a reflection on what you've learned and guidance on the next steps in your Flutter journey.

Get a Free eBook

We hope you are enjoying your recently purchased book! Your feedback is incredibly valuable to us, and to all other readers looking for great books.

If you found this book helpful or enjoyable, we would truly appreciate it, if you could take a moment to leave a short review with a 5 star rating on Amazon. It helps us grow, and lets other readers discover our books.

As a thank you, we would love to send you a free digital copy of this book, and a **30%** discount code on your next cart value on our official websites:

www.orangeava.com

www.orangeava.in (For Indian Subcontinent)

☑ **Here's how:**

Leave a review for the book on Amazon.

Take a screenshot of your review, and send an email to **info@orangeava.com** (it can be just the confirmation screen).

Once, we receive your screenshot, we will send you the digital file, within 24 hours.

Thank you so much for your support – it means a lot to us!

Downloading the code bundles and colored images

Please follow the links or scan the QR codes to download the **_Code Bundles and Images_** of the book:

https://github.com/ava-orange-education/Ultimate-Flutter-for-Cross-Platform-App-Development

The code bundles and images of the book are also hosted on ***https://rebrand.ly/295b9e***

In case there's an update to the code, it will be updated on the existing GitHub repository.

Errata

We take immense pride in our work at **Orange Education Pvt Ltd,** and follow best practices to ensure the accuracy of our content to provide an indulging reading experience to our subscribers. Our readers are our mirrors, and we use their inputs to reflect and improve upon human errors, if any, that may have occurred during the publishing processes involved. To let us maintain the quality and help us reach out to any readers who might be having difficulties due to any unforeseen errors, please write to us at :

errata@orangeava.com

Your support, suggestions, and feedback are highly appreciated.

DID YOU KNOW

Did you know that Orange Education Pvt Ltd offers eBook versions of every book published, with PDF and ePub files available? You can upgrade to the eBook version at **www.orangeava.com** and as a print book customer, you are entitled to a discount on the eBook copy. Get in touch with us at: **info@orangeava.com** for more details.

At **www.orangeava.com**, you can also read a collection of free technical articles, sign up for a range of free newsletters, and receive exclusive discounts and offers on AVA™ Books and eBooks.

PIRACY

If you come across any illegal copies of our works in any form on the internet, we would be grateful if you would provide us with the location address or website name. Please contact us at **info@orangeava.com** with a link to the material.

ARE YOU INTERESTED IN AUTHORING WITH US?

If there is a topic that you have expertise in, and you are interested in either writing or contributing to a book, please write to us at **business@orangeava.com**. We are on a journey to help developers and tech professionals to gain insights on the present technological advancements and innovations happening across the globe and build a community that believes Knowledge is best acquired by sharing and learning with others. Please reach out to us to learn what our audience demands and how you can be part of this educational reform. We also welcome ideas from tech experts and help them build learning and development content for their domains.

REVIEWS

Please leave a review. Once you have read and used this book, why not leave a review on the site that you purchased it from? Potential readers can then see and use your unbiased opinion to make purchase decisions. We at Orange Education would love to know what you think about our products, and our authors can learn from your feedback. Thank you!

For more information about Orange Education, please visit **www.orangeava.com**.

Table of Contents

Section 1

Getting Started with Flutter

CHAPTER 1

Introduction to Flutter and its Environment

This chapter introduces Flutter, a powerful framework for developing cross-platform applications. We will delve deep into what Flutter is all about and its remarkable benefits, and we will explore the fundamental concepts of Flutter's widget-based UI development. So, without any further ado, let's embark on this exciting journey into the world of Flutter.

Structure

In this chapter, we will discuss the following topics:

- Overview of Flutter and its advantages
- Setting up the development environment
- Exploring Flutter project structure
- Introducing Flutter widgets

Overview of Flutter and its advantages

Flutter, the revolutionary cross-platform framework, has come a long way since its inception. Born out of the innovative minds at Google, Flutter was first unveiled to the world at the Dart Developer Summit in October 2015. It emerged as a result of the company's desire to address the challenges faced by developers in building high-quality and performant mobile apps for multiple platforms.

Led by a team of passionate engineers, Flutter was designed to empower developers with a robust and efficient toolkit. It aimed to enable the creation of stunning user interfaces, seamlessly blending beautiful designs with a smooth user experience. As Flutter started to gain traction, it quickly became a hot topic within the tech community, captivating developers and entrepreneurs alike (refer to *Figure 1.1*).

Figure 1.1*: Dart Developer Summit in October 2015 (source: news.dartlang.org)*

Flutter was officially released as an open-source project by Google in May 2017, signaling its commitment to fostering a vibrant developer community. This move was pivotal in attracting talented individuals worldwide to contribute to its growth and development. With each new release, Flutter continued to evolve, introducing enhancements, performance optimizations, and expanded platform support.

What truly sets Flutter apart is its unique approach to UI development. Flutter adopts a reactive framework, where the entire user interface is built using a composition of widgets, creating a highly customizable and flexible UI tree. This innovative architecture allows for rapid rendering and updates, resulting in smooth animations and fluid interactions. Flutter's ability to provide a native-like experience across platforms has positioned it as a game-changer in the world of mobile app development.

Today, Flutter has established itself as one of the leading frameworks for building multi-platform apps. Its vibrant and passionate community, combined with its extensive ecosystem of libraries and packages, has propelled Flutter to new heights. From startups to tech giants, businesses of all sizes are harnessing the power of Flutter to create stunning, performant, and engaging mobile experiences.

Flutter Under the Hood

Have you ever marveled at how some apps look and feel the same across different devices like iPhones and Android smartphones? Flutter, the cross-platform UI toolkit, is the magic behind this seamless experience. In this section, we'll explore Flutter's architectural overview and shed light on its inner workings.

Architectural Layers

Imagine you're an architect designing a house. You start with a blueprint that outlines the overall structure and layout. Similarly, Flutter follows a layered architectural model that serves as the foundation for building stunning cross-platform apps (see *Figure* 1.2).

At its core, Flutter utilizes a layered architecture that promotes extensibility and flexibility. Each layer operates independently, with no privileged access to the layer below, allowing for optional and replaceable components. This modular approach empowers developers to customize and tailor their Flutter applications to suit their specific needs. *Figure* 1.2 depicts the architectural layers in Flutter:

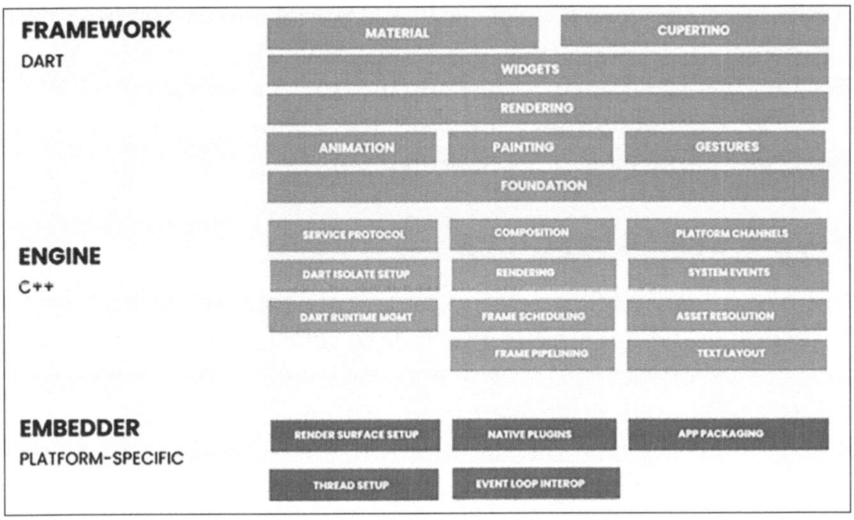

***Figure* 1.2**: *Architectural layers*

At the base of Flutter's architecture lies the operating system, where Flutter apps are packaged just like any other native application. Flutter provides a platform-specific embedder that acts as the bridge between your app and the operating system. It handles rendering surfaces, accessibility features, and user input. Think of it as the interface that connects your app to the underlying device functionalities.

Now, let's zoom in on the core of Flutter – the Flutter engine. This powerful engine is responsible for turning your code into beautiful visual experiences. It works closely with the platform-specific embedder, communicating with the operating system and handling essential tasks like graphics, text layout, file and network operations, etc. Just like a skilled artist, the Flutter engine paints every frame of your app, creating a fluid and responsive user interface.

To interact with the Flutter engine, developers like you use the Dart programming language and the Flutter framework. Dart provides a familiar and expressive syntax, making it easy to write code that defines your app's behavior. The Flutter framework, written in Dart, acts as your creative toolkit. It offers a range of tools, widgets, and libraries that empower you to craft delightful user interfaces.

Think of Flutter's framework as a set of building blocks. You can assemble these blocks, called widgets, to create the UI of your app. It's like arranging Lego bricks to construct a unique structure. The widgets layer not only helps you design visually appealing interfaces but also enables a reactive programming model. This means your app can react to user interactions, respond to data changes, and provide a dynamic user experience.

Flutter provides ready-to-use libraries like Material and Cupertino that embody the design principles of popular operating systems. These libraries offer a wealth of pre-built widgets that ensure your app looks and feels native on Android and iOS devices. By leveraging these libraries, you can easily adopt the distinctive styles and user interface patterns of each platform.

Reactive User Interfaces

Imagine you're using your Twitter app, and as you interact with a tweet, the app instantly responds and updates its interface to reflect your actions. For example, when you tap the retweet button, the button visually acknowledges your tap by changing its appearance or triggering an action. This seamless and real-time interaction is made possible through the concept of reactive user interfaces in Flutter. *Figure* 1.3 depicts a typical Twitter web interface.

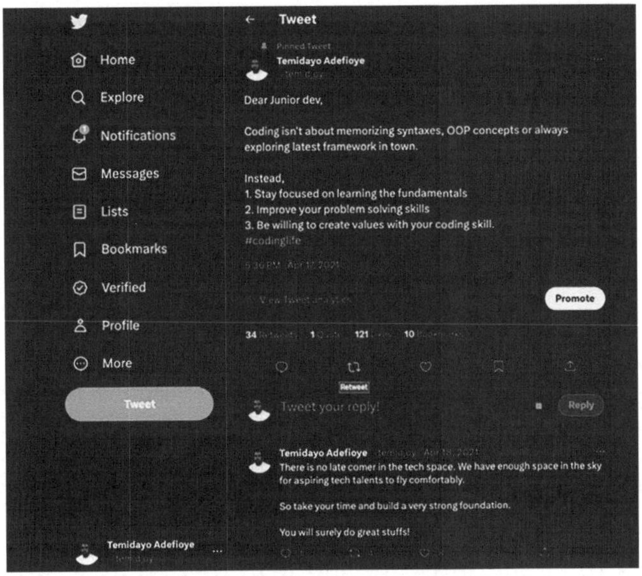

Figure 1.3: *twitter web app*

In Flutter, a reactive user interface follows a simple yet powerful principle: changes in the app's state trigger updates in the user interface. This means that when the underlying data or conditions in the app change, the UI automatically reflects those changes. This reactive nature eliminates the need for manual UI updates, making development faster and more efficient.

To achieve this reactivity, Flutter utilizes a declarative programming model. Instead of imperatively instructing the app on how to update the UI, you define what the UI should look like based on the current state of the app. Flutter's framework takes care of comparing the previous and current states, and efficiently updates only the necessary parts of the UI.

This reactive approach brings several benefits to Flutter development. It allows for a highly responsive user experience, as the UI updates in real-time, providing instant feedback to user actions. It also simplifies development by decoupling the UI logic from the underlying data and business logic, making it easier to maintain and modify the app as it evolves.

Introducing Widgets

In Flutter, widgets are the fundamental building blocks of the user interface. Think of them as the Lego bricks that you use to construct your app's UI. Widgets are the visual and interactive elements that users see and interact with on their devices, such as buttons, text fields, images, and so on. See *Figure 1.4*:

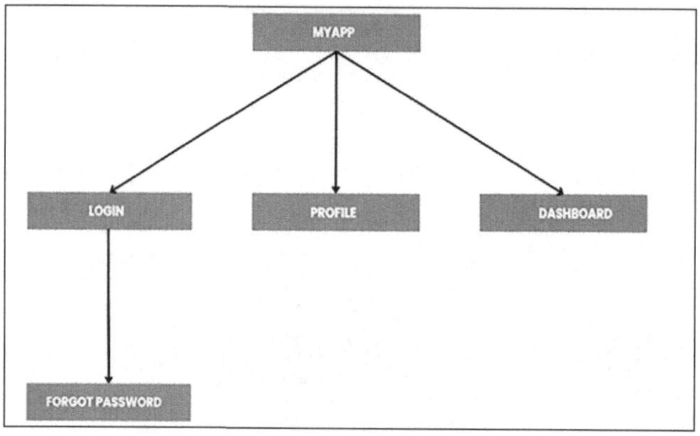

Figure 1.4: *Widget Tree*

What makes widgets powerful in Flutter is their composability. Just like how you can combine different Lego bricks to create complex structures, you can combine widgets to create intricate and feature-rich user interfaces. Widgets can be nested and arranged in a tree-like structure, forming a hierarchy where each widget serves a specific purpose and contributes to the overall UI.

Flutter follows a reactive programming model, which means that widgets are not only responsible for defining the visual elements of the UI but also for managing their own state and responding to changes. This allows widgets to be dynamic and responsive to user interactions.

Widgets in Flutter come in two flavors: stateless widgets and stateful widgets. Stateless widgets represent components that don't have any internal state and their appearance is solely determined by the properties they receive. They are useful for building UI elements that don't change based on user interactions, such as static text or icons.

On the other hand, stateful widgets are widgets that can maintain and update their internal state. They are used for UI elements that need to change dynamically based on user actions or changing data. Stateful widgets can handle events, update their state, and trigger UI updates accordingly.

One of the key advantages of using widgets in Flutter is the hot reload feature. With hot reload, you can make changes to your widget tree and see the updates instantly without restarting the app. This rapid iteration cycle greatly enhances the developer experience and allows for quick experimentation and fine-tuning of the UI.

Don't worry; there is a section in this book dedicated to widgets. We will go over everything about widgets.

The Rendering Process

The rendering process is what transforms your widget tree into the actual pixels that are displayed on the screen. It's like the magic behind the scenes that brings your app's UI to life!

When you build your app's UI using widgets, you're essentially creating a tree-like structure where each widget represents a visual element. This widget tree is a virtual representation of what your app should look like, but it's not directly visible to the user.

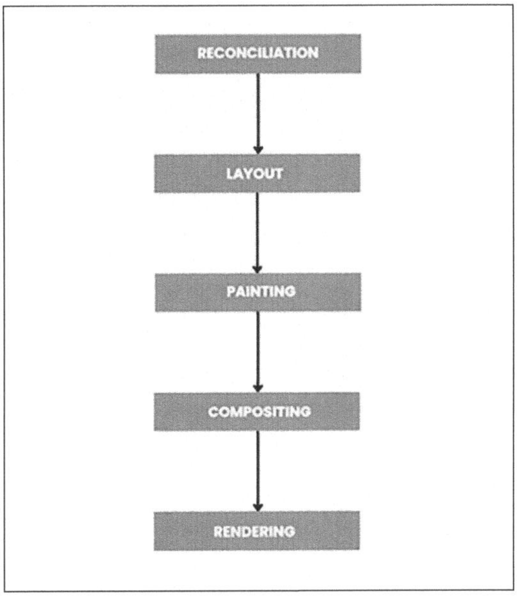

Figure 1.5: *The rendering process*

During the rendering process, Flutter takes this widget tree and performs a series of steps to convert it into pixels that can be displayed on the screen. Let's break down these steps as follows:

1. **Widget Reconciliation:** Flutter compares the new widget tree with the previous widget tree to identify any differences or updates. It figures out what needs to be added, removed, or updated in the UI based on these differences.

2. **Layout:** Once the differences are identified, Flutter performs a layout process to determine the size and position of each widget in the UI. It calculates how much space each widget should occupy and where it should be placed within the screen.

3. **Painting:** After the layout is determined, Flutter goes through a painting process where it assigns colors, gradients, and other visual attributes to each widget. It paints the widgets onto a canvas, creating the visual representation of your app's UI.
4. **Compositing:** In this step, Flutter takes the painted widgets and combines them together to create the final image that will be displayed on the screen. It considers factors like transparency, overlapping, and layering to ensure the correct rendering order.
5. **Rendering:** Finally, Flutter takes the composited image and converts it into platform-specific graphics instructions that can be understood by the underlying operating system. These instructions are sent to the GPU (Graphics Processing Unit) for rendering on the screen.

Throughout this rendering process, Flutter takes advantage of its high-performance rendering engine and advanced graphics libraries to ensure smooth animations, efficient rendering, and a visually appealing user interface.

The Platform Embedders

When you build a Flutter app, it's not just about the code you write in Dart and the Flutter framework. There's also a crucial piece called the platform embedders that enable your Flutter app to run on different operating systems like Android, iOS, and so on.

Think of the platform embedders as the bridge between your Flutter app and the underlying operating system. They handle the communication, integration, and execution of your Flutter code on the target platform.

Each platform, such as Android and iOS, has its own specific platform embedder. These embedders are written in languages like Java and C++ for Android, Objective-C/Objective-C++ for iOS and macOS, and C++ for Windows and Linux. They provide the necessary entry point for your Flutter app and handle important tasks like rendering surfaces, accessibility, and input.

The platform embedder is responsible for coordinating with the underlying operating system and providing the necessary services and resources that your Flutter app needs to run smoothly. It acts as a mediator, translating Flutter's cross-platform code into platform-specific instructions that the operating system understands.

For example, when you interact with a button in your Flutter app, the platform embedder handles the touch events, communicates with the operating system to update the UI, and ensures that the button behaves as expected on the specific platform. It ensures that your Flutter app feels native and integrates seamlessly with the underlying system.

Flutter provides a set of built-in platform embedders for common target platforms like Android, iOS, macOS, and Windows. These embedders are well-maintained and optimized for performance. However, it's worth noting that Flutter is designed to be extensible and customizable, so you can also create your own platform embedders if needed.

The platform embedders play a vital role in making Flutter a truly multi-platform framework. They enable you to write your app's UI and logic once in Flutter and deploy it to multiple platforms, ensuring a consistent user experience across different devices and operating systems.

Flutter and Third-Party Code

Flutter is a powerful framework that allows you to build stunning user interfaces and create engaging app experiences. However, there may be times when you need to integrate your Flutter app with existing codebases, libraries, or services. Flutter provides various techniques and approaches to seamlessly integrate with other codes and leverage their functionalities.

One common scenario is when you want to use a platform-specific feature or access a native API that is not directly available in Flutter. For example, you might need to use a camera, access device sensors, or interact with a specific hardware component. Flutter provides a mechanism called platform channels that allows you to establish a communication bridge between your Flutter app and the native code on the platform.

Platform channels enable you to send messages and data back and forth between your Flutter app and the platform-specific code. This allows you to leverage the capabilities of the underlying operating system and access features that are not directly exposed through Flutter's cross-platform APIs. With platform channels, you can seamlessly integrate platform-specific functionality into your Flutter app while still maintaining a unified codebase.

Another approach to integrating Flutter with other code is through the use of plugins. Flutter plugins are packages that encapsulate platform-specific code and expose it as Flutter-compatible APIs. These plugins provide a higher-level abstraction and simplify the process of integrating with platform-specific functionalities. There is a wide range of plugins available in the Flutter ecosystem, covering various domains such as camera, geolocation, database access, and so on.

Additionally, Flutter also supports the integration of web content through the use of web views. Web views allow you to embed web-based content within your Flutter app, enabling you to display web pages, web applications, or web-based components seamlessly. This integration opens up possibilities for incorporating web-based features or migrating existing web applications to Flutter while preserving their functionality.

Flutter for the Web

In addition to building apps for mobile platforms like iOS and Android, Flutter also provides support for creating web applications. This means that you can use Flutter's powerful framework and development workflow to build interactive and responsive web-based experiences.

Flutter's web support allows you to leverage your existing knowledge and skills in Flutter to create web applications that look and feel native, just like their mobile counterparts. With Flutter, you can write code once and deploy it across multiple platforms, including the web. This not only saves time and effort but also ensures a consistent user experience across different devices and screen sizes.

When it comes to building web applications with Flutter, there are a few key aspects to consider. First, Flutter uses a technology called **CanvasKit** to render the user interface elements on the web. **CanvasKit** is a web-based implementation of Flutter's rendering engine, which is responsible for converting your Flutter code into pixels on the screen. It provides a high-performance and efficient way of rendering UI components, resulting in smooth and responsive web applications. See *Figure 1.6*:

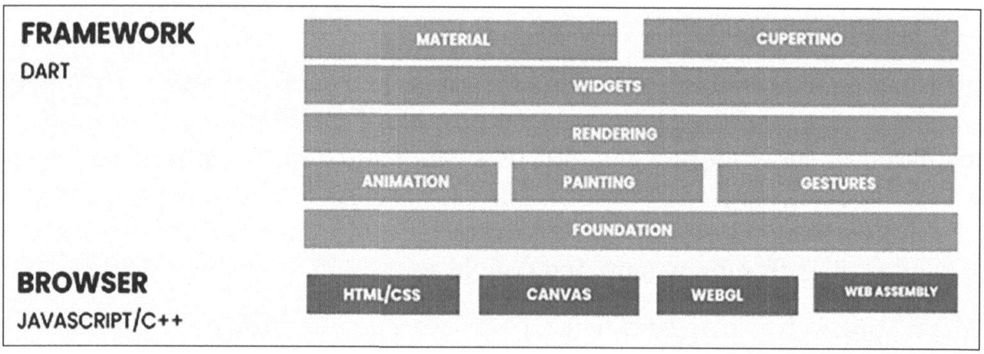

***Figure 1.6**: Flutter web support*

Flutter's web support also includes a set of widgets specifically designed for the web platform. These widgets allow you to create web-specific layouts, handle user interactions, and integrate with web services and APIs. Whether it's handling mouse events, managing browser history, or making HTTP requests, Flutter's web widgets provide the necessary tools and abstractions to build robust web applications.

When you build a Flutter web application, you can take advantage of Flutter's hot reload feature, which allows you to see your changes instantly without restarting the entire application. This rapid development workflow makes it easy to iterate and experiment with your web app's design and functionality, resulting in faster development cycles and quicker feedback loops.

It's important to note that while Flutter's web support is highly capable and allows you to build complex web applications, there might be certain platform-specific limitations or considerations to keep in mind. Since web technologies and browser capabilities can vary, it's essential to test and optimize your Flutter web app across different browsers and devices to ensure a consistent experience for your users.

With Flutter's web support, you have the flexibility to extend your app's reach to the web platform without compromising on the performance or user experience. Whether you're building a mobile app, a web app, or both, Flutter empowers you to create stunning and feature-rich applications that can delight users across multiple platforms.

So, if you're interested in exploring the world of web development with Flutter, learning Flutter is one of the best decisions you are going to make.

Reasons to Choose Flutter

When I proposed Flutter to my company as an alternative to React Native, my boss wanted to understand why we should make the switch. It wasn't about my personal preferences; it was about finding a technology that could help us deliver apps to clients quickly and efficiently. We were working with tight timelines, and I needed a solution that would enable me to achieve a certain UI without writing excessive amounts of JavaScript code. While React Native might be the right choice for other companies, it didn't align with our specific circumstances. So Let's explore some of the exciting advantages I shared with him.

Fast Development and Time-to-Market

One of the key advantages of Flutter is its fast development workflow. Flutter's hot reload feature allows developers to see instant updates to their code changes, making the development process highly efficient. This means you can iterate and refine your app quickly, reducing the time it takes to bring your product to market. With Flutter, you can meet tight deadlines and deliver high-quality apps in a shorter timeframe.

Single Codebase, Multiple Platforms

Flutter follows a *write once, run anywhere* approach, allowing you to write code once and deploy it across multiple platforms. Whether you're targeting iOS, Android, web, or even desktop platforms, Flutter enables you to maintain a single codebase. This significantly reduces development efforts and ensures consistent app behavior and UI across different devices and operating systems.

Beautiful and Customizable UI

Here is my favorite part. Flutter empowers developers to create visually stunning and highly customizable user interfaces. Flutter's rich set of pre-designed widgets, combined with its flexible UI framework, enables you to build pixel-perfect designs and create a unique app experience. With Flutter, you have full control over every aspect of your app's UI, from layout and animations to typography and themes.

High Performance

Flutter's performance is exceptional, thanks to its use of Dart, a compiled language that allows Flutter apps to run directly on the device's hardware. Flutter apps are compiled into native machine code, resulting in high-performance experiences that feel smooth and responsive. Whether it's rendering complex UIs or handling intensive animations, Flutter excels in delivering top-notch performance.

Strong Community and Ecosystem

Flutter has a vibrant and supportive community that actively contributes to its growth and development. This means you'll find a wealth of resources, tutorials, and packages to help you along your Flutter journey. The Flutter ecosystem offers numerous packages and plugins for integrating with popular services, accessing device features, and adding additional functionalities to your app.

Setting up the Development Environment

To start building amazing Flutter applications, you first need to set up your development environment. This involves preparing your system, installing the necessary tools, and configuring everything to ensure a smooth development experience.

In this section, I will guide you through the process of setting up your development environment for Flutter. We will cover the system requirements, downloading and installing the Flutter SDK, configuring your IDE, and verifying the installation.

By the end of this section, you will have a fully functional Flutter development environment ready to bring your app ideas to life. So let's dive in and get started!

Systems Requirements

Before you start developing Flutter applications, it's important to ensure that your system meets the necessary requirements. Here are the following key system requirements for setting up a Flutter development environment:

Operating System

Flutter is supported on multiple operating systems, including:

- **Windows:** Flutter works on Windows 7 or later versions. It is compatible with 64-bit systems.
- **macOS:** Flutter is compatible with macOS (Mac OS X) 10.14 (Mojave) or later versions.
- **Linux:** Flutter supports various Linux distributions, including Ubuntu, Debian, Fedora, and others.

Ensure that your operating system is up to date and meets the minimum requirements for Flutter development.

Hardware Specifications

Flutter development does not require high-end hardware. However, it's recommended to have a system with decent specifications to ensure smooth performance. Here are the following minimum hardware requirements:

- **Processor:** Any modern processor with at least two cores.
- **RAM:** At least 8 GB of RAM, although 16 GB or more is recommended for better performance.
- **Storage:** Sufficient free disk space for installing the Flutter SDK, IDE, and other development tools.

Make sure your system meets these hardware requirements to support a comfortable Flutter development experience.

Keep in mind that these requirements may change over time, so it's always a good idea to check the official Flutter documentation for the latest system requirements before starting the installation process.

Installing Flutter SDK

The Flutter SDK is the core component you need to start developing Flutter applications. It includes all the necessary tools, libraries, and frameworks to build cross-platform apps with ease. To install the Flutter SDK, follow these steps:

1. **Download the Flutter SDK:** Visit the official Flutter website (flutter.dev) and navigate to the Downloads section via the Install Flutter button. Choose the version suitable for your operating system (Windows, macOS, or Linux) and download the Flutter SDK package (as shown in *Figure 1.7*):

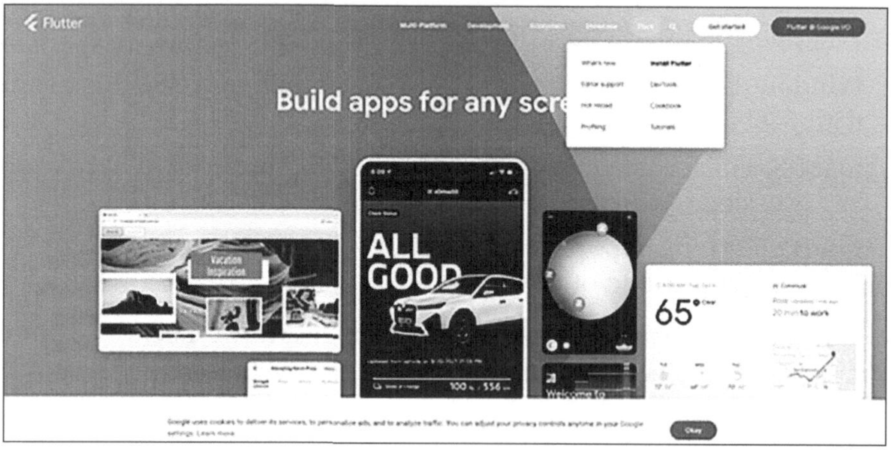

***Figure 1.7**: Flutter website*

2. **Extract the Flutter SDK:** Once the download is complete, extract the contents of the Flutter SDK package to a preferred location on your computer. This will create a folder containing the Flutter files.

3. **Configure the Flutter Environment:** Next, you need to set up the Flutter environment variables. On macOS and Linux, open your terminal and run the following command:

```
export PATH="$PATH:<path-to-flutter-sdk>/bin"
```

Click on start Windows, and search for "**`Environment Variables`**." Click on "**`Edit the system environment variables`**" and then click "**`Environment Variables`**." In the "**`System Variables`**" section, select the "**`Path`**" variable and click "**`Edit`**." Add a new entry with the path to the Flutter SDK's "**`bin`**" folder.

4. **Verify the Flutter Installation:** To ensure that Flutter is correctly installed, open a new terminal or command prompt and run the following command: See *Figure 1.8*:

```
flutter doctor
```

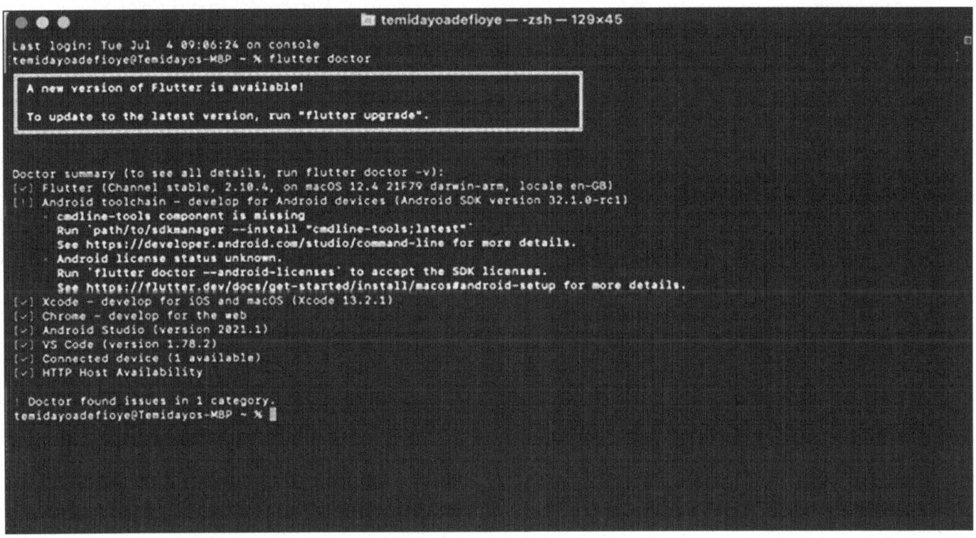

***Figure 1.8**: Flutter doctor*

This command will check your system for any necessary dependencies and display a report. Make sure all the checks pass successfully, and any issues are resolved before proceeding.

Congratulations! You have successfully installed the Flutter SDK on your system. Now you're ready to create stunning cross-platform applications using Flutter.

Configuring Visual Studio Code

VS Code, short for Visual Studio Code, is a popular lightweight source code editor developed by Microsoft. It is widely used by developers across various programming languages and platforms due to its flexibility, extensive feature set, and strong community support. VS Code provides a highly customizable and efficient development environment for writing, debugging, and managing code.

Now, to configure VS Code for Flutter, follow these steps:

1. **Install Visual Studio Code:** If you haven't already, download and install Visual Studio Code from the official website (code.visualstudio.com). Choose the version suitable for your operating system and follow the installation instructions.

2. **Install the Flutter and Dart Extensions:** Launch Visual Studio Code and open the Extensions view by clicking on the square icon on the left sidebar or by pressing `*Ctrl+Shift+X*` (`*Cmd+Shift+X*` on macOS). Search for `Flutter` and `Dart` extensions, and click on "`Install`" to install both of them. These extensions provide essential tools and features for Flutter development within VS Code (see *Figure 1.9*).

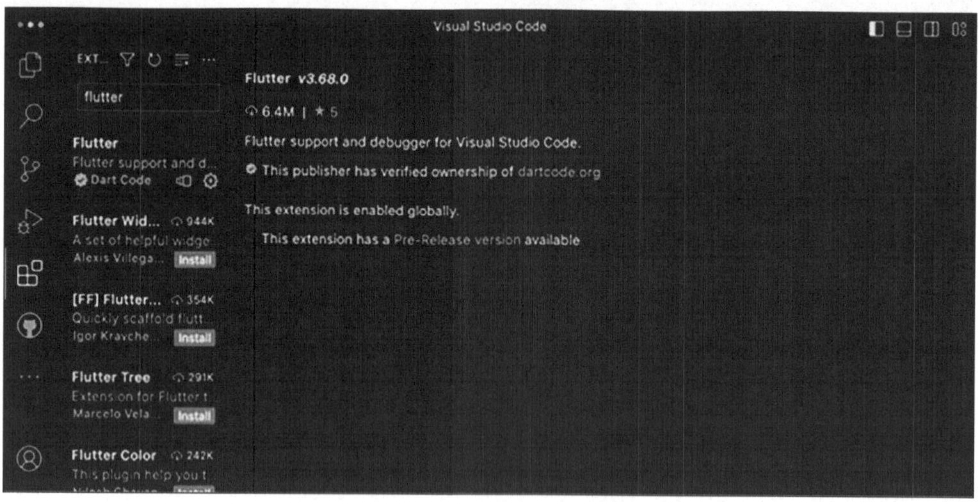

Figure 1.9: *Flutter and Dart Extensions*

3. **Set Up Flutter SDK Path:** Once the extensions are installed, you need to specify the path to the Flutter SDK in VS Code. Go to the File menu,

select **`Preferences`**, and then click on **`Settings`** (or press *Ctrl+,* (`Cmd+`, on macOS)). In the settings search bar, type **`Flutter SDK Path`** and click on **`Edit in settings.json`** to open the settings file. Add the following line, replacing **`<path-to-flutter-sdk>`** with the actual path to your Flutter SDK:

```
"dart.flutterSdkPath": "<path-to-flutter-sdk>"
```

4. **Flutter Doctor:** Run the Flutter Doctor command from the integrated terminal within VS Code to ensure that all necessary dependencies are properly configured. Open the terminal by going to the **`View`** menu and selecting **`Terminal`** or by pressing `*Ctrl+*` (backtick) (`**`Cmd+`**` (backtick) on macOS).

```
flutter doctor
```

Fix any reported issues to ensure a smooth development experience.

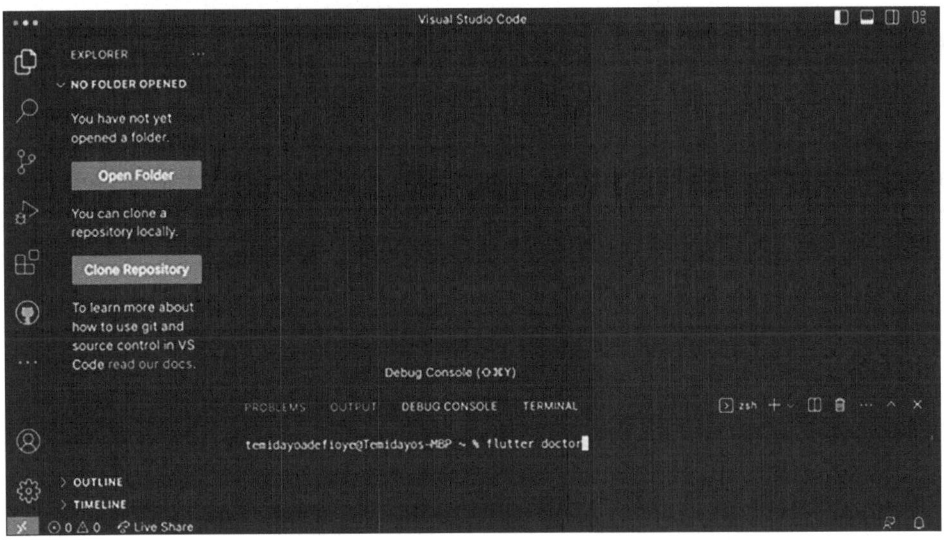

***Figure 1.10**: Flutter Terminal on VS Code*

5. **Create a Flutter Project:** Now that your development environment is set up, you can create a new Flutter project. Open the command palette in VS Code by pressing `*Ctrl+Shift+P*` (`*Cmd+Shift+P*` on macOS) and search for **`Flutter: New Project`**. Follow the prompts to provide a project name and select a directory where the project will be created.

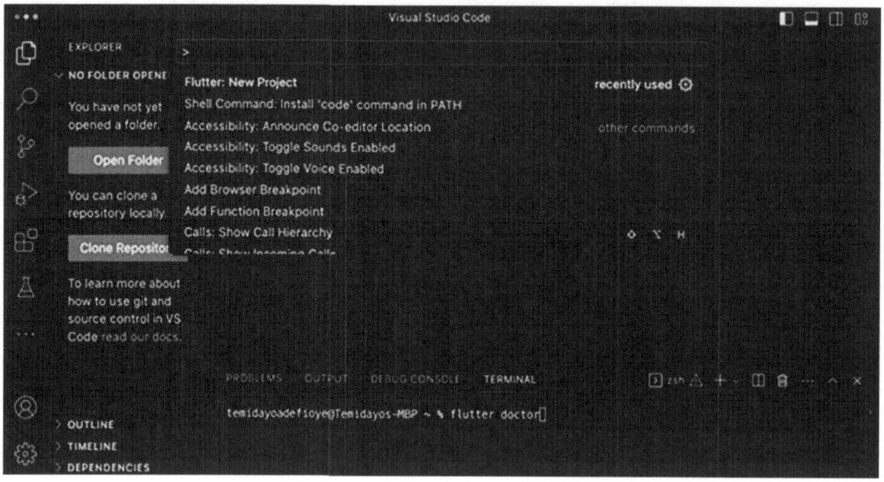

***Figure 1.11**: Flutter New Project*

Congratulations! You have successfully configured Visual Studio Code for Flutter development. You can now start coding Flutter applications using the powerful features and tools provided by VS Code.

Installing Flutter Dependencies

Before you can start developing Flutter applications, it is important to ensure that all the necessary dependencies are installed. Flutter provides a convenient command called **flutter doctor** to check and install any missing dependencies. In my case, since I already have Flutter installed and the `flutter doctor` command showed all green ticks except for Android toolchain dependencies, which can also be installed by following the instructions below the warning.

To ensure that your system is properly configured, use this checklist to verify that all Flutter dependencies have been installed:

1. **Install Flutter SDK:** If you haven't already, download and install the Flutter SDK by following the instructions provided in the official Flutter documentation for your operating system. The Flutter SDK is the core framework required for Flutter development.

2. **Set Up Flutter SDK Path:** After installing the Flutter SDK, you need to configure the system environment variables to include the Flutter SDK path. This allows your computer to locate the Flutter command-line tools. Refer to the Configuring Visual Studio Code section discussed earlier for detailed instructions on setting up the Flutter SDK path for your specific operating system.

3. **Install Dart SDK:** Flutter uses the Dart programming language for application development. Make sure you have the Dart SDK installed on your system. You can download and install the Dart SDK from the official Dart website (dart.dev).
4. **Install Android Studio**: To develop Flutter apps for Android, you need to have Android Studio installed on your system. Android Studio provides the necessary tools and resources for Android app development. Download and install Android Studio from the official Android Studio website (developer.android.com/studio) and follow the installation instructions.
5. **Set Up Android Device or Emulator:** To run and test Flutter apps on Android, you need to set up either a physical Android device or an Android emulator. If you have a physical Android device, enable USB debugging in the device settings. If you prefer to use an emulator, you can create and configure one using the AVD Manager in Android Studio.
6. **Install Xcode (For macOS):** If you're developing Flutter apps for iOS on macOS, you need to have Xcode installed. Xcode is the integrated development environment (IDE) for iOS app development. You can download Xcode from the Mac App Store or the Apple Developer website and follow the installation instructions.
7. **Set Up iOS Simulator (For macOS):** To run and test Flutter apps on iOS, you can use the iOS Simulator provided by Xcode. Open Xcode and navigate to `Preferences`. Go to the `Components` tab and install the simulator for the iOS version you want to target.

Once you have installed the Flutter SDK, Dart SDK, Android Studio, Xcode (for macOS), and set up the necessary Android and iOS devices/emulators, you are ready to start developing Flutter applications.

Troubleshooting

During the setup process for Flutter development environment, you may encounter some common issues or errors. Don't worry, many of these issues have been experienced by other developers, and there are often simple solutions available. Here are some common issues and troubleshooting tips to help you resolve them:

Flutter SDK Installation Error

If you encounter an error while installing the Flutter SDK, ensure that you have met the system requirements for Flutter and that your internet connection is stable. Sometimes, antivirus software or firewall settings may interfere with the installation process, so temporarily disabling them can help. If the error persists, refer to the official Flutter documentation and online community forums for specific troubleshooting steps.

Flutter Command Not Found

If you're unable to run Flutter commands in your terminal or command prompt, double-check that you have properly set up the Flutter SDK path in your system environment variables. Make sure the Flutter SDK directory is added to the system's PATH variable. Restart your terminal or command prompt after making changes to the environment variables.

Android Emulator Issues

If you encounter issues with running the Android emulator, ensure that you have installed the necessary Android SDK components using the Android SDK Manager in Android Studio. Make sure the emulator is properly configured, and if you're using a physical Android device, ensure that it's connected and recognized by your computer. Restarting the emulator or your computer can sometimes resolve issues.

iOS Simulator Issues (macOS)

If you're facing issues with the iOS Simulator in Xcode, make sure you have the required iOS Simulator installed for the iOS version you want to target. Verify that the iOS Simulator is correctly configured in Xcode preferences. If the issue persists, try resetting the iOS Simulator or restarting Xcode.

Dependency Management Errors

Flutter relies on various packages and dependencies to function properly. If you encounter dependency-related errors or conflicts, ensure that you have correctly specified the dependencies in your Flutter project's **`pubspec.yaml`** file. Run `` `**flutter pub get**` `` to fetch and update the required dependencies. If conflicts arise, try running `flutter pub upgrade` to update to compatible versions.

Connection Errors

Flutter requires a stable internet connection, especially during the initial setup and when fetching dependencies. If you experience connection-related errors or slow download speeds, check your network connection and try switching to a different network if available.

Community Resources

If you're unable to resolve an issue on your own, don't hesitate to seek help from the Flutter community. The Flutter website provides comprehensive documentation, FAQs, and guides that address common issues. You can also join Flutter forums, groups, or communities where experienced developers can assist you with troubleshooting and provide guidance.

Remember to consult the official Flutter documentation, search the Flutter community forums, and leverage online resources for specific troubleshooting steps related to your issue. With a little patience and persistence, most setup-related issues can be resolved, allowing you to proceed with Flutter app development smoothly.

Exploring Flutter Project Structure

Imagine you're standing in front of a magnificent building, marveling at its architectural beauty. You admire the way each component seamlessly fits together to create a functional and visually appealing structure. In many ways, building a Flutter app is similar to constructing a physical building. Just as a building requires a solid foundation and well-designed components, a Flutter app relies on a well-structured project layout and organized codebase to ensure its functionality and maintainability.

When you create a new Flutter project, Flutter automatically generates a default directory structure that serves as a foundation for your app development. Each directory has a specific purpose and helps organize your code and assets effectively. Let's explore the default directory structure of a Flutter project.

In this section, we will explore the fundamental aspects of a Flutter project structure. We'll examine how different components come together to form the building blocks of a Flutter app. Understanding the project structure is crucial for developers to effectively navigate and manage their codebase. So, let's dive into the blueprint of a Flutter project and uncover the key elements that make it a solid foundation for app development.

Directory Structure

Just like a well-designed building has different sections dedicated to specific purposes, a Flutter project consists of various directories that serve different functions. Understanding the purpose of each directory is key to organizing your code and assets effectively. Let's take a closer look at the following default directory structure of a Flutter project:

- **`lib` folder**

Figure 1.12 shows the lib folder:

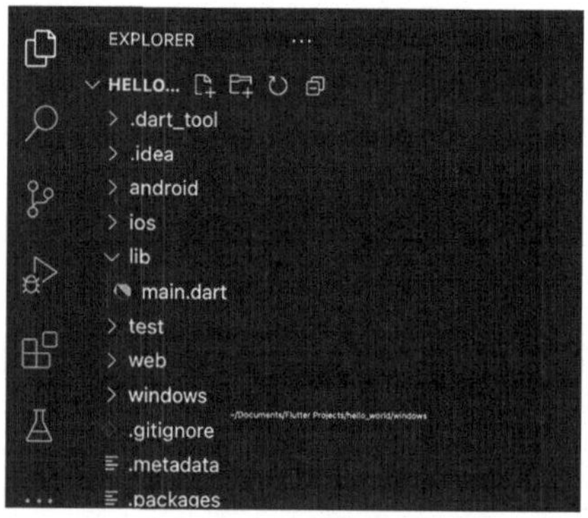

Figure 1.12: *Flutter lib folder*

This is the heart of your Flutter project. The `` `lib` `` directory contains all the Dart code files that make up your app's logic, user interface, and functionality. You'll spend most of your development time working within this directory, creating or modifying Dart files to build your app.

- **`test` folder**

Figure 1.13 shows the `test` folder:

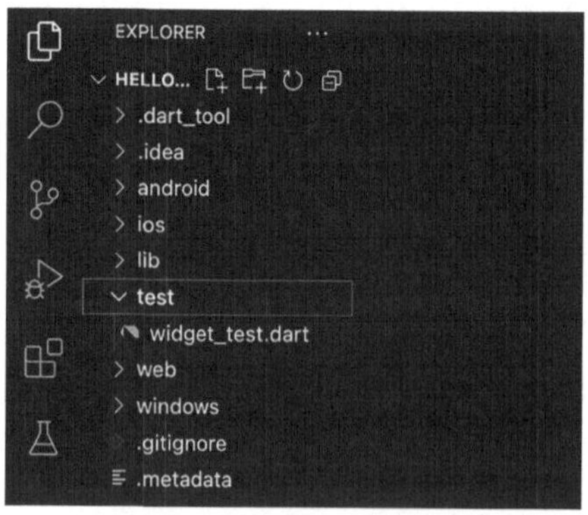

Figure 1.13: *Flutter test folder*

The `test` directory is where you write unit tests for your Flutter app. It's crucial to include tests in your development process to ensure the reliability and stability of your app. Writing tests helps identify and fix bugs early on, improving the overall quality of your app.

- **`android` folder**

Figure 1.14 shows the **`android`** folder:

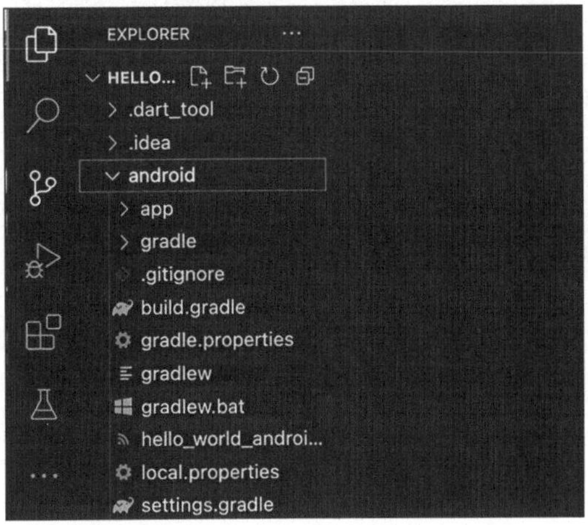

***Figure 1.14**: Flutter android folder*

This directory is specific to Android development. It contains the necessary files and configurations for building, running, and packaging your Flutter app for the Android platform. You'll find files such as `build.gradle` and `AndroidManifest.xml` within this directory.

- **`ios` folder**

Figure 1.15 shows the **`ios`** folder:

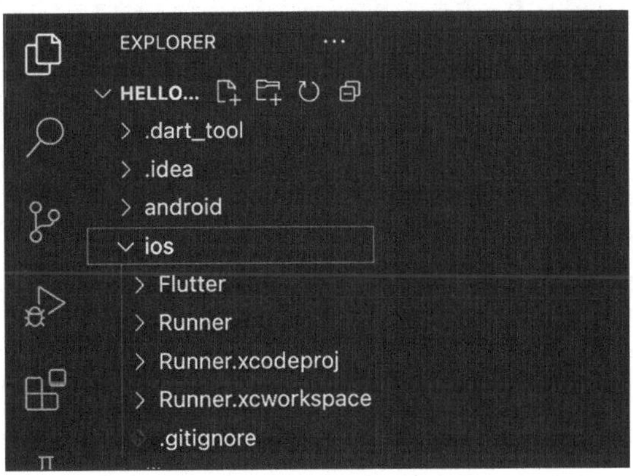

***Figure 1.15**: Flutter ios folder*

The **ios** directory is dedicated to iOS development. It houses the necessary files and configurations for building, running, and packaging your Flutter app for the iOS platform. Files like **Podfile** and **Info.plist** can be found here.

- **assets folder**

Figure 1.16 shows the **assets** folder:

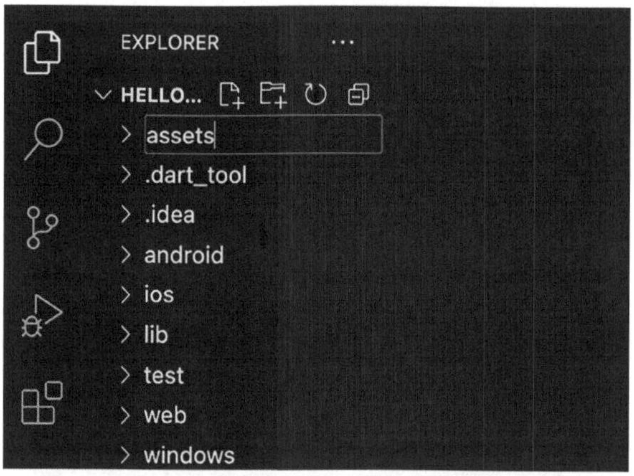

***Figure 1.16**: Flutter assets folder*

The **assets** directory is used to store static files, such as images, fonts, and other resources that your app may require. You can organize your assets into subdirectories within the `**assets**` directory to maintain a structured approach to asset management. This directory is not created when you create your Flutter project, but it is expected that you create it at the root of your project.

- **web (optional) folder**

Figure 1.17 shows the **web** folder:

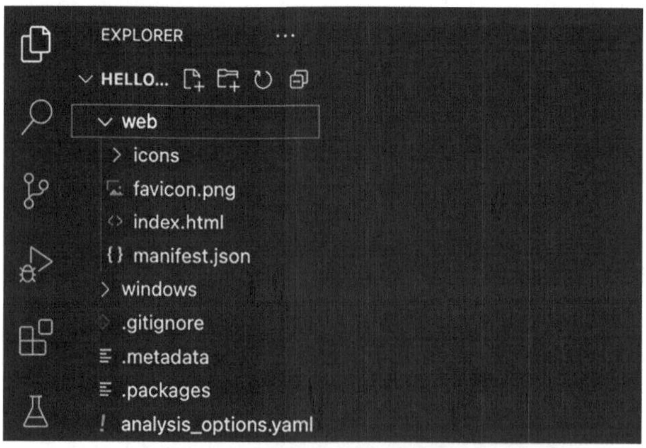

***Figure 1.17**: Flutter web folder*

If you're targeting the web platform with your Flutter app, you'll find a `**web**` directory. It contains files and configurations specific to web deployment, allowing you to build and run your app in a web browser.

The `**index.html**` file located inside the `**web**` folder serves as the entry point for your web application, providing a starting point for building and rendering your Flutter project on the web platform.

- **windows (optional) folder**

Figure 1.18 shows the **windows** folder:

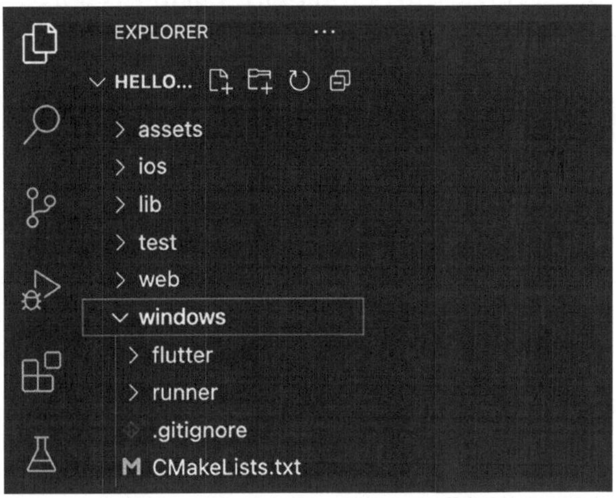

***Figure 1.18**: Flutter windows folder*

If you're targeting the Windows operating system with your Flutter app, you'll find a `**windows**` directory. It contains files and configurations specific to Windows deployment, allowing you to build and run your app on the Windows operating system.

In the `**windows**` directory of your Flutter project, you'll find various files and folders meant for creating and running your app on Windows computers. Some of the important ones include:

1. **Runner:** This folder holds the essential code for your app to start running on a Windows device.
2. **Generated Files:** Inside this directory, you might see generated files that help connect your Flutter code to Windows-specific functionalities.
3. **Configuration Files:** These are files like `**CMakeLists.txt**` and `**windows.CMake.props**`, which configure how your app interacts with Windows components during building.

4. **Resources:** Here, you might store images, icons, or other resources specific to the Windows platform that your app might use.
5. **Other Supporting Files:** Depending on your project setup, you might also see additional files or folders catering to specific needs, like debugging tools or custom configurations.

The essence of explaining each folder is to help you understand the purpose of each directory and navigate your project with ease. It also promotes code organization and separation of concerns, making your project more maintainable and scalable. As your app grows in complexity, having a well-structured directory layout becomes increasingly important.

Configuration Files

Just as a building requires a blueprint to define its structure and specifications, a Flutter project relies on configuration files to define various settings and behaviors. These configuration files play a crucial role in shaping your app and enabling it to interact with the underlying platforms. Let's explore the following important configuration files you'll encounter in a Flutter project:

- **`pubspec.yaml`**

Figure 1.19 shows the **`pubspec`** file:

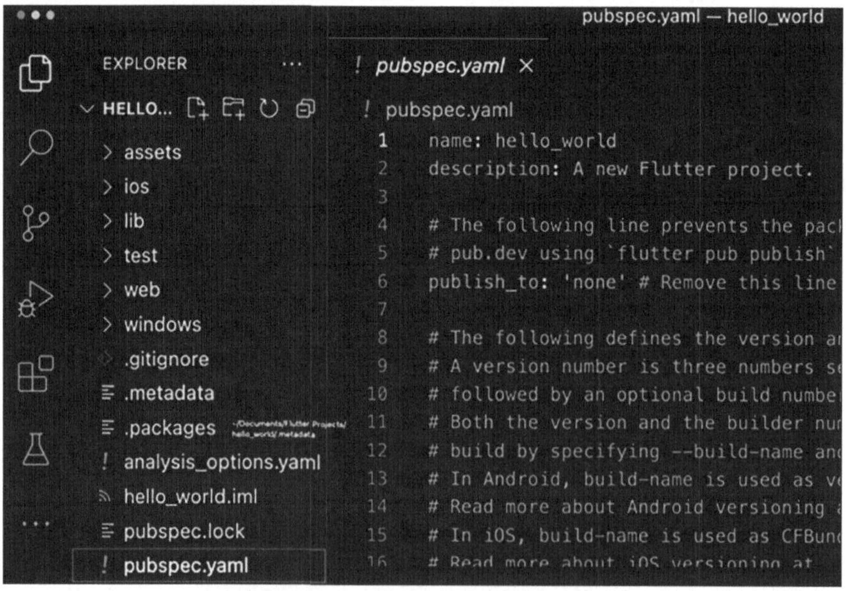

Figure 1.19: *Flutter pubspec.yaml file*

Consider this file the project's manifest. It is written in YAML (Yet Another Markup Language) and defines the dependencies, assets, metadata, and other specifications for your Flutter app. In real-life terms, think of it as the ingredients list and recipe for your app. You specify the external packages your app requires, any custom assets to include, as well as the app's name, version, and other metadata.

- **AndroidManifest.xml**

Figure 1.20 shows the **`AndroidManifest`** file:

***Figure 1.20**: Flutter AndroidManifest file*

This file is specific to Android development and resides within the `**android/app**` directory. It is an XML file that provides essential information about your app to the Android operating system. It includes details such as the app's package name, permissions, activity declarations, and so on. In real-life terms, consider it as the detailed plan that tells the Android system how your app should be presented and behave.

- **Info.plist**

Figure 1.21 shows the **`info.plist`** file:

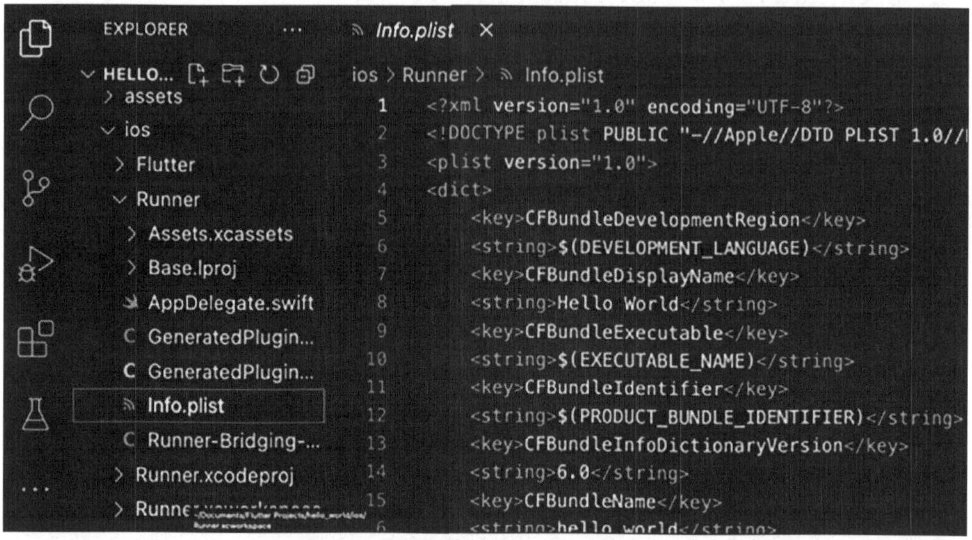

Figure 1.21: *Flutter info.plist file*

This file is specific to iOS development and resides within the **`ios/Runner`** directory. It is a property list file in XML format that contains configuration details for your app on the iOS platform. It includes information such as the app's bundle identifier, supported device orientations, background modes, and so on. In real-life terms, think of it as a document that provides instructions to the iOS system about your app's characteristics and capabilities.

These configuration files allow you to define crucial aspects of your app, such as its dependencies, assets, permissions, and platform-specific settings. Understanding and customizing these files according to your app's requirements is essential for a successful Flutter project.

In addition to these configuration files, you may also encounter other platform-specific files within the **`android`** and **`ios`** directories, such as **`build.gradle`** for Android or **`Podfile`** for iOS. These files enable you to customize various aspects of your app's behavior on each platform.

As you embark on your Flutter journey, familiarize yourself with these configuration files and their role in shaping your app. Just as a well-designed blueprint ensures a successful construction project, these configuration files pave the way for a robust and functional Flutter app.

Important Files

A Flutter project relies on a set of crucial files that bring your app to life. These files are integral to the development process and contribute to the functionality and behavior of your Flutter app. Let's explore some of the key files you'll encounter in a Flutter project:

main.dart

Figure 1.22 shows the **`main.dart`** file:

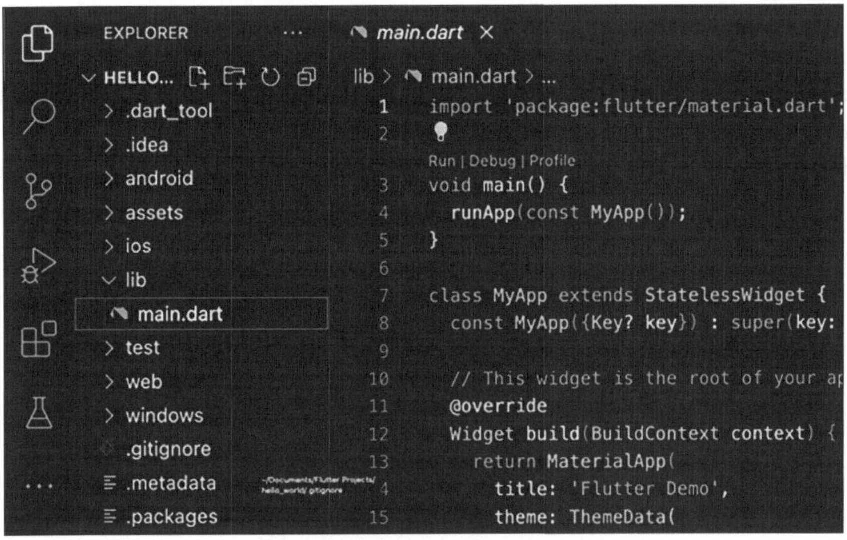

***Figure 1.22**: Flutter main.dart file*

This file serves as the entry point to your Flutter app. It contains the **`main`** function, which is the starting point of your app's execution. In this file, you'll define the root widget of your app, which represents the user interface and structure of your application. Think of **`main.dart`** as the front door to your app, where everything begins.

pubspec.yaml

We've mentioned this file before in the section on configuration files. In addition to specifying dependencies and assets, the `**pubspec.yaml**` file also manages Flutter SDK versions, provides additional metadata about your app, and allows you to define scripts and other project-specific configurations. This file acts as a central hub for managing your app's dependencies and other project-related settings.

build.gradle (Android) and Podfile (iOS)

These files are platform-specific and are used to configure and customize your app's behavior on each platform. The `build.gradle` file is located in the `android/app` directory, while the `Podfile` resides in the `ios` directory. These files allow you to define additional dependencies, configure build settings, specify version requirements, and perform various platform-specific configurations.

AppDelegate.swift (iOS) and MainActivity.kt (Android)

These files are platform-specific entry points for your Flutter app on iOS and Android, respectively. They provide a bridge between the Flutter framework and the platform-specific code. In these files, you can handle platform-specific initialization tasks, configure plugins, and set up specific behaviors or features for each platform.

These are just a few of the important files you'll often encounter in a Flutter project. Each file plays a vital role in the development, functionality, and customization of your app.

Conclusion

This chapter has taken us on an exciting journey into the world of Flutter. We've explored the history and background of Flutter, gained insights into its core concepts and principles, and learned about the importance of setting up the development environment. Along the way, we've seen the power and potential of Flutter to create stunning cross-platform apps with ease.

We've connected on a deeper level, understanding the challenges and decisions that developers must make. We've discovered how Flutter can be a game changer by providing a streamlined and efficient way to create modern and functional user interfaces.

However, this is only the beginning. Flutter opens up a whole new world of possibilities, allowing us to create apps that are not only visually appealing but also performant and responsive. We have the tools to bring our app ideas to life, thanks to Flutter's-rich ecosystem of widgets, themes, and plugins.

As we progress through this book, we'll delve deeper into the complexities of Flutter development. We'll look at advanced UI design techniques, cross-platform development strategies, and best practices for testing and debugging.

Together, we will unlock Flutter's full potential and be able to create remarkable cross-platform applications.

So buckle up and get ready for the exciting journey ahead.

Remember, Flutter is not just a technology – it's a pathway to innovation and limitless possibilities.

In the next chapter, we will delve into the core basics of Dart, how it can help you create stunning and interactive UI for your next project.

Points to Remember

- Flutter is a powerful cross-platform UI toolkit that allows you to build beautiful and functional apps for multiple platforms.
- Widgets are the building blocks of a Flutter app, representing the various elements of the user interface.
- Flutter follows a declarative programming model, where you describe the desired UI state, and Flutter takes care of updating the UI to reflect that state.
- Understanding the core concepts of Flutter, such as the widget tree and the reactive nature of UI development, is essential for creating dynamic and responsive apps.
- Flutter offers an extensible and layered architecture, allowing developers to customize and replace different parts of the framework as needed.
- Setting up the Flutter development environment involves installing the Flutter SDK, configuring VS Code or any other preferred IDE, and installing necessary dependencies.
- Troubleshooting is a common part of the setup process, and it's important to address any issues or errors that may arise. Resources and troubleshooting tips can help overcome these challenges.
- Familiarize yourself with the directory structure of a Flutter project, including important files and configuration files, to better understand the organization of your app.
- Flutter's compatibility with different platforms is made possible through platform embedders, which provide the necessary interface and communication with the underlying operating systems.
- Flutter's web support enables you to deploy your Flutter apps on the web, expanding your app's reach and accessibility.

Multiple Choice Questions

1. What are Flutter widgets?
    a. Visual elements that make up the user interface
    b. Tools used for debugging and testing Flutter apps
    c. Libraries for managing state and data in Flutter
    d. Configuration files required for setting up Flutter projects
2. Which of the following accurately describes the Flutter architecture?
    a. A layered and extensible system with no dependencies between layers
    b. A tightly coupled system with privileged access between layers
    c. A monolithic structure with limited flexibility for customization
    d. A framework with no clear separation of concerns between layers
3. How does Flutter handle UI updates?
    a. By manually triggering UI updates with explicit code
    b. By relying on the operating system to handle UI updates
    c. Through a reactive programming model that automatically updates the UI based on state changes
    d. By requiring developers to write platform-specific code for each UI update
4. What is an essential step in setting up the Flutter development environment?
    a. Installing the Flutter SDK and configuring the IDE
    b. Creating a new project directory for Flutter apps
    c. Installing third-party libraries and dependencies
    d. Connecting physical devices or emulators for testing

Answers

1. a
2. a
3. c
4. a

Questions

1. What is Flutter and how does it differentiate itself from other cross-platform frameworks?
2. Explain the concept of reactive user interfaces in Flutter. How does it contribute to a dynamic and responsive app?
3. Discuss the importance of Flutter's widget-based architecture in UI development. How does it enable code reusability and composability?
4. What are the advantages of Flutter's hot reload feature during app development? How does it enhance the developer's productivity?
5. Describe the Flutter rendering process. How does Flutter convert UI code into pixels on the screen?
6. How does Flutter integrate with different platforms through platform embedders? Explain the role of platform-specific embedders in running Flutter apps.
7. Discuss the significance of the Flutter engine in the overall Flutter framework. What core functionalities does it provide?
8. Explain Flutter's web support and its implications for developers. How does Flutter enable the creation of web applications alongside mobile apps?

Key Terms

- **YAML:** A human-readable data serialization format commonly used in Flutter for configuring project settings and defining the structure of files like `pubspec.yaml`, which contains metadata and dependencies for a Flutter project.

- ***AndroidManifest***: An XML file in Android projects that provides essential information about the app to the Android operating system, such as app permissions, activities, services, and hardware requirements.
- **`lib`**: The "**`lib`**" directory in a Flutter project holds the main source code files, including Dart files, where developers write the logic and implement the functionality of their Flutter app.
- ***Flutter Engine:*** The core engine of Flutter responsible for rendering the UI, managing input events, and providing access to platform-specific services.
- ***Platform Embedders***: Components that enable Flutter apps to run on different platforms, providing the necessary interface and communication with the underlying operating systems.
- ***Reactive User Interfaces:*** UIs that automatically update in response to changes in data or state, ensuring a dynamic and synchronized user experience.
- ***Hot Reload***: It is a powerful feature of Flutter that allows for real-time code changes and updates without restarting the app, enhancing developer productivity and speeding up the development process.
- **`Info.plist`**: A property list file in iOS projects that contains essential configuration information about the app, including bundle identifier, app name, supported device orientations, and permissions.
- **`Podfile`**: A file used in Flutter projects with native iOS dependencies, specifically for integrating third-party libraries and frameworks using CocoaPods. The **`Podfile`** specifies the required dependencies and manages their installation and configuration.

CHAPTER 2

Introduction to Dart Programming

Dart, the programming language used in Flutter development, has an interesting history that dates back to 2011. It was initially conceived by Google as a modern language for web development, with the goal of overcoming the limitations of JavaScript and enabling developers to build high-performance web applications. Over time, Dart evolved and expanded its scope to encompass not just web development but also mobile and desktop application development.

Structure

In this chapter, the following topics will be covered:

- Introduction to Dart language syntax and features
- Variables, data types, and operators in Dart
- Control flow statements (if-else, loops)
- Functions and parameter passing in Dart
- Dart packages and libraries

Introduction to Dart

The history of Dart can be traced back to the early days of the web, when JavaScript was the de facto programming language for client-side scripting. Although JavaScript served its purpose well, developers often encountered challenges related to its performance, scalability, and maintainability. Recognizing the need for a more robust language, Google embarked on a mission to develop Dart.

The Genesis

Dart was officially announced by Google in October 2011, with the primary objective of providing a better language for web development. It aimed to address the shortcomings of JavaScript while embracing the same principles that made JavaScript popular – an interpreted, dynamically typed language that could be executed across different platforms.

The early versions of Dart focused on compiling JavaScript, allowing developers to leverage their existing knowledge of JavaScript while benefiting from Dart's additional features and improvements. However, Google soon realized that Dart had the potential to be more than just a language for web development. With its strong performance characteristics and versatility, Dart could be used to build native applications across multiple platforms.

As Dart continued to evolve, Google introduced Flutter in 2017, an open-source UI toolkit built using Dart. Flutter embraced the concept of reactive UI programming and allowed developers to build beautiful, cross-platform applications with a single codebase. The combination of Dart and Flutter proved to be a powerful duo, enabling developers to create high-quality, performant apps for iOS, Android, the web, and desktop platforms.

Today, Dart has gained significant traction in the developer community and is widely recognized as a powerful and expressive language for building mobile and web applications. Its growing ecosystem of libraries and tools, coupled with its strong integration with Flutter, makes Dart a compelling choice for developers seeking to create modern, cross-platform apps.

Overview of the Dart Language

Now that we have explored the history of Dart, let's dive into what Dart is.

Dart is a modern, object-oriented programming language designed to be fast, productive, and scalable. It was developed with the aim of providing an efficient language for building a wide range of applications, including web, mobile, and desktop. Dart combines the best aspects of statically typed and dynamically typed languages, offering developers a flexible and expressive coding experience.

When we talk about statically typed and dynamically typed languages, we are referring to how the language handles variable types and type checking. In statically typed languages like Dart, the type of variable is known and checked at compile time. This means that the compiler verifies the types of variables and ensures that they are used correctly throughout the code. Statically typed languages offer benefits, such as early error detection and enhanced code reliability.

On the other hand, dynamically typed languages do not enforce strict type-checking at compile time. Instead, the type of variable is determined at runtime. This provides more flexibility in terms of assigning different types of values to variables, but it can also lead to potential errors if the wrong types are used.

One of the key features of Dart is its focus on productivity. The language is designed to make developers more efficient by providing features like concise syntax, strong type inference, and a rich set of built-in libraries. Dart encourages clean and readable code, allowing developers to express their ideas straightforwardly.

Dart supports both just-in-time (JIT) and ahead-of-time (AOT) compilation, providing flexibility and performance optimization. During development, the Dart virtual machine (VM) uses JIT compilation to provide fast feedback with its hot reload feature, allowing developers to see the changes instantly without the need for a full application restart. For production releases, Dart code can be compiled into a highly optimized machine code using AOT compilation, resulting in fast startup times and efficient execution.

The language follows an object-oriented paradigm, where everything is an object and classes define the blueprint for creating objects. Dart supports features such as inheritance, interfaces, mixins, and abstract classes, enabling developers to write modular and reusable code. It also provides support for generics, allowing for the creation of data structures and algorithms that are type-safe and reusable across different data types.

Another notable aspect of Dart is its strong asynchronous programming support. Dart incorporates the concepts of futures and async/await syntax, making it easy to handle asynchronous operations, such as network requests and file I/O, without blocking the application's execution. This asynchronous programming model allows for the development of responsive and efficient applications.

Dart has a rich standard library that includes modules for working with collections, files, networking, asynchronous programming, and more. Additionally, the Dart ecosystem offers a wide range of third-party packages and libraries that extend the capabilities of the language and simplify common development tasks.

With its combination of productivity, performance, and flexibility, Dart has become a preferred language for Flutter development. Its ability to create beautiful user interfaces, handle complex business logic, and integrate seamlessly with Flutter's UI framework makes Dart an ideal choice for building cross-platform applications.

Dart Under the Hood

To truly understand Dart and its significance in Flutter's development, it's important to explore how Dart works under the hood. Having a deeper understanding of Dart's operations will provide valuable insights into its performance, memory management, and execution model.

Dart is a general-purpose programming language that employs a combination of interpreted and compiled execution. When developing Flutter applications, Dart code goes through different stages of execution, optimizing performance and ensuring efficient resource utilization.

At the core of Dart's execution model is its virtual machine (VM). The Dart VM is responsible for running Dart code and provides a runtime environment that enables the execution of Dart programs. The VM interprets Dart code during the initial development and debugging phases, allowing for quick iterations and easier troubleshooting.

As a Flutter application progresses toward release, Dart utilizes a technique called Just-in-Time (JIT) compilation. JIT compilation dynamically translates Dart code into machine code as the application runs. This process optimizes the execution speed by generating highly optimized machine code specific to the target platform. JIT compilation allows for faster development cycles, as developers can see the immediate impact of code changes through Flutter's hot reload feature.

For production-ready Flutter applications, Dart employs Ahead-of-Time (AOT) compilation. AOT compilation precompiles Dart code into efficient machine code ahead of time, reducing startup time and enabling faster execution. The AOT-compiled code is platform-specific, resulting in improved performance and native-like behavior on the target platform.

Dart's execution model also incorporates a garbage collector that manages memory allocation and deallocation. The garbage collector automatically detects and reclaims memory that is no longer in use, freeing up resources and preventing memory leaks. This automatic memory management helps simplify memory management for developers, allowing them to focus more on building the application's logic and user experience.

Additionally, Dart supports asynchronous programming through its native support for asynchronous operations and the **`async/await`** syntax. Asynchronous programming in Dart enables developers to handle time-consuming tasks, such as network requests or file operations, without blocking the main UI thread. This ensures that the user interface remains responsive and prevents the application from becoming unresponsive during long-running operations.

Dart Syntax Basics

A few years ago, a tech newbie curiously asked me, "Why does a computer need a language, and what's up with this thing called syntax?" He was puzzled by the idea that computers can't understand human languages like French, English, Yoruba, Igbo, or Hausa. Intrigued by his curiosity, I smiled and decided to give him an illustration to demystify the concept.

I asked him to imagine human languages, where there are over 7100 languages spoken in the world today. Each language has its own unique rules and grammar, and to communicate effectively, you must adhere to those rules. Any attempt to use the language in an improper way would result in native speakers pointing out your mistakes.

Similarly, in the computer world, there are thousands of programming languages, each with its own set of rules and syntax. Syntax serves as the language's grammar, defining the combinations of symbols and words that are considered correctly structured statements or expressions.

So, what exactly is the syntax? In simple terms, it is like the language's rulebook – a set of guidelines that dictates how you should construct your code. Just as a proper sentence follows the grammar rules of a language, a correctly structured statement in a programming language adheres to its syntax.

Dart's Most Commonly Used Keywords

Dart comes with a set of carefully chosen keywords that serve as the building blocks for writing code. These keywords are like special commands that tell the computer what to do, and they are essential for instructing your program on how to perform different tasks. Understanding these keywords is crucial for becoming proficient in Dart programming.

In this section, we'll explore some of the most commonly used keywords in Dart, such as '**`var`**,' '**`if`**,' '**`else`**,' '**`for`**,' '**`while`**,' '**`switch`**,' and '**`return`**.' Each keyword has its own function, just like every word in any human language.

- **var**: The **'var'** keyword is used to declare variables in Dart. Variables are containers that temporarily store data, allowing you to manipulate and work with different values throughout your program.
- **if/else**: These conditional keywords are used for decision-making in your code. With 'if,' you can check whether a certain condition is true or false, and, based on the result, execute specific blocks of code. **'else'** is used in conjunction with **'if'** to provide an alternative set of instructions when the condition is false.
- **for**: The **'for'** keyword is essential for creating loops in Dart. It allows you to repeat a block of code a specific number of times or iterate over elements in a collection.
- **while**: Similar to **'for**,' the **'while'** keyword is used for creating loops. However, with 'while,' the loop continues to execute as long as a specified condition remains true.
- **switch**: The **'switch'** keyword facilitates multi-way branching in Dart. It provides an elegant way to handle multiple cases based on the value of an expression.
- **return**: The **'return'** keyword is crucial in functions, where it specifies the value to be sent back to the caller when the function is executed.
- **function**: The **'function'** keyword is used to define reusable blocks of code in Dart. Functions can take input arguments, perform specific tasks, and return results. They play a significant role in structuring and organizing code, promoting code reusability and modularity.
- **class**: The **'class'** keyword is employed to define a class in Dart, with '**class_name**' representing the name of the class. Inside the class body, you can include fields to store data, constructors to initialize the class, getter methods to retrieve values, and setter methods to update values.
- **print**: The **'print'** keyword is not only a keyword, but also a function that allows you to display output on the console. It is commonly used for debugging purposes, providing insights into variable values, execution flow, and other important information during program execution.

Dart Comments

Comments are like little notes or explanations you write within your code to provide additional information for yourself and other developers who read your code. Imagine you are creating a presentation slide, and you want to include some comments to help you remember some key points you want to discuss during a presentation. These comments will not be part of the actual slides, but they make it easier for you to flow with your slides.

There are two types of comments: single-line comments and multi-line comments.

- **Single-line Comments:**

```
// This is a single-line comment.
// It starts with two forward slashes.
```

Single-line comments are used for short explanations or notes that fit within a single line. They start with two forward slashes (//) and continue until the end of the line. Dart ignores everything after the // symbols, so the comments do not affect the program's functionality.

- **Multi-line Comments:**

```
/* This is a multi-line comment.
   It can span multiple lines, making it useful for longer
explanations or section headings.
*/
```

Multi-line comments, also known as block comments, are used for longer explanations or section headings that span multiple lines. They start with `/*` and end with `*/`. Everything between the `/*` and `*/` symbols is treated as a comment by Dart.

Comments are essential for adding clarity to your code. They help you and other developers understand the purpose of different sections of the code, explain complex algorithms, or provide reminders for future improvements. While comments don't affect the program's execution, they are valuable for making your code more readable and maintainable.

Here's an example of how comments can be used in Dart code:

```
// This function calculates the area of a rectangle.
double calculateArea(double length, double width) {
  // The area formula is length * width.
  double area = length * width;
  return area; // Return the calculated area.
}
```

In this example, we have used comments to describe what the function does and how it calculates the area of a rectangle. These comments provide valuable information to anyone reading the code and help them understand the logic behind the function.

As you continue to write Dart code and explore Flutter development, comments will become an essential part of your coding practices, aiding you in writing clean, well-documented, and organized code.

The Entry Point

Every program needs a starting point, and that starting point is the `main()` function. Just like a football match begins with the sound of the referee's whistle, every Dart program starts with the `main()` function.

Imagine you are about to watch an exciting football game. The players are on the field, the stadium is buzzing with anticipation, and the referee stands in the center of the pitch. As soon as the referee blows the whistle, the game begins. But what happens if the referee refuses to blow the whistle? Well, the game will not begin.

Similarly, the **main()** function in Dart serves as the entry point for your code. When you run a Dart program, the Dart runtime looks for the **main()** function and starts executing the code from there. It's the starting signal that gets your program up and running.

Now, let's take a closer look at the structure of the `main()` function:

```
void main() {
  // Your code goes here
  // This is where the action begins!
}
```

In this example, `main()` is defined with a return type of `void`, indicating that it doesn't return any value. The opening and closing curly braces `{}` enclose the code block where you can write your Dart instructions.

Every Dart program must have a **main()** function. Without it, the game won't start, and your program won't run. As we delve deeper into Dart programming, you'll discover how to use this crucial function to create powerful and interactive applications with Flutter. Let's continue our journey into the world of Flutter UI development, where **main()** will play a significant role in bringing your creative ideas to life, just like the referee's whistle starts an exhilarating football match.

DartPad Playground

DartPad is a powerful online tool that allows you to write, run, and experiment with Dart code directly in your web browser. It's a beginner-friendly environment that provides a simple interface to practice coding without the need to set up a local development environment.

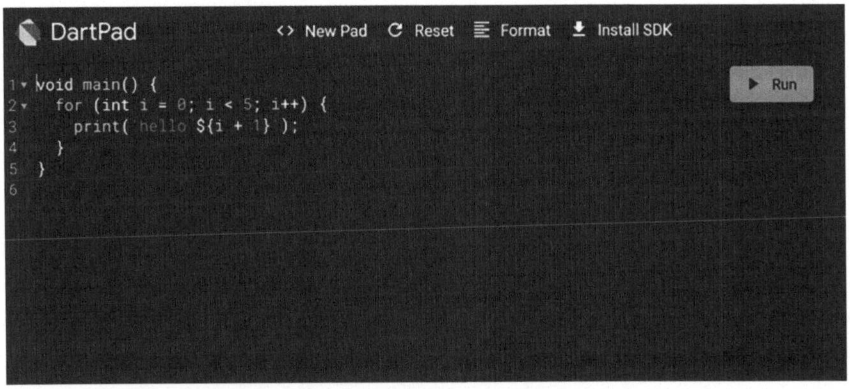

***Figure 2.1**: DartPad Playground(dartpad.dev)*

Imagine you have just started learning Dart and want to practice writing some code. Instead of installing any software on your computer, you can use DartPad to start coding right away. It's like having a virtual playground for Dart where you can test and explore various code snippets.

You can write Dart code in the main editor window. For example,

Let's print a simple `Hello World`.

```
void main() {

  print(“Hello World”);
}
```

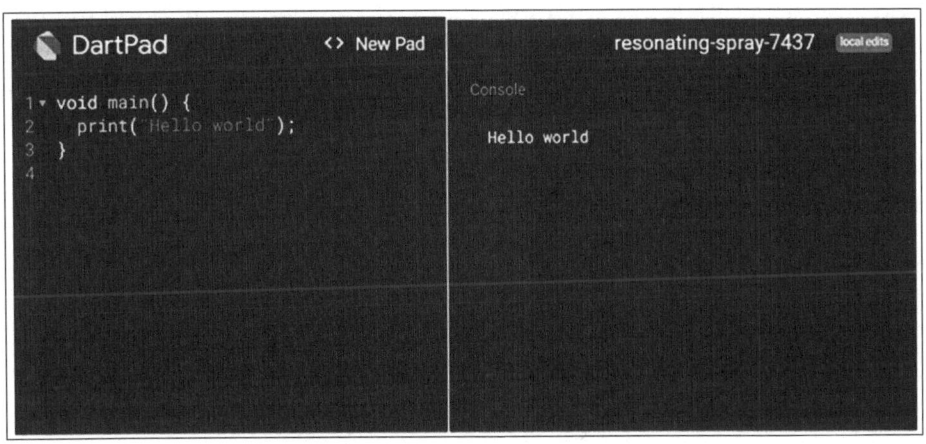

***Figure 2.2**: Dart hello world output*

In this example, Let's write another simple program to add two numbers together:

```
void main() {
  int num1 = 10;
  int num2 = 20;
  int sum = num1 + num2;
  print("The sum of $num1 and $num2 is $sum");
}
```

In this example, we declare two integer variables, `num1` and `num2`, and assign them the values 10 and 20, respectively. Then, we calculate their sum and store it in the variable `sum`. Finally, we use the `print()` function to display the result of the sum to the console.

To run the code and see the output, click the **Run** button in DartPad. The output will be displayed in the **Console** area below the editor.

Don't worry if you don't fully understand the code snippet right now. We will dive deeper into each concept and explain everything step by step in subsequent sections. The purpose of this example is to show you how DartPad can be used to write and run Dart code easily in your web browser. As we progress, you'll gain a better understanding of Dart and be able to write more complex and exciting code to build amazing Flutter applications.

Understanding Variables and Data Types in Dart

During one of my Dart basics lectures with a tech newbie, I wanted to explain the concept of variables in a relatable way, so I recalled a childhood memory. In our native language, there is something called **Kolo**, which translates to a saving box. Back in the early 2000s, we used Kolo to keep our money. Whenever we wanted to use the money, we opened up the box and took back our savings. The fascinating thing was that we couldn't withdraw more than we had put into it. If we saved ₦500, we couldn't withdraw more than that.

This is exactly how a variable works in programming. Just like the Kolo, you temporarily store a value in a variable so that whenever the computer needs it, it can access and use it. The value can be a number, a text, or any other data type, and you can change or update the value of the variable as needed.

Variables

Variables are like containers that store data, much like a "**Kolo**" (a savings box) that you use to keep your money safe. Just as you can retrieve and use your money from the Kolo whenever you need it, variables allow you to temporarily store and manipulate different values in your code. They play a crucial role in programming, enabling you to work with data and create dynamic and interactive applications.

Here's a closer look at how variables work in Dart:

Declaring Variables

To use a variable, you must first declare it with a specific name. Think of the variable name as the label on your Kolo, helping you identify what you've saved inside. In Dart, you can declare a variable using the '`var`' keyword, followed by the variable name.

```
var age; // Declaration of a variable named 'age'
```

Assigning Values

Once you've declared a variable, you can assign a value to it. Consider this as putting money into your Kolo. You can store various types of data in a variable, such as numbers, text, or even complex data structures.

```
age = 25; // Assigning the value 25 to the variable 'age'
```

Type Inference

Dart is a type of computer language that needs you to tell it what kind of data (like numbers, letters, etc.) you're using with different variables. However, Dart has a cool feature where you can just assign a value to a variable, and it will guess what type of data you're using–no need for you to specifically tell it. This makes your coding more simple and less wordy.

```
var name = 'Temidayo'; // Dart infers that the data type is String
```

Constants

While variables can change their values during program execution, you can also declare constants whose values remain fixed. Think of constants as a Kolo that, once locked, cannot be opened or modified. In Dart, you can use the **final** or **const** keywords to declare constants.

```
final pi = 3.14; // Declaring a final constant 'pi'
const appName = 'MyApp'; // Declaring a constant 'appName'
```

Dynamic Typing

In contrast to static typing, Dart also supports dynamic typing, where a variable can change its data type during runtime. It's like having a magic Kolo that can transform its contents. While dynamic typing provides flexibility, it's essential to use it judiciously to avoid potential issues.

```
dynamic dynamicValue = 42; // The variable 'dynamicValue' initially
holds an integer
dynamicValue = 'Hello'; // Now, 'dynamicValue' holds a string
```

Data Types

As we've seen, variables act as containers to store and recall data during program execution. However, to make sense of this data, the computer needs to know its type, just like you would distinguish between coins and paper notes in your Kolo (savings box). In Dart, data types help the computer understand the nature of the information stored in each variable, ensuring the integrity and reliability of the data.

Let's take a look at some common data types in Dart and how they are used:

Integer (`int`)

In Dart, the integer data type represents whole numbers without any fractional or decimal parts. It allows you to work with numbers in a straightforward manner, just like counting objects or measuring quantities. Imagine you are managing a fruit stall, and you want to keep track of the number of oranges you have in stock. In Dart, you would use the 'int' data type to store this information.

Here's how you can declare and use integers in Dart:

```
int numberOfOranges = 50;
```

In this example, we have declared a variable named `**numberOfOranges**` of type **'int'** and assigned it a value of 50. Now, Dart understands that this variable should only store whole numbers and will raise an error if you try to assign a non-integer value to it.

Integers come in various forms, such as positive and negative numbers, including zero. You can perform common mathematical operations like addition, subtraction, multiplication, and division with integer variables.

```
int apples = 10;
int bananas = 5;

int totalFruits = apples + bananas; // totalFruits will be 15
```

You can also use integers to represent quantities, counts, and many other numeric aspects in your Dart programs. The integer data type is essential for a wide range of applications, from simple calculations to more complex algorithms.

Remember that Dart integers have a fixed size, which means they can represent a specific range of values based on their bit length. For example, a 32-bit integer can represent values from approximately -2 billion to +2 billion.

Double (double)

The double data type is used to represent numbers with fractional parts. It's ideal for dealing with values that require more precision, such as measurements, currency, or any real-world data that includes decimal points. Imagine you are working on a finance app, and you need to calculate the total amount due for a shopping cart. You would use the **`double`** data type to store the prices of items that may have fractions of a cent.

Here's how you can declare and use double values in Dart:

```
double priceOfItem = 49.99;
```

In this example, we've declared a variable named `` `priceOfItem` `` of type **'double'** and assigned it a value of 49.99. Dart automatically recognizes this variable as a double, and you can perform various arithmetic operations with it, such as addition, subtraction, multiplication, and division.

```
double taxRate = 0.075;
double subtotal = 100.00;

double totalAmount = subtotal + (subtotal * taxRate); // totalAmount
will be 107.50
```

Double values are particularly useful when handling real-world data that can be represented as fractions, percentages, or decimals. The double data type provides the precision needed for accurate calculations in these scenarios.

It's essential to be cautious when working with double values due to potential floating-point errors. These errors can arise from the internal representation of floating-point numbers in computers. Rounding errors can occur when you perform multiple arithmetic operations with double values. For critical financial calculations or scenarios where high precision is required, you may need to use additional techniques to mitigate floating-point errors.

String

The string data type is used to represent sequences of characters, such as text or words. Strings are essential for handling textual data, user inputs, messages, and much more. Imagine you are building a messaging app, and you need to store and display text messages between users. You would use the 'String' data type to handle these messages.

Here's how you can declare and use string values in Dart:

```
String firstName = 'John';
String lastName = "Doe";
String fullName = firstName + " " + lastName; // fullName will be "John
Doe"
```

In this example, we've declared three variables, **firstName**, **lastName**, and **fullName**, all of type 'String'. Dart allows you to create strings using single quotes or double quotes. You can concatenate strings using the '+' operator to build more complex strings, as demonstrated by the **fullName** variable.

Strings can also contain special characters, escape sequences, and placeholders for dynamic values. Here's an example of using an escape sequence to include a newline character in a string:

```
String message = "Hello, \nWelcome to our app!";
```

The '**\n**' escape sequence inserts a new line in the string, resulting in the message being displayed with a line break.

Moreover, you can use string interpolation to embed dynamic values within a string. Dart allows you to use the '**$**' symbol, followed by the variable name inside a string, to include the value of the variable:

```
int age = 30;
String greeting = "Hello, I am $age years old!";
```

In this case, the variable **'age'** is embedded in the **'greeting'** string, and its value will be dynamically inserted when the string is evaluated.

Boolean (bool)

The boolean data type is used to represent two values: **true** and **false**. Booleans are essential for making decisions in programming. They allow us to create conditions and control the flow of our code based on whether certain conditions are true or false.

Imagine you are building a simple weather app, and you want to display a message depending on whether it's sunny or rainy. You would use a boolean variable to represent the weather condition:

```
bool isSunny = true;
bool isRainy = false;
```

Here, we've declared two boolean variables, **isSunny** and **isRainy**. The `**true**` value in **isSunny** indicates that it's sunny, while the **false** value in **isRainy** means it's not raining.

Booleans are often used in conditional statements like `**if**`, `**else**`, and `**while**` to control the flow of code execution. Here's an example of using a boolean variable in a simple if statement:

```
void main() {
bool isRaining = true;

print(isRaining);

}
```

In this code, we display the value of the `**isRaining**` Boolean variable.

Boolean variables are useful in a wide range of scenarios, from simple decision-making to complex logic. Understanding how to work with boolean data types is essential for writing effective and dynamic Dart code that responds to changing conditions and user inputs.

List

This is a powerful and versatile way to store collections of items. You can think of it as a container that holds multiple elements in a specific order. Lists are dynamic, meaning their size can change, and they can store elements of different data types.

For instance, imagine you are managing a shopping list. You can create a Dart list to represent the items you need to buy:

```
List<String> shoppingList = ['Apples', 'Bananas', 'Milk', 'Bread'];
```

In this example, we declared a list called `shoppingList`, which can hold strings. It currently contains four items: **'Apples'**, **'Bananas'**, **'Milk'**, and **'Bread'**. Lists are zero-indexed, so you can access individual items using their index, like `**shoppingList[0]**`, which would return **'Apples'**.

One of the most powerful features of lists is their ability to be modified. You can add new elements, remove existing ones, or update the values of specific items.

Let's say you want to add **'Eggs'** to your shopping list:

```
shoppingList.add('Eggs');
```

Now, the list will include **'Eggs'** as the last item.

You can also remove items from the list using the `**remove**` method:

```
shoppingList.remove('Bananas');
```

This will remove **'Bananas'** from the list. You can also update an item by accessing it using its index and assigning a new value:

```
shoppingList[2] = 'Orange Juice';
```

Now, **'Milk'** is replaced with 'Orange Juice'.

Lists are incredibly versatile and are widely used in Dart programming to manage collections of data efficiently. Whether you're handling shopping lists, to-do lists, or any other type of data that requires grouping, Dart lists will prove to be an essential tool in your programming journey.

Map

This is a fundamental way to store key-value pairs. Think of it as a real-world dictionary, where each word (key) has a corresponding definition (value). Maps are dynamic and unordered collections, meaning they don't have an inherent order, and you can add or remove key-value pairs as needed.

Let's use a practical example to illustrate the concept of a map. Imagine you are building a simple contacts application, and you want to store the phone numbers of your friends. You can use a Dart map to represent each friend's name as the key and their phone number as the value:

```
Map<String, String> contacts = {
  'John': '+2348012321244',
  'Jane': '+987654321',
  'Demilade': '+2347012873646',
};
```

In this example, we created a map called `**contacts**`, which maps names (strings) to phone numbers (strings). Each entry is enclosed in curly braces `**{}**` and consists of key-value pairs separated by a colon. The keys and values are separated by a comma.

You can access the phone number of a specific friend by using their name as the key:

```
String johnPhoneNumber = contacts['John']; // Returns '+2348012321244'
```

If you want to add a new contact or update an existing one, you can simply assign a new value to the corresponding key:

```
contacts['Mandela'] = '+2348012321244'; // Adds a new contact with name
Mandela and phone number '+555555555'
contacts['John'] = '+999999999'; // Updates John's phone number to
'+999999999'
```

To remove a contact, you can use the `remove` method:

```
contacts.remove('Jane'); // Removes the contact with the name 'Jane'
```

Maps are incredibly versatile and are widely used in Dart programming to store and manage data in a structured manner. They provide a flexible way to organize information, making them an essential tool for various applications, from simple data management to complex data structures.

Understanding Dart Operators

Operators are symbols or keywords that perform various operations on data or variables. Dart provides a wide range of operators that allow you to manipulate and process data efficiently. These operators help you perform tasks such as arithmetic calculations, comparisons, and logical operations, making them essential for building robust and dynamic applications.

Arithmetic Operators

These allow you to perform basic arithmetic calculations on numeric data. Dart supports all the standard arithmetic operators, including addition (+), subtraction (-), multiplication (*), division (/), and modulo (remainder) (%).

Here are some examples of using arithmetic operators in Dart:

- **Addition** (+): Adds two numbers together.

```
int num1 = 10;
int num2 = 20;
int sum = num1 + num2;
print("Sum: $sum"); // Output: Sum: 30
```

- **Subtraction** (-): Subtracts the second number from the first number.

```
int num1 = 25;
int num2 = 15;
int difference = num1 - num2;
print("Difference: $difference"); // Output: Difference: 10
```

- **Multiplication** (*): Multiplies two numbers together.

```
int num1 = 5;
int num2 = 6;
int product = num1 * num2;
print("Product: $product"); // Output: Product: 30
```

- **Division** (/): Divides the first number by the second number. Note that if both numbers are integers, the result will also be an integer.

```
int num1 = 20;
int num2 = 4;
double quotient = num1 / num2;
print("Quotient: $quotient"); // Output: Quotient: 5.0
```

- **Modulo** (%): Returns the remainder of the division of the first number by the second number. One of the popular uses of this operator is to identify even or odd numbers in a set of numbers.

```
int num1 = 25;
int num2 = 7;
int remainder = num1 % num2;
print("Remainder: $remainder"); // Output: Remainder: 4
```

These arithmetic operators can be used with different numeric data types, such as integers and doubles, allowing you to perform various calculations in your Dart programs. Remember to use parentheses when necessary to control the order of operations and ensure the correct result in complex calculations.

Assignment Operators

These are used to assign values to variables. They are shortcuts for performing an operation and assigning the result to the same variable. Dart supports several assignment operators, including the basic assignment operator (=) and compound assignment operators like +=, -=, *=, /=, and %=.

Here are some examples of using assignment operators in Dart:

- **Basic Assignment (=):** Assigns the value on the right-hand side to the variable on the left-hand side.

```
int num1 = 10;
int num2;
num2 = num1;
print("num2: $num2"); // Output: num2: 10
```

- **Compound Assignment (+=):** Adds the value on the right-hand side to the variable on the left-hand side and assigns the result to the variable.

```
int num1 = 5;
int num2 = 10;
```

```
num1 += num2;
print("num1: $num1"); // Output: num1: 15
```

- **Compound Assignment (-=):** Subtracts the value on the right-hand side from the variable on the left-hand side and assigns the result to the variable.

```
int num1 = 20;
int num2 = 5;
num1 -= num2;
print("num1: $num1"); // Output: num1: 15
```

- **Compound Assignment (*=):** Multiplies the variable on the left-hand side by the value on the right-hand side and assigns the result to the variable.

```
int num1 = 4;
int num2 = 3;
num1 *= num2;
print("num1: $num1"); // Output: num1: 12
```

- **Compound Assignment (/=):** Divides the variable on the left-hand side by the value on the right-hand side and assigns the result to the variable.

```
double num1 = 20;
double num2 = 4;
num1 /= num2;
print("num1: $num1"); // Output: num1: 5.0
```

- **Compound Assignment (%=):** Computes the remainder of dividing the variable on the left-hand side by the value on the right-hand side and assigns the result to the variable.

```
int num1 = 25;
int num2 = 7;
num1 %= num2;
print("num1: $num1"); // Output: num1: 4
```

Assignment operators are useful for simplifying code and making it more concise, especially when performing repetitive operations on the same variable. They allow you to update the value of a variable in a single line of code, which can improve readability and maintainability in your Dart programs.

Comparison Operators

Comparison operators in Dart are used to compare two values and return a boolean result (true or false) based on the comparison. Dart supports several comparison operators, including equal to (==), not equal to (!=), greater than (>), less than (<), greater than or equal to (>=), and less than or equal to (<=).

Here are some examples of using comparison operators in Dart:

- **Equal to (==):** This checks if the values on both sides are equal.

```
int num1 = 5;
int num2 = 5;
bool result = num1 == num2;
print("result: $result"); // Output: result: true
```

This is true because the value of num1 is the same as num2.

- **Not equal to (!=):** Checks if the values on both sides are not equal.

```
int num1 = 5;
int num2 = 10;
bool result = num1 != num2;
print("result: $result"); // Output: result: true
```

- **Greater than (>):** Checks if the value on the left-hand side is greater than the value on the right-hand side.

```
int num1 = 10;
int num2 = 5;
bool result = num1 > num2;
print("result: $result"); // Output: result: true
```

- **Less than (<):** Checks if the value on the left-hand side is less than the value on the right-hand side.

```
int num1 = 5;
int num2 = 10;
bool result = num1 < num2;
print("result: $result"); // Output: result: true
```

- **Greater than or equal to (>=):** Checks if the value on the left-hand side is greater than or equal to the value on the right-hand side.

```
int num1 = 10;
int num2 = 10;
bool result = num1 >= num2;
print("result: $result"); // Output: result: true
```

- **Less than or equal to (<=):** Checks if the value on the left-hand side is less than or equal to the value on the right-hand side.

```
int num1 = 5;
int num2 = 10;
bool result = num1 <= num2;
print("result: $result"); // Output: result: true
```

Comparison operators are commonly used in conditional statements, such as if statements and while loops, to make decisions based on the relationship between two values. They are essential for implementing logic and flow control in Dart programs and are widely used in various programming scenarios.

Dart Statements

Statements are like individual instructions that tell the computer what to do step by step. Imagine you are giving directions to a friend to bake a cake. Each step you provide is a statement, guiding them on what actions to take. Similarly, in Dart, statements are used to perform specific actions and make decisions in the code.

Let's look at some examples of Dart statements and how they work.

Control Statements

Control flow statements in Dart are used to change the flow of program execution based on certain conditions or criteria. They allow us to make decisions and repeat blocks of code as needed. In this subsection, we'll explore three essential control flow statements: if-else, switch, and loops.

Imagine you are driving a car, and you come across a traffic light. The traffic light changes color from green to yellow and then red. What do you do in each situation? When the light is green, you proceed forward. When it turns yellow, you slow down and prepare to stop. And when it turns red, you stop your car completely.

Similarly, in programming, we encounter situations where we need to make decisions based on certain conditions. The if-else statement is like the traffic light for our code. It helps us determine which path to take based on whether a condition is true or false.

The switch statement, on the other hand, is like a junction with multiple routes. Depending on the value of a variable or expression, we can choose different paths to execute.

Lastly, loops are like driving on a circular road. We repeat a specific set of instructions until a certain condition is met. Just as you keep driving on a circular road until you decide to exit, loops keep executing code until a particular condition becomes false.

If-else Statement

The if-else statement is a fundamental control flow statement that allows you to make decisions in your code. It helps you choose between two or more alternatives based on whether a given condition is true or false.

Imagine you are planning to go out for a walk. Before you leave your house, you check the weather outside. If it's raining, you decide to take an umbrella with you. Otherwise, if it's a sunny day, you leave the umbrella at home.

In Dart, you can achieve the same decision-making process using the if-else statement. Here's how it works:

```
void main() {
  bool isRaining = true;

  if (isRaining) {
    print("Take an umbrella with you!");
  } else {
    print("Leave the umbrella at home!");
  }
}
```

In this example, we have a boolean variable called `**isRaining**`, which is set to `**true**`. When we use the **if-else** statement, the code inside the if block will be executed if the condition `**isRaining**` is true, and the code inside the else block will be executed if the condition is false.

So, if `**isRaining**` is true, the output will be "**Take an umbrella with you!**", and if `**isRaining**` is false, the output will be "**Leave the umbrella at home!**".

You can also use multiple conditions with **else-if** statements to create more complex decision-making scenarios. The **if-else** statement is a powerful tool that allows you to control the flow of your program based on various conditions, making your code more flexible and responsive to different situations. A standalone '**if**' without '**else**' can also work when you only have one condition to check.

Here is an example:

```
void main() {
  int number = 10;

  if (number > 0) {
    print("The number is positive.");
  } else if (number < 0) {
    print("The number is negative.");
  } else {
    print("The number is zero.");
  }
}
```

In this example, the program checks the value of the number variable. If it's greater than 0, it prints "**The number is positive**." If it's less than 0, it prints "**The number is negative**." If neither of these conditions is true, it means the number is zero, and it prints "**The number is zero.**" The else-if statements allow you to create a chain of conditions, and only the block corresponding to the first true condition will be executed.

Switch Statement

The `**switch**` statement is a control flow statement that allows you to execute different blocks of code based on the value of a variable or expression. It is a powerful alternative to multiple `**if-else**` statements when dealing with multiple cases.

The syntax for the `switch` statement is as follows:

```
switch (expression) {
  case value1:
    // Code to execute if the expression is equal to value1
    break;
  case value2:
    // Code to execute if the expression is equal to value2
    break;
  // Add more cases as needed
```

```
  default:
    // Code to execute if none of the cases match the expression
}
```

Here's an example to illustrate how `switch` works:

```
void main() {
  String grade = 'A';

  switch (grade) {
    case 'A':
      print('Excellent!');
      break;
    case 'B':
      print('Good!');
      break;
    case 'C':
      print('Average.');
      break;
    case 'D':
      print('Poor.');
      break;
    default:
      print('Invalid grade.');
  }
}
```

In this example, we use the `switch` statement to check the value of the `grade` variable and print a corresponding message based on the grade. If `grade` is 'A', it will print '**Excellent!**'; if it's '**B**', it will print '**Good!**', and so on. If none of the cases matches the value of `grade`, it will execute the code under the `default` label.

The `break` statement is used to exit the `switch` block after a case is matched and executed. Without `break`, the execution will continue to the next case, leading to unexpected behavior.

Remember to use `switch` when you have a finite number of cases to consider, and it will help make your code more concise and readable. They cannot be used for complicated conditions where AND and OR operators are involved. For that, we need to implement else-if. Switch only works for a simple comparison of one variable with finite different possible values.

Loop Statements

These are like magic when you have to perform repetitive tasks without writing the same code over and over again.

Imagine you have a list of products in your online store, and you want to display each product's name to your customers. Instead of writing the code for each product one by one, you can use loop statements to automate this process.

In Dart, loop statements allow you to perform repetitive tasks with ease. There are two main types of loop statements: the `for` loop and the `while` loop.

The `for` loop

The `for` loop is used when you know the number of times you want to repeat a task. For example, if you have 100 products, you can use a `for` loop to display each product's name:

```
void main() {
  List<String> products = ['Product A', 'Product B', 'Product C', ...];
// Add all your product names here

  for (int i = 0; i < products.length; i++) {
    print('Product ${i + 1}: ${products[i]}');
  }
}
```

In this example, we have a list called `products`, which contains all the product names. The `for` loop goes through each item in the list and prints the product's name along with its index in the list.

The `while` loop

The `while` loop is used when you want to repeat a task until a specific condition is met. For instance, you might want to display products until their price exceeds a certain value:

```
void main() {
  List<double> prices = [20.0, 25.0, 30.0, ...]; // Add all your product
prices here
  int productNumber = 1;

  while (productNumber <= prices.length && prices[productNumber - 1] <=
50.0) {
```

```
    print('Product $productNumber: ${prices[productNumber - 1]}');
    productNumber++;
  }
}
```

In this example, we have a list called `**prices**`, which contains the prices of the products. The `**while**` loop checks if the product price is less than or equal to $50 and displays the product number and price. The loop continues until either the condition is no longer met or all products have been displayed.

Loop statements are powerful tools in programming that help you efficiently handle large datasets or repetitive tasks, saving you time and effort when writing code.

Functions

Functions are an essential part of programming and play a crucial role in organizing and reusing code. Think of a function as a set of instructions that perform a specific task. Instead of writing the same code over and over, you can define a function and call it whenever you need that task to be executed.

You can create a function using the `**void**` keyword (if it doesn't return any value) followed by the function name, parentheses for parameters (if any), and curly braces to enclose the function body.

Let's look at an example to understand functions better:

```
// Function to greet a person
void greetPerson(String name) {
  print('Hello, $name! How are you today?');
}
// Function to calculate the sum of two numbers
int calculateSum(int a, int b) {
  return a + b;
}

void main() {
  // Calling the greetPerson function
  greetPerson('John');

  // Calling the calculateSum function and storing the result in a
variable
  int result = calculateSum(10, 20);
  print('The sum is: $result');
}
```

In this example, we have defined two functions: `greetPerson` and `calculateSum`. The `greetPerson` function takes a `name` as a parameter and greets the person using their name. The `calculateSum` function takes two parameters `a` and `b`, calculates their sum, and returns the result. The `return` keyword here is like a messenger that allows a function to send back a specific result or value after it has completed its task. It's like the function saying, "Here's what I found or calculated, and now you can use this information elsewhere in your code."

In the `main` function, we call the `greetPerson` function with the argument 'John', which prints 'Hello, John! How are you today?' to the console. Then, we call the `calculateSum` function with arguments 10 and 20 and store the result in the variable `result`. Finally, we print 'The sum is: 30' to the console.

As a note, a function argument in programming is like a special instruction or piece of information that you can give to a function, helping it perform a specific task or calculation.

Functions make code more organized, easier to maintain, and promote code reusability. You can define functions for various tasks in your program, making it more efficient and modular.

While functions have a wide range of use cases and are fundamental to programming, we won't go into a deep dive into them in this book. Our primary focus is on modern UI development using Flutter.

However, understanding functions is essential for building interactive and dynamic user interfaces. Functions play a significant role in organizing your code and making it more maintainable, efficient, and reusable. As we progress through this book, we'll utilize functions when necessary to enhance the UI development process and create engaging user experiences.

Object-Oriented Programming

Object-Oriented Programming (OOP) is a programming paradigm that allows us to model real-world entities as objects in our code. These objects have attributes (data) and behaviors (functions/methods) that define their characteristics and what they can do.

Think of objects as things you can see and interact with in the real world. For example, you can think of a car as an object. A car has attributes like color, model, and speed, and it can perform actions like accelerating and braking. In OOP, we can create a Car class that represents the blueprint for creating individual car objects.

A class is like a blueprint or a template for creating objects. It defines the attributes and behaviors that all objects of that class will have. Objects created from a class are known as instances.

Let's create a simple example to illustrate OOP in Dart:

```
// Define a Car class
class Car {
  String color;
  String model;
  int speed;

  // Method to accelerate the car
  void accelerate() {
    speed += 10;
    print('The car is now traveling at $speed km/h.');
  }

  // Method to brake the car
  void brake() {
    speed -= 5;
    print('The car is now traveling at $speed km/h.');
  }
}

void main() {
  // Create an instance of the Car class
  Car myCar = Car();
  myCar.color = 'Red';
  myCar.model = 'Sedan';
  myCar.speed = 60;

  // Call methods on the car instance
  myCar.accelerate(); // Output: The car is now traveling at 70 km/h.
  myCar.brake();      // Output: The car is now traveling at 65 km/h.
}
```

In this example, we define a `Car` class with attributes `color`, `model`, and `speed`, and two methods `accelerate` and `brake`. We create an instance of the `Car` class called `myCar` and set its attributes. Then we call the methods on the `myCar` instance to simulate the car accelerating and braking.

OOP allows us to organize our code into logical and reusable units, making it easier to understand, maintain, and extend. It's a powerful concept that forms the foundation of many modern programming languages, including Dart.

Exception Handling

This is a crucial concept in Dart programming that allows you to handle errors and unexpected situations in your code. Let's imagine a scenario where you are driving a car, and suddenly you encounter a roadblock. Instead of panicking, you follow a detour indicated by the road signs and safely reach your destination. Exception handling works similarly, providing a detour for your program to recover from unexpected errors and continue its execution.

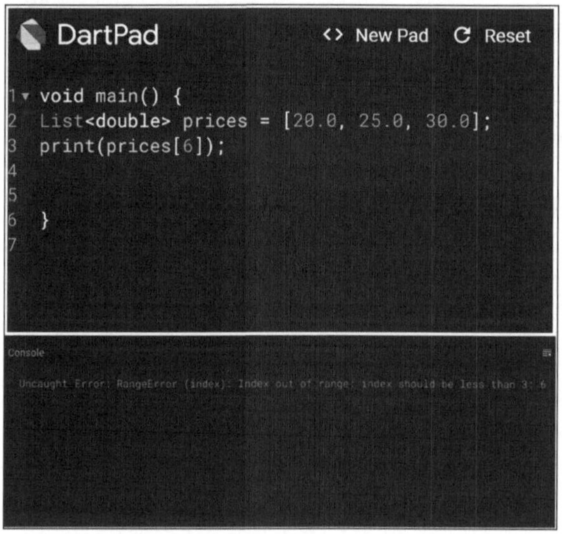

***Figure 2.3**: Dart index out of range*

Exceptions occur when something goes wrong during the program's execution, such as division by zero, accessing an invalid index on a list, or attempting to open a file that doesn't exist. When an exception occurs, it can disrupt the normal flow of your code and cause your program to crash.

Throw

`throw` is a powerful feature that allows you to raise exceptions in your code when an unexpected situation occurs. Imagine you are driving home, and suddenly you encounter serious traffic ahead. If you love your colleagues taking the same route, you will most likely alert them about the gridlock, so they can take the necessary actions. Throwing an exception in Dart is like signaling gridlock ahead to prevent the program from continuing under abnormal circumstances.

When you encounter an error or an exceptional condition in your code that you didn't anticipate, you can use the `throw` keyword to raise an exception. This signals to the Dart runtime that something unexpected has occurred, and the program cannot continue executing as usual.

Here's an example of how to use `throw` in Dart:

```
void depositMoney(double amount) {
  if (amount <= 0) {
    throw Exception('Invalid amount. Amount must be greater than 0.');
  }

  // Code to deposit the money into an account goes here.
  // ...
}
```

In this example, we have a function called `depositMoney` that takes an `amount` as a parameter. Before depositing the money, we check if the `amount` is greater than 0. If it's not, we use the `throw` keyword to raise an `Exception` with a specific error message.

When the `throw` statement is executed, it immediately stops the normal flow of the program and looks for an exception handler (try-catch block) to handle the raised exception. If no handler is found, the program will terminate and display the error message.

This approach allows you to gracefully handle error scenarios and provide meaningful feedback to users when something goes wrong. It's a critical tool for writing robust and reliable code, ensuring that your programs can handle unexpected situations with clarity.

Catch

This keyword is used in exception handling. Just like in my personal experience with cooking my special jollof rice recipe at home, there are times when the gas cooker temperature is too high. In such situations, instead of risking the food getting burned and causing a disaster in the kitchen, I quickly take action to adjust the temperature and prevent any mishaps.

In Dart, `catch` comes into play when an error, also known as an exception, occurs in your code. The `catch` keyword is used in conjunction with `try` and `finally` to handle exceptions and provide a safe fallback or alternative action when something goes wrong.

Here's an example of how to use `catch` in Dart:

```
void cookJollofRice() {
  try {
    // Code for cooking jollof rice
    measureIngredients();
    adjustGasCookerTemperature();
    stirPot();
    // ... other cooking steps
  } catch (e) {
    // Handle any cooking issues
    print('Oops! Something went wrong: $e');
    adjustCookingTechnique();
  }
}

void measureIngredients() {
  // Code to measure and add the ingredients
}

void adjustGasCookerTemperature() {
  // Code to adjust the gas cooker temperature
}

void stirPot() {
  // Code to stir the pot during cooking
}

void adjustCookingTechnique() {
  // Code to adjust the cooking technique
}
```

In this example, the try block contains the cooking steps for making jollof rice. If there's any problem during the cooking process, such as incorrect ingredient measurements or a sudden increase in gas cooker temperature, the catch block will handle the issue. It prints an error message, indicating that something went wrong, and suggests adjusting the cooking technique.

With this approach, your Jollof rice cooking experience becomes more robust. Instead of letting any mishaps ruin the meal, you can handle unexpected situations and make sure your delicious jollof rice turns out perfect every time!

Using `catch` in exception handling allows you to prevent your program from crashing when an unexpected situation arises. Instead of letting the program terminate abruptly, you can easily handle errors, provide meaningful feedback to users, or log the errors for debugging purposes.

Finally

In the context of cooking jollof rice, the `finally` block can be likened to the final steps you take after the cooking process is complete, regardless of whether everything went smoothly or if any issues occurred. Imagine that after you finish cooking the jollof rice and serve it on the dining table, there are still some essential tasks you need to attend to, like turning off the gas cooker, cleaning up the kitchen, and ensuring everything is set for a delightful meal.

In Dart, the `finally` block serves a similar purpose. It allows you to specify a code block that will always be executed, regardless of whether an exception occurred in the `try` block or if the code executed successfully without any issues.

Here's how the `finally` block works in Dart:

```
void cookJollofRice() {
  try {
    // Code for cooking jollof rice
    measureIngredients();
    adjustGasCookerTemperature();
    stirPot();
    // ... other cooking steps
  } catch (e) {
    // Handle any cooking issues
    print('Oops! Something went wrong: $e');
    adjustCookingTechnique();
  } finally {
    // Code that will always be executed
    cleanUpKitchen();
    turnOffGasCooker();
  }
}

void cleanUpKitchen() {
  // Code to clean up the kitchen after cooking
}

void turnOffGasCooker() {
  // Code to turn off the gas cooker after cooking
}
```

The `finally` block contains the functions `cleanUpKitchen` and `turnOffGasCooker`, which represent the final steps you take after cooking jollof rice. Regardless of whether there was any issue during the cooking process (in the `try` block) or if the code executed successfully without any exceptions, the code inside the `finally` block will always be executed.

This way, you can ensure that critical tasks are performed after the cooking process, just like turning off the gas cooker and cleaning up the kitchen after preparing a delicious meal. The `finally` block adds robustness to your code and allows you to handle various scenarios, making your Dart programs more reliable and maintainable.

Dart Null Safety

Let's imagine you're organizing a party, and you have a list of your friends who might attend. Each friend can either confirm they're coming (a definite value) or not say anything (null).

In the world of Dart without null safety, it's like preparing party jollof rice for each friend without knowing if they're actually coming or not. Sometimes, you might be giving jollof rice to someone who didn't even show up, leading to confusion.

Now, Dart's null safety is your party planner's assistant. It makes sure you only prepare party jollof rice for friends who confirmed they're coming. No more wondering if you're giving a favor to someone who's not there!

Here's how it looks in Dart code:

```
void main() {
  String? friendName; // This friend might come or might not (null).

  // Uncomment the next line to see Dart saying: "Hey, be careful,
friendName could be null!"
  // print(friendName.length);

  // But Dart is smart. If you check first, it's all good.
  if (friendName != null) {
    print('Party jollof rice for ${friendName} is ready!');
  } else {
    print('No party jollof rice because the friend is not confirmed.');
```

```
  }

  // Now, no matter if the friend is confirmed or not, your code won't
crash due to null issues.
}
```

Dart Best Practices

Best practices and coding style are essential to writing clean and maintainable Dart code. They help improve code readability, consistency, and collaboration among developers. Just like following a recipe with clear instructions, adhering to coding standards ensures that your Dart code is easy to understand, modify, and maintain.

Naming Conventions

Naming conventions help us choose meaningful and descriptive names for variables, functions, classes, and other identifiers in our code. This makes it easier for others (and ourselves) to understand the purpose and role of different elements in the code.

Here are some common naming conventions in Dart:

Variable Names

Use descriptive names that indicate the purpose or content of the variable. Use camelCase for variables, starting with a lowercase letter, and capitalize the first letter of each subsequent word.

```
// Good naming convention
int studentAge = 20;

// Avoid using single-letter or unclear names
int a = 20;
int sAge = 20;
```

Constant Names

Use uppercase letters and separate words with underscores for constants.

```
// Good naming convention
const double PI = 3.14;
```

```
// Avoid using lowercase or unclear names
const double pi = 3.14;
const double Pi = 3.14;
```

Function Names

Use verbs or verb phrases to indicate the action the function performs. Use camelCase for function names, starting with a lowercase letter.

```
// Good naming convention
int calculateSum(int a, int b) {
  return a + b;
}

// Avoid using unclear or unrelated names
int s(int a, int b) {
  return a + b;
}
```

Class Names

Use nouns or noun phrases to represent classes. Use PascalCase for class names, starting with an uppercase letter.

```
// Good naming convention
class Person {
  String name;
  int age;
}

// Avoid using verb or unclear names
class getName {
  String name;
}
```

The use of consistent and descriptive naming conventions makes the code more readable and easier to understand, which is especially important when collaborating with other developers on larger projects.

Code Formatting

This is an essential aspect of writing clean and maintainable Dart code. It refers to the consistent arrangement of code elements, such as indentation, line breaks, spacing, and alignment. Proper code formatting makes your code more readable and helps you and other developers understand the structure of the code at a glance.

Imagine you are organizing your shoe rack, and all the shoes are neatly arranged, aligned, and spaced evenly. This makes it easy for you to decide what shoes you will be wearing for an outing. Similarly, in Dart programming, code formatting ensures that your code is well-organized and easy to read, making it a breeze to navigate and understand. To make formatting simpler for developers, code editors such as Android Studio and Visual Studio Code have integrated an inbuilt code formatting feature with one click.

Let's explore some best practices for code formatting in Dart:

Indentation

Use two spaces for indentation. This helps visually separate code blocks and improves readability. Avoid using tabs, as they may cause inconsistencies across different text editors.

```
void main() {
  if (condition) {
    // Code block
  } else {
    // Another code block
  }
}
```

Line Breaks

Use line breaks to separate different logical sections of your code. This makes it easier to understand the flow of the program.

```
void main() {
  print('Hello, world!');

  // Some other code here

  print('Goodbye, world!');
}
```

Spacing

Add a single space after commas in function arguments and between operators. This enhances readability.

```
void printNumbers(int num1, int num2) {
  print('Number 1: $num1, Number 2: $num2');
}

int addNumbers(int a, int b) {
  return a + b;
}
```

Function Naming

Use meaningful names for functions that accurately describe their purpose. This makes your code more self-explanatory.

```
// Good naming
int calculateSum(int num1, int num2) {
  return num1 + num2;
}

// Avoid vague naming
int calc(int a, int b) {
  return a + b;
}
```

As you continue your journey in Dart programming, adhering to these coding style guidelines will become second nature, resulting in a cleaner and more elegant code.

Conclusion

Congratulations on completing this chapter! You've taken the first step towards becoming a skilled Dart developer and mastering the art of modern UI development with Flutter.

As you dive deeper into Dart, remember that learning a new programming language can be a challenging yet rewarding experience. You have to embrace the journey with curiosity and determination, just like the thrill of exploring new cities. Each line of code you write is a step towards creating beautiful and functional applications that will delight users and leave a lasting impact.

The road ahead may have its twists and turns, but the knowledge and skills you gain will empower you to bring your creative ideas to life and build innovative solutions. As you continue your learning journey, remember that every great developer starts with the basics.

Onward to the next chapter, where we'll dive into the captivating world of building beautiful and responsive UI designs with Flutter. Happy coding!

Assessment

Calculate the Perimeter of a Square

Given a rectangle with a length of 5.0 units and a width of 3.0 units, what is the area of the rectangle?

Steps to Complete the Task on DartPad:

1. **Open DartPad:**

   Go to https://dartpad.dev/ to access DartPad in your web browser.

2. **Define Variables:**

   Inside the `main()` function, declare two variables for the length and width of the rectangle and assign their values. For example:

   ```
   void main() {
     double length = 5.0;
     double width = 3.0;
   }
   ```

3. **Calculate the Area:**

   Add another variable to store the area of the rectangle. Use the formula `area = length * width` to calculate the area. For example:

   ```
   void main() {
     double length = 5.0;
     double width = 3.0;

     double area = length * width;
   }
   ```

4. **Display the Result:**

   Use the `print()` function to display the calculated area on the console. For example:

```
void main() {
  double length = 5.0;
  double width = 3.0;

  double area = length * width;
  print('The area of the rectangle is: $area');
}
```

5. **Run the Code:**

   Click the **`Run`** button on DartPad to execute the code. Take a screenshot of your solution and share it on social media, tagging me (@ temidayoadefioye). Let the world see your first solution on DartPad!

   That's it! You've successfully completed the task of calculating the area of a rectangle using DartPad. You can make changes to the output by adjusting the values stored in the length and width variables, running the code again, and seeing the new result.

Find the Sum of Even Numbers using Dart

Write a Dart program that calculates the sum of all even numbers from 1 to 10 and displays the result.

Steps to Complete the Task on DartPad:

1. **Open DartPad:**

   Go to https://dartpad.dev/ to access DartPad in your web browser.

2. **Define Function:**

   Create a function called `` `sumOfEvenNumbers` `` to find the sum of even numbers. The function should take no parameters and return an integer value.

3. **Calculate Sum:**

   Inside the function, use a `` `for` `` loop to iterate through numbers from 1 to 10. For each number, check if it is even (divisible by 2), and if so, add it to a running sum.

4. **Display the Result:**

   After the `` `for` `` loop, use the `` `print()` `` function to display the calculated sum of even numbers on the console.

5. **Run the Code:**

   Click the **`Run`** button on DartPad to execute the code. Take a screenshot of your solution and share it on social media, tagging me (@ temidayoadefioye). Let the world see your first solution on DartPad!

Points to Remember

- Dart is a modern, object-oriented programming language designed for creating web, mobile, and server applications.
- The `main()` function serves as the entry point for a Dart program, just like the referee's whistle starts a football match.
- DartPad is an online tool that allows you to write, run, and experiment with Dart code directly in your web browser.
- Dart has various data types, such as integers, doubles, strings, booleans, lists, and maps, that are used to store different types of data.
- Dart supports various operators, such as arithmetic, assignment, comparison, logical, and bitwise operators to perform different operations.
- Control flow statements like `if-else` and loops (`for` and `while`) help control the flow of the program based on conditions.
- Comments in Dart are used to provide explanations and notes within the code to make it more readable and understandable.
- The `try`, `catch`, and `finally` blocks are used for exception handling to gracefully handle errors and perform cleanup tasks when necessary.

Answers

Question 2

```
// Function to find the sum of even numbers from 1 to 10
int sumOfEvenNumbers() {
  // Initialize a variable to hold the sum
  int sum = 0;

  // Use a for loop to iterate through numbers from 1 to 10
  for (int i = 1; i <= 10; i++) {
    // Check if the number is even
    if (i % 2 == 0) {
      // If it's even, add it to the sum
      sum += i;
    }
```

```
  }

  // Return the final sum
  return sum;
}

void main() {
  // Call the function to find the sum of even numbers from 1 to 10
  int sum = sumOfEvenNumbers();

  // Display the result
  print('The sum of even numbers from 1 to 10 is: $sum');
}
```

In this code, we define a function called `sumOfEvenNumbers` that finds the sum of even numbers from 1 to 10 using a `for` loop and conditional statements. We then call this function from the `main()` function and display the result using the `print()` function.

Key terms

- **Main Function:** The entry point for Dart programs which are automatically executed when the program starts running.
- **DartPad:** An online tool that allows you to write, run, and experiment with Dart code directly in your web browser.
- **Data Types:** The different categories of data that can be stored in variables, such as integers, doubles, strings, booleans, lists, and maps.
- **Comments:** Annotations or notes written within code to provide explanations, documentation, or reminders for developers.
- **Operators:** Symbols used to perform operations on data, including arithmetic, assignment, comparison, logical, and bitwise operators.
- **Control Flow Statements:** Statements that determine the flow of execution in a program, such as `if`, `else`, and loops (`for`, `while`).
- **Asynchronous Programming:** Allows concurrent execution of tasks without blocking other code, used for time-consuming operations.
- **JIT (Just-In-Time):** Compiles Dart code to machine code at runtime for fast development and debugging.
- **AOT (Ahead-Of-Time):** Compiles Dart code to machine code ahead of time for optimized and faster execution in production.

- **Futures:** Represents the result of potentially asynchronous operations and handles delayed values.
- **Async/Await Syntax:** Modern way of writing readable asynchronous code, using `async` and `await` keywords.
- **Dart VM (Virtual Machine):** Runtime environment executing Dart code on various platforms.
- **Garbage Collector:** Mechanism automatically managing memory, preventing leaks, and ensuring efficient memory usage.

Further Reading

- Operators
  - https://dart.dev/language/operators
- Dart Object Oriented Programming
  - https://dart-tutorial.com/object-oriented-programming/
- Asynchronous programming: futures, async, await
  - https://dart.dev/codelabs/async-await

CHAPTER 3

Exploring Flutter Widgets and UI Elements

In the previous chapter, we briefly explored Flutter widgets as a core concept. Now, in this chapter, we're going to dive into the world of Flutter widgets in much greater detail. We'll uncover their versatility, understand their functionalities, and explore how to use them effectively to craft beautiful and responsive user interfaces.

Widgets are the fundamental building blocks of user interfaces. Everything you see on the screen, from buttons and text fields to complex layouts and animations, is represented by widgets. Whether you're creating a simple app or a sophisticated user interface, understanding widgets is essential.

Widgets can be compared to LEGO bricks. Just as you use LEGO bricks to construct various structures and shapes, you use widgets in Flutter to design and construct your app's user interface. Each widget is a self-contained component that can be combined and nested with other widgets to create more complex and interactive elements.

The beauty of widgets lies in their flexibility and reusability. Flutter comes with a rich set of pre-built widgets that you can use as building blocks, and you can also create your own custom widgets to suit your specific needs.

Structure

In this chapter, the following topics will be covered:

- Introduction to different types of Flutter widgets
- Working with basic layout widgets (Container, Row, and Column)
- Exploring text and image widgets
- Handling user input with Flutter widgets (Button, TextField)
- Introduction to stateful and stateless widgets

Introducing Flutter Widgets

Imagine you're building a house, and each room represents a different part of your app's user interface. In Flutter, these rooms are called widgets. Just like in a house where you have different furniture and decorations in each room, Flutter widgets are the visual and interactive elements that make up your app's UI.

Widgets in Flutter are like building blocks that you can assemble to create your desired app design. They range from simple components like buttons and text fields to more complex layouts and animations. Think of widgets as the tools in your toolbox that allow you to craft beautiful and functional user interfaces.

What makes Flutter widgets exciting is their ability to be dynamic and responsive. Just like you can rearrange furniture or change the color of a room, widgets can adapt and respond to user interactions or changes in data. They give your app a lively and interactive feel, making it more engaging for users.

In Flutter, widgets follow a parent-child relationship, forming a hierarchical structure known as the widget tree. The root widget acts as the foundation, and each child widget builds upon it, creating a structured and organized UI. This tree-like structure allows you to easily manage and control the flow of information and actions within your app.

The beauty of Flutter widgets lies in their declarative nature. Rather than specifying the exact steps to create a UI, you describe what you want the UI to look like based on the current state of your app. Flutter takes care of the rest, automatically updating the UI to reflect any changes in the state.

As a Flutter developer, it's essential to grasp the concept of widgets early on because they play a central role in the Flutter framework. With widgets, you can build visually appealing and responsive UIs that work seamlessly across multiple platforms.

Exploring the Widget Catalog

This is a treasure trove of pre-built widgets that cater to various functionalities, designs, and user interactions. These widgets are categorized based on their specific purposes, making it easier for developers to find the right components for their app's user interface. As the Flutter framework evolves, the widget catalog continues to expand, introducing new widgets to enhance the capabilities of your applications.

Basic Widgets

As we dive deeper into Flutter, it's essential to understand the basic building blocks that form the foundation of your app's user interface. These basic widgets are the fundamental elements that enable you to create engaging and interactive layouts. In this section, we will explore the Basics widget catalog, which comprises widgets that are crucial for building user interfaces. These widgets serve as the starting point for crafting your app's layout, structure, and interaction. Let's take a closer look at some of the essential widgets within this category:

Scaffold

Imagine building a house. Before you add all the details and furnishings, you need a solid foundation. In Flutter, the `Scaffold` widget plays the role of the foundation for your app's user interface. It provides the basic structure and layout that forms the backbone of your app's screens.

The `Scaffold` widget acts as a container for various components that make up your app's UI, such as the `AppBar`, body content, floating action button, and more. It brings together these elements to create a cohesive and organized user interface.

Let's break down the key components and features of the `Scaffold` widget:

See *Figure 3.1: Sections marked in rectangles are scaffold components.*

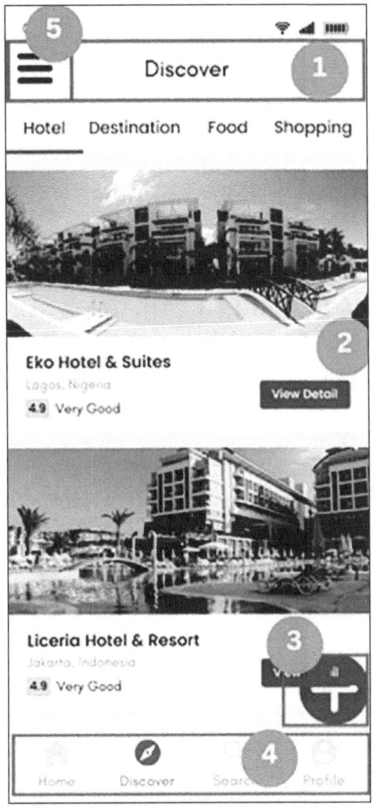

***Figure 3.1**: Scaffold components*

1. **AppBar**

   The `AppBar` sits at the top of the screen and often contains the app's title, navigation icons, and other actions. The `Scaffold` widget lets you easily include an `AppBar` as its top section.

2. **Body Content**

   The main content of your screen resides within the body of the `Scaffold`. It can hold various widgets like text, images, lists, and even other layout structures. This is where you present the core information and interactions to your users.

3. **Floating Action Button (FAB)**

   The `Scaffold` also provides a dedicated spot for the floating action button (FAB). This button is usually circular and prominently placed to trigger a primary action, such as adding a new item or initiating a key interaction in your app.

4. **Bottom Navigation Bar**

   If your app uses a bottom navigation bar to switch between different sections or views, the `Scaffold` supports integrating this navigation element as well. The bottom navigation bar is commonly used in apps with multiple screens or functionalities.

5. **Drawer**

   The `Scaffold` can also include a side drawer, accessible through a menu icon. The drawer provides additional navigation options or settings that users can access without leaving the current screen.

6. **Styling and Theming**

   Through the `Scaffold` widget, you can easily apply consistent styling and theming to your app's UI elcments. This ensures that your app maintains a cohesive look and feel across different screens and interactions. Don't worry, later in this book, we will discuss styling and theming in depth.

AppBar

The `AppBar` stands as a versatile and fundamental element for creating effective navigation and enhancing the functionality of your app. Think of it as a navigational hub that holds various components to improve the user experience and interaction.

The `AppBar` widget typically resides at the top of the screen and provides users with quick access to essential actions, navigation, and information. It often includes features like the app's title, navigation icons, and optional widgets like a `TabBar` or a `FlexibleSpaceBar`.

Let's break down the key components and features of the `AppBar` widget:

See *Figure 3.2: App widget marked in rectangles.*

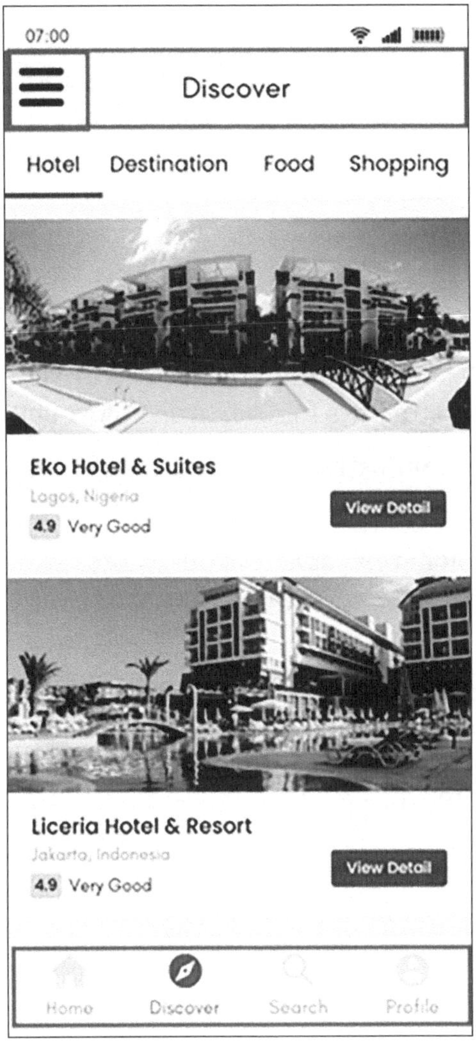

***Figure 3.2**: Appbar widget*

1. **App Title**

   The app title is the main text displayed on the `AppBar`, indicating the name or purpose of the app. It helps users identify the app they are using and sets the context for the content.

2. **Leading and Trailing Icons**

   The `AppBar` can accommodate icons on both the leading and trailing sides. These icons are often used for navigation, actions, or menus. For example, the back arrow icon (leading icon) is commonly used to navigate back to the previous screen.

3. **Actions**

   Actions are additional icons placed on the `AppBar` for performing specific tasks or actions within the app. These can include actions like searching, settings, sharing, and more. Actions provide users with convenient shortcuts to common functionalities.

4. **Bottom Area Widgets**

   The bottom area of the `AppBar` is perfect for accommodating additional widgets, such as a `TabBar` or a `FlexibleSpaceBar`. The `TabBar` allows users to switch between different sections or views of the app, while the `FlexibleSpaceBar` allows for creative and dynamic design elements.

5. **Styling and Customization**

   You can customize the appearance of the `AppBar` by adjusting its background color, text styles, icon colors, and more. This flexibility enables you to create an `AppBar` that matches your app's branding and design.

To implement the `AppBar` widget, you typically include it as part of the `Scaffold` widget, which provides the overall structure of your app's layout. By using the `AppBar`, you enhance your app's navigation and user experience, making it easier for users to interact with your app's features and content.

Container

Over the past few years, I've been fortunate to collaborate with interior designers, and there's a distinct flair to their approach to crafting captivating interiors. It's not just about arranging furniture randomly; they meticulously plan layouts, select colors, and ensure a cohesive design. In Flutter, think of the `Container` widget as your design palette–a tool that empowers you to elegantly structure and embellish your UI components, much like an interior designer does.

The `Container` widget is incredibly versatile, serving as a fundamental building block for your app's layout and visual appearance. Let's dive into its capabilities and features:

1. **Layout Control**

   At its core, the `Container` widget provides control over how your child widget is positioned within it. You can use properties like `alignment`, `margin`, `padding`, and `constraints` to determine the placement and spacing of your content.

2. **Size Control**

   Need to set specific dimensions for your widget? The `Container` widget allows you to define the width and height of your child widget. You can also use constraints to create responsive designs that adapt to different screen sizes.

3. **Decoration**

   A beautiful room isn't complete without paint and decorations. Similarly, the `Container` widget allows you to apply visual enhancements through its `decoration` property. You can set background colors, gradients, borders, shadows, and more to create a visually appealing UI.

4. **Child Alignment**

   Inside a `Container`, you can align its child widget using properties like `alignment` and `childAlignment`. This ensures that your content is positioned precisely where you want it within the container.

5. **Child Constraints**

   The `Container` widget also provides the option to constrain its child widget's size using the `constraints` property. This can be particularly useful when you want to limit the size of your content within a certain space.

6. **Transformations**

   Just as a room might need rearranging, you can transform the contents of a `Container` using properties like `transform` and `transformAlignment`. This allows you to rotate, scale, or translate your child widget.

7. **Alignment and Padding Shorthand**

   To make your code more concise, the `Container` widget offers shorthand properties like `alignment`, `padding`, `margin`, and more. This makes it easier to quickly adjust the layout and spacing of your UI.

The `Container` widget's flexibility and range of features make it an essential tool for creating well-organized, visually pleasing UIs. As we delve into various sections of this chapter, you'll have the opportunity to witness the `Container` widget in action. We'll use it to craft engaging UI elements, structure layouts, and enhance the overall visual appeal of our app components. So, keep an eye out for how the `Container` widget takes center stage in creating beautifully designed and well-organized Flutter interfaces.

Column

Imagine you're stacking books on a shelf. Each book is a different piece of information, yet they all need to fit neatly within the shelf's space. Similarly, in Flutter, the `Column` widget serves as a vertical arrangement tool for your UI elements.

When you use a `Column`, you're essentially creating a vertical list of widgets that are stacked on top of each other, one after the other. Just like how books have different heights, each widget in a `Column` can have its own size and proportions. This arrangement is particularly useful when you want to present information in a structured and readable format, such as a list of messages, user details, or navigation options.

See *Figure 3.3: Column widget Marked in rectangle*:

***Figure 3.3**: Column widget Marked in red rectangle*

Flexible Layouts and Alignment

Much like adjusting the spacing between your books on a shelf, you can control the spacing between widgets within a `Column`. You can also align these widgets to your liking–be it at the start, center, or end of the column–using alignment properties.

Widgets within Widgets

Don't forget that you can place any widget you like within a `Column`. Whether it's text, images, buttons, or even other containers, you can stack them up for a clear and organized presentation.

As you progress through this chapter, we'll take a deeper dive into the `Column` widget, exploring its various properties and use cases. So, if you're curious to learn more about how to fine-tune your vertical layouts, you're in for a ride! Keep an eye out for upcoming sections where we'll explore the intricacies of the `Column` widget and its versatile applications.

Row

Let's take a closer look at the `Row` widget with a relatable illustration. Imagine you have a shoe rack where you neatly arrange your shoes in a row. Each pair of shoes occupies a designated spot, and you can easily add or remove shoes as needed. In the world of Flutter, the `Row` widget functions in a similar way—it allows you to arrange UI elements horizontally, just like those shoes on a rack.

Here's a comprehensive explanation of how the `Row` widget works:

1. **Horizontal Arrangement:** The primary purpose of the `Row` widget is to place its child widgets in a horizontal line. This is particularly useful when you want to display items side by side, such as buttons, text, or images.
2. **Main Axis Alignment:** You have the power to define how the children are aligned along the main axis, which runs horizontally for a `Row`. This alignment can be set to the start, center, end, or even space evenly between the items.
3. **Cross Axis Alignment:** Similar to the main axis, the cross-axis alignment determines how the children align vertically. This ensures that your items are not only arranged side by side but also consistently aligned in a straight line vertically.
4. **Distributing Space:** When dealing with varying sizes of UI elements, you can use the `Expanded` or `Flexible` widgets to distribute available space among the children. This is akin to having adjustable shelves on your shoe rack for larger or smaller shoes.
5. **Adding Spacing:** Using the `mainAxisAlignment` and `crossAxisAlignment` properties, you can control the spacing between the children. Think of it as arranging your shoes with uniform gaps to ensure they look neat and well-organized.

Much like the meticulous arrangement of shoes on a rack, the `Row` widget in Flutter allows you to create visually pleasing and responsive layouts.

As we delve further into this chapter, we'll take a deeper dive into the `Row` widget, exploring its properties, customization options, and practical examples.

Image

Visual content is crucial for engaging users. This is where the `Image` widget steps in. The `Image` widget in Flutter allows you to display various types of images, from local assets to network images, enhancing your app's visual appeal.

See *Figure 3.4: Image widget displaying image assets*

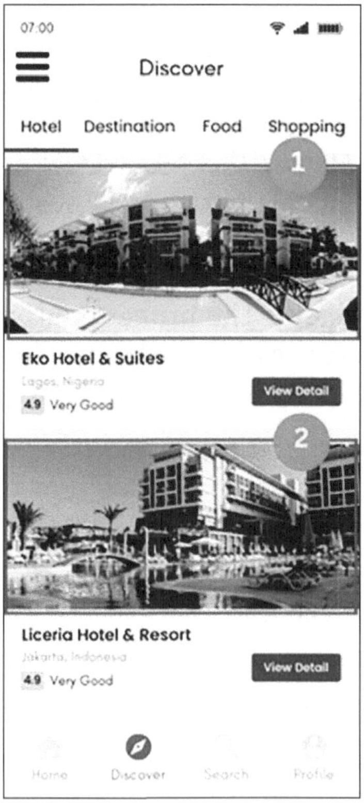

Figure 3.4: *Image widget*

Local Assets:

You can use the `Image.asset` constructor to display images stored locally within your app's assets directory. These assets can include images, icons, and more. The `Image.asset` constructor requires you to provide the asset's path as a string.

Network Images:

For images hosted on the internet, the `Image.network` constructor is your go-to option. By providing the image URL as a string, this constructor fetches and displays the image directly from the web.

Memory Images:

In some cases, you might want to display images directly from memory. The `Image.memory` constructor is designed for this purpose. It takes a `Uint8List` as its argument, allowing you to display images stored in bytes.

Fit and Alignment:

The `fit` property of the `Image` widget lets you control how the image should be fitted within its parent widget. You can choose from options like `BoxFit.cover`, `BoxFit.contain`, and more. Additionally, the `alignment` property helps you align the image within its container.

Placeholder and Error Handling:

To handle scenarios when the image isn't available or is still loading, you can use the `Image.asset` or `Image.network` constructors' `placeholder` and `errorBuilder` properties. These allow you to display placeholders or custom error messages when needed.

Performance Optimization:

Images can consume a significant amount of resources, impacting app performance. To optimize this, consider using tools like the `flutter_svg` package for scalable vector graphics or cached image solutions like the `cached_network_image` package for efficient loading of network images.

As you continue your journey through this chapter, you'll have the opportunity to work with images and these tools in practical scenarios that bring your UI to life.

Text

Text is a fundamental component of any app's user interface. The `Text` widget is your tool to display textual content, such as titles, labels, descriptions, and more. It allows you to control various aspects of text presentation, such as font, style, alignment, and more.

See *Figure 3.5: Texts displayed using text widget*

***Figure* 3.5**: *Text widget*

Basic Usage:

The `Text` widget is straightforward to use. You provide the text content as a string in its `text` property. This string is what will be displayed on the screen.

Styling:

Textual content in an app often requires specific styling to enhance its readability and visual appeal. The `style` property of the `Text` widget allows you to customize various aspects of the text, including font size, color, weight, and more.

Text Alignment:

The `textAlign` property lets you control the alignment of the text within its container. You can choose from options like left, center, right, and justify.

Text Direction:

In languages that are read from right to left, you can use the `textDirection` property to ensure the text is displayed correctly.

Text Overflow:

When the available space is limited, text may be truncated. The `overflow` property helps you manage how text overflow is handled, whether by clipping, ellipsis, or fading.

Rich Text:

For more complex text layouts, such as inline formatting or mixed styles, you can use the `RichText` widget. This widget allows you to apply different styles to different parts of the text.

Accessibility:

Text is not just about visual presentation; it's also about making content accessible to all users. You can use the `Semantics` widget to provide a description or label for screen readers, ensuring your app is inclusive.

Internationalization (i18n):

When building apps for a global audience, you might need to display text in different languages. The `intl` package can assist you in managing the internationalization and localization of text.

The `Text` widget serves as the foundation for displaying textual content in your app. As you continue your journey through this chapter, you'll have opportunities to work with the `Text` widget in practical scenarios that demonstrate its flexibility and utility.

ElevatedButton

User interfaces are built not only for displaying information but also for user interaction. The `ElevatedButton` widget in Flutter serves as a core component for creating interactive buttons that users can tap or click. These buttons are often used to trigger actions, navigate to other screens, or submit forms.

See *Figure 3.6: Login button using* **ElevatedButton** *widget*

Figure 3.6: *ElevatedButton widget*

Basic Usage:

The `ElevatedButton` widget is straightforward to use. You define its child widget, which is typically a `Text` widget, to display the label of the button. When the user taps or clicks the button, it triggers an action that you specify through its `onPressed` property.

Styling:

Just like the `Text` widget, you can customize the appearance of the `ElevatedButton` using the `style` property. You can adjust properties like text style, background color, padding, and more to match your app's design.

Elevation:

The name "ElevatedButton" implies a sense of depth, and that's exactly what the elevation property controls. You can adjust how much the button stands out from its surroundings by setting the elevation value.

Focus and Accessibility:

Interactive elements should provide a good user experience for all users, including those who navigate with a keyboard or assistive technologies. The `ElevatedButton` automatically handles focus, making it easier for keyboard users to interact with your app. To enhance accessibility, consider providing a label or description for the button using the `Semantics` widget.

Disabled State:

Buttons might need to be disabled in certain scenarios, such as when the user hasn't provided the required input. The `ElevatedButton` supports a `disabled` state that visually indicates to users that the button cannot be interacted with.

Customization:

While the default styling of `ElevatedButton` is suitable for many scenarios, you can also create highly customized buttons by wrapping the `ElevatedButton` with other widgets like `Container`, `Ink`, or `ClipRRect`.

Tap Feedback:

When the user taps an `ElevatedButton`, it provides visual feedback by changing its appearance temporarily. This visual feedback helps users understand that their interaction was registered.

As you progress through this chapter, you'll have the opportunity to see the `ElevatedButton` in action and explore how it can enhance your app's interactivity.

SizedBox

The **SizedBox** widget is a simple yet powerful tool for adjusting the dimensions and spacing of your UI elements. Let's explore its functionality and how it can be used effectively.

What is the `SizedBox` Widget?

The `SizedBox` widget is used to define a fixed size for its child widget. It's particularly useful when you need to create precise spacing between elements or enforce specific dimensions for UI components.

How Does it Work?

The `SizedBox` widget takes two main parameters: `width` and `height`. By specifying these parameters, you can control the size of the `SizedBox` and consequently, the size of its child widget.

Common Use Cases

- **Spacing:** You can use a `SizedBox` to create consistent spacing between UI elements. For instance, if you want to place a fixed gap between two buttons, you can wrap them in a `Row` and insert a `SizedBox` between them.
- **Enforcing Dimensions:** When you need to ensure that a widget occupies a specific space on the screen, the `SizedBox` is your go-to solution. For example, you can use it to guarantee that an image maintains a certain height and width.
- **Layout Alignment:** To achieve a balanced layout, you might use `SizedBox` to add empty space around a central widget. This is particularly useful when designing responsive interfaces.

When to Use `SizedBox`

The `SizedBox` widget is handy in scenarios where you want to exert precise control over spacing and dimensions. However, it's important to use it thoughtfully and avoid excessive usage, as it can hinder the natural flexibility of Flutter's layout system.

While `SizedBox` is great for creating fixed dimensions, Flutter also offers flexible layout widgets like `Row`, `Column`, and `Container` that adapt to different screen sizes and orientations. It's crucial to strike a balance between fixed and flexible layout components for optimal responsiveness.

Input Widgets

User interaction plays a pivotal role in creating engaging and dynamic applications. Users expect more than just static screens; they want to interact with your app, provide input, and see meaningful responses. This is where input widgets come into play.

Imagine a messaging app without a text input field or a fitness app without a way to record your workouts. These are scenarios where input widgets shine. Flutter, with its versatile and comprehensive set of input widgets, empowers developers to build interactive and responsive user interfaces with ease.

Autocomplete Widget

In many applications, user input is a key element. However, as the complexity of the app and the potential input options increase, providing a smooth and efficient input experience becomes crucial. The `Autocomplete` widget in Flutter addresses this challenge by offering a way to suggest and complete user input based on a predefined set of options.

See *Figure 3.7: A basic app with Autocomplete widget*

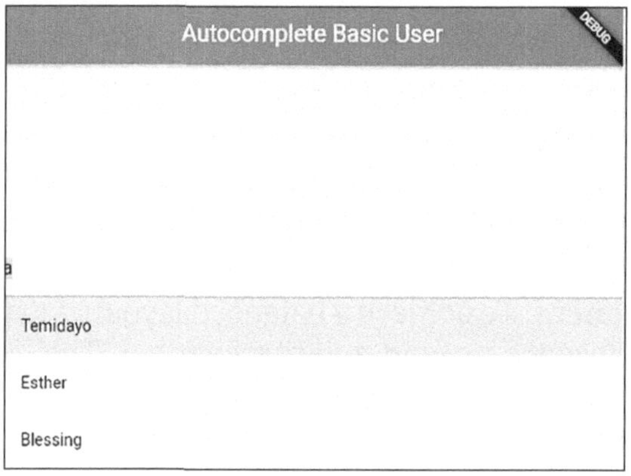

***Figure 3.7**: Autocomplete widget*

Functionality

The `Autocomplete` widget is designed to work with text input fields. As the user types, the widget presents a dropdown-like menu of suggested completions based on the entered text. This feature is particularly useful when dealing with a long list of items or complex input patterns. Users can select a suggestion from the dropdown, which can be directly inserted into the input field, saving them time and reducing the risk of errors.

Usage

Implementing the `Autocomplete` widget involves providing a list of possible completions (`options`) and a callback function that filters and sorts these options based on the current input. You can customize the appearance of the suggestions list, control the maximum number of suggestions shown, and determine how the selected completion is displayed in the input field.

User Experience

The `Autocomplete` widget enhances the user experience by offering real-time suggestions that help users find the right input quickly. It's particularly useful when dealing with data that users might not be familiar with, such as selecting a location from a list of cities, choosing a product from an inventory, or picking a contact from an address book.

Accessibility

When implementing the `Autocomplete` widget, consider accessibility. Ensure that the suggestions list is navigable using keyboard controls, and provide appropriate labels or descriptions for the suggestions using the `Semantics` widget.

Customization

While the basic functionality of the `Autocomplete` widget serves a wide range of scenarios, you can also customize its behavior and appearance. For instance, you can control how the suggestions are sorted, highlight matches in the suggestions, and even provide your own custom widget for each suggestion.

Practical Examples

Think of an app that allows users to search for books by entering the author's name. As the user types, the `Autocomplete` widget can offer a list of author names that match the input, helping the user quickly find the desired author without typing the full name.

The `Autocomplete` widget simplifies user input by providing real-time suggestions based on a predefined list of options. With the use of this widget, you can improve the accuracy and efficiency of data entry in your app, resulting in a more user-friendly and intuitive experience. As you continue exploring this chapter, you'll gain hands-on experience with the `Autocomplete` widget and discover its potential for enhancing your app's input capabilities.

Form

In any app that requires user input, data validation, and management play a critical role in maintaining data integrity and providing a seamless user experience. The

`Form` widget in Flutter serves as a fundamental building block for creating forms that efficiently handle user input, validate data, and manage form submissions.

See *Figure 3.8: A sign-in form with a Form widget*

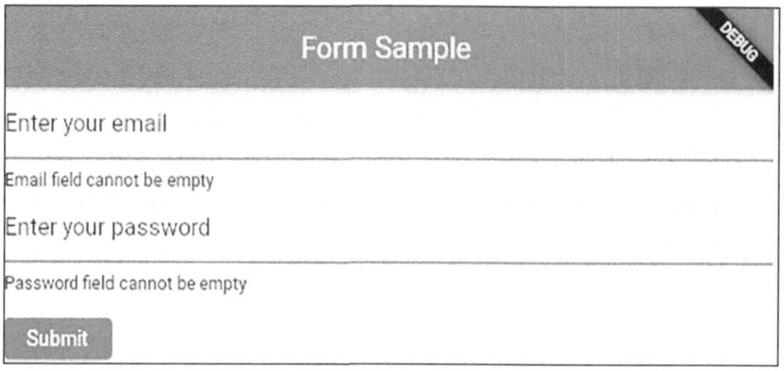

***Figure 3.8**: Form widget*

Purpose and Functionality

The primary purpose of the `Form` widget is to manage the state and validation of multiple input fields collectively. It enables developers to group related form fields and applies validation logic to ensure the correctness of user-provided data. When a user submits the form, the `Form` widget aggregates the data from its fields and exposes it to the app for processing.

Usage

To implement a `Form`, you typically wrap the form's input fields (such as text fields, checkboxes, and radio buttons) within the `Form` widget. Each input field is associated with a unique `FormField` widget, which encapsulates the logic for validation, error handling, and data submission. The `Form` widget also provides mechanisms to trigger validation and submission, either through user interaction or programmatic control.

Validation

The `Form` widget integrates seamlessly with Flutter's validation framework. Each `FormField` widget can define its own validation rules by providing a validation function. When the user interacts with the form, the `Form` widget automatically validates the input data and displays error messages if needed. This helps users understand and correct input errors before submitting the form.

User Experience

The `Form` widget significantly improves the user experience by ensuring that the data entered is accurate and consistent. As users interact with the form, real-time validation and error messages guide them toward correct input. This eliminates the need for users to correct mistakes after form submission and reduces frustration.

Practical Examples

Imagine you're building a registration form for an event. The form may include fields like name, email address, phone number, and a checkbox to accept terms and conditions. By using the `Form` widget, you can manage the input fields' state, validate the email address format, require all fields to be filled, and present error messages to users if they forget to enter a required field or provide an invalid email.

Accessibility

When creating forms, accessibility considerations are crucial. Ensure that error messages are conveyed clearly to users with visual impairments and that interactive elements, like checkboxes and radio buttons, are properly labeled for screen readers.

In summary, the `Form` widget plays a crucial role in managing user input, data validation, and form submission in your Flutter apps. As you continue exploring Flutter's UI elements, mastering the `Form` widget will enable you to create robust and well-structured forms that enhance your app's usability and reliability.

Accessibility Widgets

Imagine you are a Flutter developer, tasked with creating a cutting-edge music streaming app for a client. You invest your time and expertise in building an app with stunning visuals and an exceptional user experience. The app looks fantastic, and you're confident it will be a hit among users.

As the app enters the beta testing phase, the team receives valuable feedback. Unfortunately, some users encountered challenges while using the app. Upon investigation, you discover that the app lacks accessibility features, making it difficult for visually impaired users to navigate and interact with the interface effectively.

To ensure that your app is inclusive and user-friendly for all users, including those with disabilities, you'll need to leverage accessibility widgets.

So what are accessibility widgets? They are a set of powerful tools designed to make your app accessible to all users, regardless of their abilities or disabilities. These widgets enhance the user experience for individuals with visual, auditory, cognitive, or motor impairments, allowing them to interact with your app effectively.

With the help of these widgets, you can add semantic information to your user interface, enabling screen readers to describe the content accurately. This is particularly helpful for users with visual impairments who rely on screen readers to navigate apps.

The story of the music streaming app just reinforced the essence of having accessibility as part of requirements from the outset of the development process. Neglecting accessibility can lead to the exclusion of a significant portion of potential users, resulting in negative feedback and potentially lost business opportunities.

As an app developer, it's your responsibility to ensure that all users can enjoy a seamless experience, regardless of their abilities. Accessibility widgets empower you to meet this goal and provide a positive and meaningful user experience for everyone.

Semantics

This is a fundamental component of accessibility in Flutter. It provides a way to add semantic information to your app's user interface, making it accessible to users with visual impairments who rely on screen readers.

With the `` `Semantics` `` widget, you can assign a label, hint, and other properties to various UI elements, such as buttons, text fields, images, and more. When a screen reader encounters a `` `Semantics` `` widget, it can read the assigned label and hint, enabling users to understand the purpose and functionality of the element.

ExcludeSemantics

While `` `Semantics` `` widgets are essential for providing useful information to screen readers, some UI elements may not require explicit descriptions. In such cases, you can use the `` `ExcludeSemantics` `` widget to prevent the inclusion of unnecessary semantics for specific widgets.

MergeSemantics

When combining multiple UI elements that share the same semantics, you can use the `` `MergeSemantics` `` widget to merge their accessibility semantics into a single entity. This prevents screen readers from reading repetitive information, improving the overall user experience.

Reconciliation and Hot Reload

Imagine you're rearranging the furniture in your living room. You decide to swap the positions of the sofa and the coffee table. As you move them around, you're making sure that the room's new layout matches your vision. Similarly, in Flutter, the process of keeping your UI in sync with your logic is known as reconciliation.

When you update your app's state or trigger a change in your UI, Flutter's reconciliation mechanism kicks into action. This process involves comparing the new version of your Widget Tree (representing your updated UI design) with the existing Element Tree (the runtime representation of your UI on the screen).

During this process, Flutter identifies the differences between the two trees. It figures out which parts of your UI need to be updated, added, or removed. This orchestration is vital for maintaining a consistent and efficient user experience. Flutter's smart reconciliation ensures that only the necessary changes are applied to your UI, minimizing unnecessary re-renders and improving performance.

Hot Reload is one of Flutter's most remarkable features. It allows you to see the impact of your code changes in real-time, without restarting your app. When you make alterations to your code and trigger Hot Reload, Flutter efficiently updates the Widget Tree, applies reconciliation, and refreshes the UI accordingly.

It empowers developers to iterate and experiment swiftly. It's like having a direct line of communication between your code and the UI. Whether you're adjusting the layout, tweaking colors, or fine-tuning animations, Hot Reload accelerates your development process by providing instant feedback.

This dynamic workflow encourages creativity, experimentation, and rapid refinement. It's akin to the freedom an artist has to explore different strokes on a canvas without the hindrance of constant setup.

Reconciliation and Hot Reload are like good friends. The former ensures that your UI remains synchronized with your logic, while the latter grants you the power to observe changes instantly and to iterate faster.

Working with Containers: Building Your Layouts

The `Container` widget is your design toolkit. It's like the master builder that helps you structure and style your UI elements with precision. Whether you're creating simple designs or complex layouts, the `Container` is your trusty tool for the job.

Step 1: Set Up Your Environment

Before we dive into creating a `Container`, make sure you have a Flutter project set up. If you don't have one, create a new project or use an existing one.

Step 2: Creating a Basic Container

Let's start by creating a basic `Container`. Imagine you're designing a card element for a weather app. You want a card that displays the temperature for the day. Here's how you can use a `Container` to achieve this:

***Figure 3.9**: Basic Container*

1. Open your Flutter project in your preferred code editor.
2. Locate the main function in your **main.dart** file.

Step 3: Add the Code Snippet

Replace or add the following code snippet in your **main.dart** file:

```
import 'package:flutter/material.dart';

void main() {
  runApp(const MyApp());
}

class MyApp extends StatelessWidget {
  const MyApp({Key? key}) : super(key: key);

  @override
  Widget build(BuildContext context) {
    return MaterialApp(
      home: Scaffold(
```

```
        appBar: AppBar(
          title: const Text('Product Catalog'),
        ),
        body: Container(
          width: 200, // Set the width of the Container
          height: 100, // Set the height of the Container
          color: Colors.blue, // Set the background color of the Container
          child: const Text(
            'Today\'s Temperature: 25°C', // Text to display inside the
Container
            style: TextStyle(
              color: Colors.white, // Text color
              fontSize: 18, // Text font size
            ),
          ),
        ),
      ),
    );
  }
}
```

Step 4: Customize Your Container

The power of the `Container` lies in its customization options. You can tweak various properties to achieve the desired design:

- `alignment`: Align the child within the `Container`.
- `padding`: Add space inside the `Container`.
- `margin`: Set spacing around the `Container`.
- `decoration`: Apply visual effects like borders and shadows.

Here's an example of customizing your `Container`:

```
import 'package:flutter/material.dart';

void main() {
  runApp(const MyApp());
}

class MyApp extends StatelessWidget {
  const MyApp({Key? key}) : super(key: key);

  @override
  Widget build(BuildContext context) {
    return MaterialApp(
      home: Scaffold(
```

```
          appBar: AppBar(
            title: const Text('Product Catalog'),
          ),
          body: Container(
            width: 200,
            height: 100,
            padding:
                const EdgeInsets.all(16), // Add padding inside the
Container
            margin: const EdgeInsets.symmetric(
                vertical: 10), // Add margin around the Container
            decoration: BoxDecoration(
              color: Colors.blue,
              borderRadius: BorderRadius.circular(10), // Add rounded
corners
              boxShadow: const [
                BoxShadow(
                  color: Colors.black26,
                  blurRadius: 5,
                  offset: Offset(0, 3), // Add a shadow
                ),
              ],
            ),
            child: const Text(
              'Today\'s Temperature: 25°C',
              style: TextStyle(
                color: Colors.white,
                fontSize: 18,
              ),
            ),
          )),
    );
  }
}
```

See *Figure 3.12: The output of the updated code.*

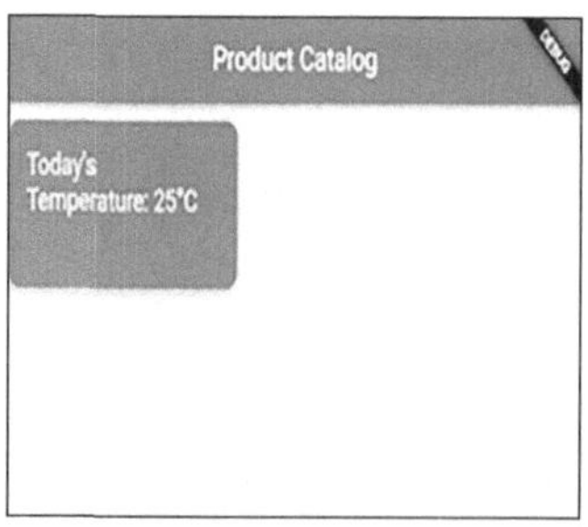

Figure 3.10: *Basic Container with Borders*

You might have noticed the const modifier applied to the widgets. This is a powerful optimization technique in Flutter. When a widget is declared as const, Flutter ensures that the widget is created only once during the lifetime of the app. This can significantly improve your app's performance by reducing unnecessary widget recreations.

Step 5: Embrace Responsive Design

Flutter's `` `Container` `` is your partner in responsive design. You can use properties like `` `width` `` and `` `height` `` to set fixed dimensions, but you can also use `` `MediaQuery` `` to make your `` `Container` `` responsive to different screen sizes:

```
Container(
  width: MediaQuery.of(context).size.width * 0.8, // 80% of screen width
  height: 100,
  // ... other properties and child
)
```

Step 6: Play and Experiment

Now that you've created a basic `` `Container` `` with some customization, don't hesitate to experiment. Change colors, sizes, and styles to see the impact on your design.

Step 7: Run Your App

Save your changes and run your Flutter app using the command in your terminal:

```
flutter run
```

Remember, the `` `Container` `` is just one of the many layout widgets Flutter offers. As you explore further, you'll discover widgets like `` `Column` ``, `` `Row` ``, and `` `Stack` ``, which allow you to build complex and dynamic layouts.

So go ahead, harness the power of the `` `Container` `` to design stunning UI elements in your Flutter app. Your creativity is the limit, and Flutter's layout widgets are your tools to bring your vision to life. Happy coding!

Feel free to share a screenshot of your design on social media and tag me—I'd love to see your creations!

Working with Row Widgets

In this section, we'll continue our exploration by combining the `` `Row` `` and `` `Container` `` widgets to create more complex layouts. Let's dive in!

Scenario: Creating a Row of Colored Boxes

Imagine you're designing a dashboard for a productivity app. You want to display quick access buttons in a row, each represented by a colored box. Here's how you can achieve this using the `Row` and `Container` widgets:

See *Figure 3.13: Creating colored boxes using Row widgets*

Figure 3.11: *Row of Colored boxes*

Step 1: Set Up Your Project

1. Create a new Flutter project.
2. Open the `main.dart` file in your project.

Step 2: Add the Row with Containers

Replace the default code in your `main.dart` file with the following:

```
import 'package:flutter/material.dart';

void main() {
  runApp(const MyApp());
}

class MyApp extends StatelessWidget {
  const MyApp({Key? key}) : super(key: key);

  @override
  Widget build(BuildContext context) {
    return MaterialApp(
      home: Scaffold(
        appBar: AppBar(
```

```
          title: const Text('Quick Access'),
        ),
        body:  Center(
          child: Row(
            mainAxisAlignment: MainAxisAlignment.center,
            children: <Widget>[
              Container(
                width: 100,
                height: 100,
                color: Colors.blue,
              ),
              const SizedBox(width: 20),
              Container(
                width: 100,
                height: 100,
                color: Colors.green,
              ),
              const SizedBox(width: 20),
              Container(
                width: 100,
                height: 100,
                color: Colors.orange,
              ),
            ],
          ),
        ),
      ),
    );
  }
}
```

Step 3: Run Your App

Save your changes and run your Flutter app using the command:

```
flutter run
```

You'll see three colored boxes displayed in a row at the center of the screen.

Step 4: Adjust Container Colors

Now, let's customize the colors of the boxes. Change the color property values of the Container widgets to experiment with different colors. For example, you can use **`Colors.red`**, **`Colors.purple`**, and **`Colors.teal`** for the boxes.

Step 5: Run Your App

Save your changes and run your Flutter app using the command:

```
flutter run
```

What do you see? Magic!

Explanation

In this scenario, we've combined the `Row` widget with the `Container` widgets to create a row of colored boxes. Each `Container` represents a quick access button with a specific color. We've used the `color` property of the `Container` to define the background color of each box. The `SizedBox` widgets with a width of 20 pixels provide spacing between the boxes.

Congratulations! You've successfully used the Row widget to create a horizontal arrangement of widgets. You don't need to worry about concepts like `StatelessWidget` or `StatefulWidget` for now. As you continue your Flutter journey, you'll gradually dive deeper into these topics.

By combining different layout widgets like `Row` and `Container`, you can create more intricate and visually appealing UIs. Don't hesitate to experiment with various properties to achieve the desired look and functionality.

Working with Column Widget

In this section, we'll explore the `Column` widget, a fundamental tool for arranging widgets vertically in Flutter. We'll dive into its functionality and guide you through using it effectively to create well-organized and visually appealing layouts.

Understanding the `Column` Widget

The `Column` widget is designed to arrange its children vertically, one below the other. It's an excellent choice when you want to create a list of widgets that need to be stacked on top of each other.

How Does it Work?

A `Column` can contain multiple child widgets, each of which occupies its designated space within the layout. The column will take the width of its widest child and distribute the available vertical space evenly among its children.

Why Use `Column`?

The `Column` widget comes in handy when you need to organize widgets vertically. It's particularly useful for creating lists, forms, and other components that require a linear arrangement of content.

Scenario: Using `Column` with `Container`

Imagine you're building a product catalog page for an e-commerce app. Each product is displayed as a `Container` within a `Column`, ensuring they are stacked one after another.

Here's a step-by-step guide on how to achieve this:

1. **Create a New Flutter Project:** Begin by creating a new Flutter project using your preferred development environment.
2. **Navigate to `lib/main.dart`:** Open the `main.dart` file in the `lib` directory of your Flutter project.
3. **Import Required Packages:**

   ```
   import 'package:flutter/material.dart';
   ```

4. **Build the UI with a `Column` of `Container` Widgets:**

   Replace the existing `build` method with the following code snippet:

   ```
     @override
   Widget build(BuildContext context) {
     return MaterialApp(
       home: Scaffold(
         appBar: AppBar(
           title: const Text('Product Catalog'),
         ),
         body: Column(
           crossAxisAlignment: CrossAxisAlignment.start,
           children: [
             Container(
               width: double.infinity,
               height: 200,
               color: Colors.blue,
               child: const Center(child: Text('Product 1')),
             ),
             Container(
               width: double.infinity,
               height: 200,
   ```

```
                color: Colors.green,
                child: const Center(child: Text('Product 2')),
              ),
              Container(
                width: double.infinity,
                height: 200,
                color: Colors.orange,
                child: const Center(child: Text('Product 3')),
              ),
            ],
          ),
        ),
      );
    }
```

In this example, we've created a `**Column**` containing three `**Container**` widgets, each representing a product. The `**crossAxisAlignment**` is set to `**CrossAxisAlignment.start**` to align the children to the left.

5. **Run the App:** Save your changes and run the app. You'll see a vertically stacked list of colorful containers, simulating a product catalog.

See *Figure* 3.14: Vertically stacked list of colorful containers

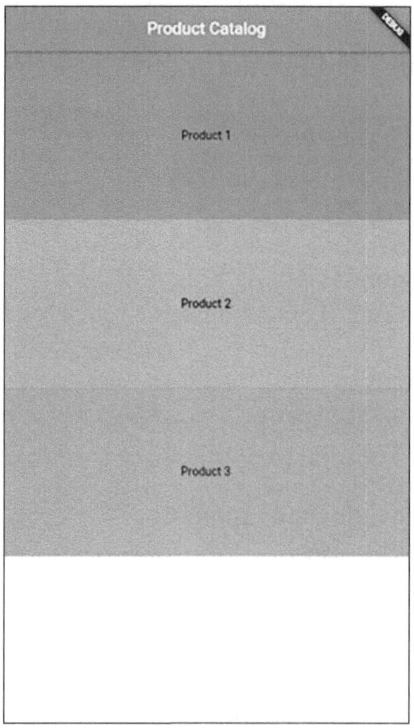

***Figure 3.12**: Containers within a column widget*

Experiment and Customize

Feel free to customize the example by changing the colors, text, and dimensions of the containers. Additionally, you can explore other properties of the `Column` widget to further enhance your layout.

Creating a Stunning UI with Text and Image Widgets

In this section, we'll go through the process of building a user interface that showcases a product using the `Text` and `Image` widgets. We'll follow Flutter's best practices to ensure a clean and effective UI structure.

Setting Up Your Project

1. **Create a New Flutter Project**: If you don't have an existing Flutter project, begin by creating a new one using the following command in your terminal:

```
flutter create product_catalog
```

2. **Prepare an Image:** Download an image that represents your product. If you can't find an assets folder, create one at the root of your project and call it `assets`. Save this image in the `assets` folder within your project.

See *Figure 3.15: Flutter assets folder*

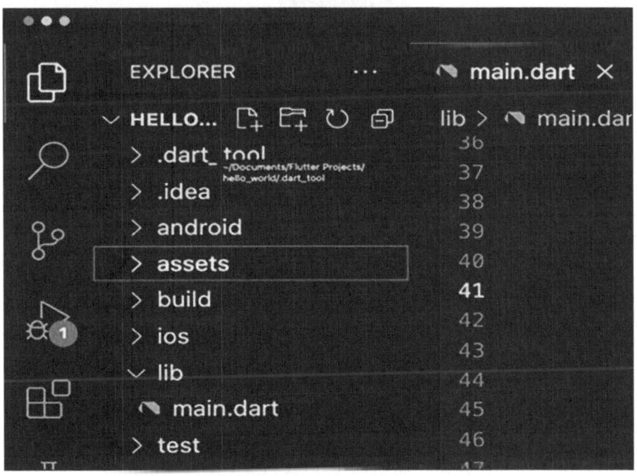

Figure 3.13: *Flutter assets folder*

3. **Update `pubspec.yaml`:** Open your `pubspec.yaml` file and add the following lines under the `flutter` section to declare your image asset:

```
assets:
  - assets/product_image.jpg
```

Building the UI

In this example, we'll construct a simple UI layout that displays an image of the product along with its description using the `Text` and `Image` widgets.

See *Figure 3.16: UI layout that displays an image and details of a product*

Figure 3.14: Product Catalog UI

1. **Open `lib/main.dart`**: Replace the default code in the `lib/main.dart` file with the following code:

```
import 'package:flutter/material.dart';

void main() {
  runApp(const MyApp());
}

class MyApp extends StatelessWidget {
const MyApp({Key? key}) : super(key: key);

  @override
  Widget build(BuildContext context) {
    return const MaterialApp(
      title: 'Product Catalog',
      home: ProductScreen(),
    );
  }
}

class ProductScreen extends StatelessWidget {
const ProductScreen({Key? key}) : super(key: key);

  @override
  Widget build(BuildContext context) {
    return Scaffold(
      appBar: AppBar(
        title: const Text('Product Catalog'),
      ),
      body: Center(
        child: Column(
          mainAxisAlignment: MainAxisAlignment.center,
          children: <Widget>[
            Image.asset(
              'leather.jpg',
              width: 200,
              height: 200,
            ),
            const SizedBox(height: 20),
            const Text(
              'Premium Quality Leather Bag',
              style: TextStyle(
                fontSize: 20,
                fontWeight: FontWeight.bold,
              ),
```

```
                ),
                const SizedBox(height: 10),
                const Text(
                  'Elevate your style with our exquisite leather
bag. Perfect for both casual and formal occasions.',
                  textAlign: TextAlign.center,
                ),
              ],
            ),
          ),
        );
      }
    }
```

Code Explanation

- We begin by importing the required `flutter/material.dart` package.
- The `main()` function is the entry point of our application. It runs the `MyApp` widget.
- The `MyApp` widget is a `MaterialApp` which defines the title of the app and sets the `ProductScreen` as the home screen.
- The `ProductScreen` widget is where the main UI is constructed. It returns a `Scaffold` widget containing an `AppBar` and the main content.
- Within the `Column` widget, we use the `Image.asset` widget to display our product image. We specify the width and height of the image to control its dimensions.
- We add some space below the image using the `SizedBox` widget.
- The first `Text` widget displays the product name with a larger font size and bold style.
- Another `SizedBox` widget adds spacing between the two text elements.
- The final `Text` widget presents a detailed description of the product. We use the `textAlign` property to center-align the text.

Running the App

1. **Run Your App:** Save the changes and run your app using the command:

   ```
   flutter run
   ```

2. **Observe the UI:** When the app launches, you'll see an AppBar with the title "**Product Catalog**" and a centered layout containing the product image and its description.

Customization and Beyond

This example illustrates how to create an appealing UI using the `Text` and `Image` widgets. You can further enhance the UI by experimenting with different fonts, colors, and layouts. As you explore Flutter's widget library, remember that a well-structured UI, clear typography, and strategically placed images contribute to an engaging user experience.

Exploring TextField and Button Widgets

In this section, we'll go through building a basic login screen using the `Button` and `TextField` widgets. We'll follow a step-by-step approach, allowing you to code along and understand each part of the process. Let's get started!

Scenario: Creating a Login Screen

Imagine you're building a mobile app that requires user authentication. You want users to be able to log in securely, so you need to design a login screen. This screen should include fields for users to enter their username and password, along with a "`Login`" button to initiate the authentication process. Additionally, you want to ensure that the password remains hidden as users type it.

See *Figure 3.17: A login screen for user authentication.*

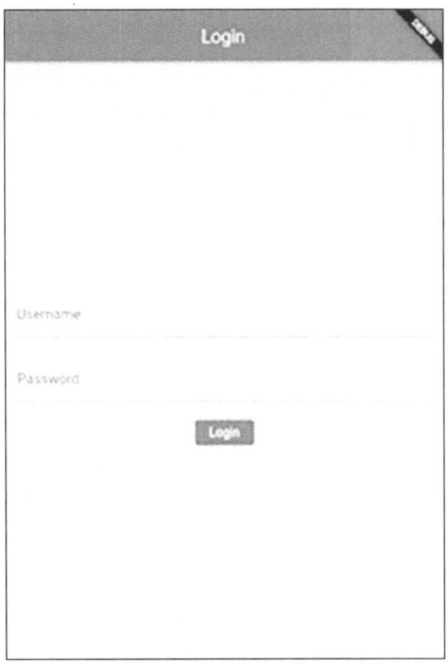

Figure 3.15: Login Screen

Step 1: Setting Up Your Project

Before we begin, make sure you have your Flutter project set up. If you haven't done this yet, refer to previous sections for guidance.

Step 2: Building the Login Screen

1. **Open `lib/main.dart`:** Open the `lib/main.dart` file in your project.
2. **Import Required Packages:** Make sure you have the necessary package imports at the top of the file:

```
import 'package:flutter/material.dart';
```

3. **Create the Main Function:** Replace the existing `main` function with the following code:

```
void main() {
  runApp(MyApp());
}
```

4. **Create MyApp Class:** Define the `MyApp` class as follows:

```
class MyApp extends StatelessWidget {
  @override
  Widget build(BuildContext context) {
    return MaterialApp(
      title: 'Login Screen',
      home: LoginScreen(),
    );
  }
}
```

5. **Create `LoginScreen` Class:** Now, let's create the `LoginScreen` class inside the `lib` folder. This will be the main screen of our app:

```
class LoginScreen extends StatelessWidget {
  @override
  Widget build(BuildContext context) {
    return Scaffold(
      appBar: AppBar(
        title: Text('Login'),
      ),
```

```
          body: Center(
            child: Padding(
              padding: const EdgeInsets.all(16.0),
              child: Column(
                mainAxisAlignment: MainAxisAlignment.center,
                children: <Widget>[
                  // Widgets will be added here
                ],
              ),
            ),
          ),
        );
      }
    }
```

6. **Add TextFields and Button:** Inside the `Column` widget, add the following code to create two `TextField` widgets for username and password inputs, and an `ElevatedButton` for login:

```
Column(
  mainAxisAlignment: MainAxisAlignment.center,
  children: <Widget>[
    TextField(
      decoration: InputDecoration(labelText: 'Username'),
    ),
    SizedBox(height: 20),
    TextField(
      decoration: InputDecoration(labelText: 'Password'),
      obscureText: true,
    ),
    SizedBox(height: 20),
    ElevatedButton(
      onPressed: () {
        // Add your login logic here
      },
      child: Text('Login'),
    ),
  ],
),
```

Step 3: Exploring the Code

a. Inside the **LoginScreen** widget, we've added two **TextField** widgets for username and password input, along with a **SizedBox** to create spacing.

b. **`TextField` (Username Input):** The first **`TextField`** widget allows users to enter their username. We've used the decoration property with the **`InputDecoration`** class to provide a visual hint (label) inside the text field. The **`labelText`** parameter sets the label for the text field, helping users understand what to enter.

c. **`TextField` (Password Input):** The second **`TextField`** widget is used for password input. For security reasons, we've set the **`obscureText`** property to true. This property hides the entered text, displaying it as dots, asterisks, or other obscured characters. This way, sensitive information like passwords remains hidden.

d. **`SizedBox`:** This widget creates a space between the text fields and the button, providing visual separation and improving the layout. The height parameter in **`SizedBox`** sets the amount of vertical space between widgets.

e. **`ElevatedButton`:** This widget serves as the login button. For now, the **`onPressed`** property is empty. You can later add your login logic here.

Step 4: Run Your App

Save your changes and run the app using the command:

```
flutter run
```

Step 5: Exploring the Login Screen

As the app launches, you'll see a simple login screen with fields for entering a username and password, along with a "**`Login`**" button. Although the button doesn't currently perform any action, this example provides a foundation for adding authentication logic and creating a functional login experience.

Stateless and Stateful Widgets

In our exploration of Flutter widgets, we've encountered a variety of powerful tools for building dynamic and responsive user interfaces. As we delve deeper into the world of Flutter development, we come across an essential concept that adds a new layer of versatility to our UI components: the state of a widget. Imagine a dynamic poster that changes its content based on user interaction. Picture a button that alters its appearance after being clicked. These interactive and adaptive behaviors are made possible by understanding and managing the state of widgets.

The concept of "**state**" is at the heart of user interfaces that react to user input, data changes, and other dynamic events. In Flutter, understanding how widgets manage their state empowers us to create apps that feel alive, responsive, and engaging. Just as a football fan's mood changes when their club scores, the state of a widget determines how it behaves in response to user actions.

Understanding the `StatelessWidget`

The term "**widget**" doesn't just refer to UI elements like buttons or text. It's a broader concept that encompasses any part of the user interface, even the parts that don't visually change. A **`StatelessWidget`** is one of the fundamental building blocks. As its name implies, it represents a widget that doesn't have any internal state that can change after it's built.

How does it work?

Imagine a painting on a canvas. Once the artist has completed the painting, it doesn't change on its own. Similarly, a **`StatelessWidget`** is like a canvas with a beautiful illustration that remains constant. These widgets are excellent for displaying static content, such as text labels, icons, or images. They're lightweight and efficient because Flutter doesn't need to monitor any internal changes.

Format of a `StatelessWidget`

Creating a **`StatelessWidget`** involves defining a class that extends **`StatelessWidget`** and implementing the required **`build`** method. The `build` method is where you define the structure of your widget, specifying how it should look based on its input parameters (also known as "**props**" in some other UI frameworks).

Here's a simplified format of a `StatelessWidget`:

```
class MyStatelessWidget extends StatelessWidget {
  // Properties, such as text and color, can be passed as parameters
  final String text;
  final Color color;

  // Constructor to initialize the properties
  MyStatelessWidget({required this.text, required this.color});

  // The build method defines the widget's appearance
  @override
  Widget build(BuildContext context) {
    return Container(
      color: color,
```

```
      child: Text(text),
    );
  }
}
```

In this example, `MyStatelessWidget` takes in `text` and `color` as parameters and uses them to build a `Container` with the specified text and background color. Once built, this widget won't change its appearance even if the input parameters change. It's a static snapshot of the UI.

When to Use `StatelessWidget`

`StatelessWidget` is your go-to choice when you need to display content that won't change or respond to user interaction. It's perfect for UI components that remain the same throughout the lifetime of your app. Think of it as a tool for building the "building blocks" of your interface.

Understanding the `StatefulWidget`

Several UI elements are dynamic and change based on user interaction, data updates, or other events. This is where the `StatefulWidget` comes into play. Unlike the `StatelessWidget`, a `StatefulWidget` has an internal state that can change over time. This makes it a powerful tool for creating interactive and responsive user interfaces.

How does it work?

Think of a `StatefulWidget` as a living organism that can respond to its environment. Just like how a chameleon changes its color to blend with its surroundings, a `StatefulWidget` can change its appearance based on the changes in its internal state. For example, a button that toggles between "**on**" and "**off**" states is a classic use case of a `StatefulWidget`.

Format of a `StatefulWidget`

Creating a `StatefulWidget` involves two classes: one for the widget itself and another for its corresponding state. The widget class extends `StatefulWidget` and returns an instance of the state class in its `createState` method. The state class extends `State` and holds the mutable data for the widget.

Here's a simplified format of a `StatefulWidget`:

```
class MyStatefulWidget extends StatefulWidget {
  @override
  _MyStatefulWidgetState createState() => _MyStatefulWidgetState();
```

```
}

class _MyStatefulWidgetState extends State<MyStatefulWidget> {
  // Properties that can change over time
  bool isActive = false;

  // Method to update the state
  void toggleActive() {
    setState(() {
      isActive = !isActive;
    });
  }

  @override
  Widget build(BuildContext context) {
    return ElevatedButton(
      onPressed: toggleActive,
      child: Text(isActive ? 'Active' : 'Inactive'),
    );
  }
}
```

In this example, `**MyStatefulWidget**` creates an instance of `_**MyStatefulWidgetState**` as its internal state. The state class holds the `**isActive**` property, which changes when the button is pressed. The `**toggleActive**` method updates the state and triggers a rebuild of the UI. The UI responds to the state change by displaying either "**Active**" or "**Inactive**" text on the button.

When to use `StatefulWidget`?

You can use a `**StatefulWidget**` when you need to create UI elements that can change, react to user actions, or display dynamic content. It's the perfect choice for building forms, interactive buttons, sliders, and any component that should update in response to user interactions or data changes.:

The `setState` Function in a `StatefulWidget`

You often need to update the internal state of the widget to trigger a rebuild of the UI and reflect the changes. This is where the `**setState**` function comes into play. It's a vital method that ensures that your UI is updated properly when the state changes.

Imagine watching a Premier League football match where the score is updated in real-time as the game is ongoing. The excitement of seeing those score changes happen on screen is similar to how the **setState** function operates in Flutter.

How `setState` works?

When you call the `**setState**` function, Flutter schedules a rebuild of the widget's UI. Here is how it works:

1. Changing State: When a part of your widget's state changes, you call the `**setState**` function. For instance, you might update a counter, change a boolean value, or modify any other state-related data.
2. Mark for Rebuild**: The `**setState**` function notifies the Flutter framework that the widget's internal state has changed and that it needs to be rebuilt.
3. Build Method Called**: The framework then calls the widget's `**build**` method again. Inside the `build` method, you create the updated UI based on the new state.
4. UI Update**: The new UI is then rendered on the screen, reflecting the changes you made to the state.

Using `setState`

Here's a practical example of how to use `**setState**` in a `**StatefulWidget**`:

```
class CounterWidget extends StatefulWidget {
  @override
  _CounterWidgetState createState() => _CounterWidgetState();
}

class _CounterWidgetState extends State<CounterWidget> {
  int _count = 0;

  void _incrementCounter() {
    setState(() {
      _count++;
    });
  }

  @override
  Widget build(BuildContext context) {
    return Column(
      children: <Widget>[
        Text('Count: $_count'),
```

```
        ElevatedButton(
          onPressed: _incrementCounter,
          child: Text('Increment'),
        ),
      ],
    );
  }
}
```

In this example, the `_incrementCounter` method uses `setState` to increase the `_count` value by one. This change triggers a rebuild of the UI, and the updated count is reflected in the `Text` widget.

When to use `setState`?

Use `setState` whenever you need to modify the internal state of a `StatefulWidget`. It's crucial for keeping your UI in sync with the data changes. Keep in mind that `setState` should only be used within the widget that extends `State`.

Caution and Performance

While `setState` is a powerful tool, excessive use of it can lead to performance issues. Since `setState` rebuilds the entire widget, using it too frequently can slow down your app. For more complex state management, you might explore state management solutions like Provider, **Riverpod**, or **BLoC**. Don't worry, we will explore state management as we build more complex Uis in this book.

Using `const` for Improved Performance

Throughout this chapter, you might have noticed the use of the `const` keyword in front of some immutable classes. This seemingly small addition plays a significant role in optimizing the performance of your Flutter apps. But what exactly does it do, and why is it recommended by Flutter?

Defining Immutable Classes

An immutable class is a class whose instances, once created, cannot be modified. In Flutter, many basic widget classes are immutable, meaning that their properties and values are set when the instance is created and remain unchanged throughout the app's life cycle. This immutability has several benefits, including simpler code, fewer bugs related to mutable state, and enhanced performance.

The Power of 'const'

When you prefix a class instantiation with the `const` keyword, you're indicating to Dart that you want the instance to be created as an immutable object if the class supports it. For example, when you use `const` with basic Flutter widget classes like `Text`, `Icon`, or `Container`, you're signaling that the properties of the widget won't change after creation.

Performance Boost

Using `const` in front of classes, especially those from the Flutter framework, can lead to improved performance for your app. Here's why:

1. **Compile-time Constant:** Dart's compiler can optimize the creation of `const` objects at compile time. This means that during the build process, Flutter can precompute certain properties and configurations, reducing the work the app has to do at runtime.

2. **Memory Efficiency:** Since `const` objects are created only once and shared across your app, they occupy less memory compared to creating new instances whenever needed. This is particularly important in Flutter, where building UI elements can be frequent and resource-intensive.

3. **Hot Reload Benefits:** When you make changes to your code and use Flutter's hot reload feature, `const` objects are more likely to retain their state, providing a smoother and faster development experience.

Flutter Recommendation

Flutter encourages the use of `const` literals as arguments to constructors of `@immutable` classes. The `@immutable` annotation indicates that the class's properties won't change after instantiation. By using `const` with `@immutable` classes, you're ensuring that Flutter's optimizations kick in, resulting in a snappier and more efficient app

Flutter makes it easy for you to identify when a class can be used with the `const` keyword. When you're writing your code in an integrated development environment (IDE) like Android Studio or Visual Studio Code, you'll notice that the code editor is quite helpful. It will underline your code and provide suggestions, including indicating when a class should be used with `const`.

So, you don't have to worry about memorizing every single immutable class in Flutter or figuring out when to use `const` by yourself. The Flutter development environment guides you along the way, making your learning and coding experience smoother.

See *Figure 3.16: VS Code displaying performance warning*

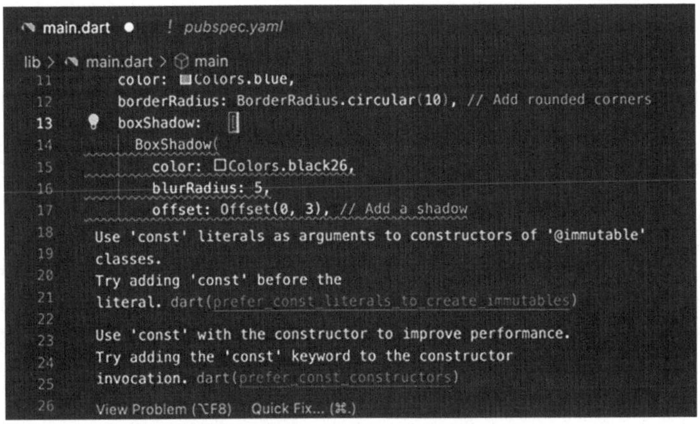

Figure 3.16: VS Code *main.dart*

As you're exploring Flutter and its vast array of widgets, keep an eye out for those subtle underlines and suggestions. They're there to assist you in writing more efficient and optimized code. Just a little blue underline can lead to a big improvement in your app's performance!

See *Figure 3.17: VS Code warning removed after implementation of the recommendation.*

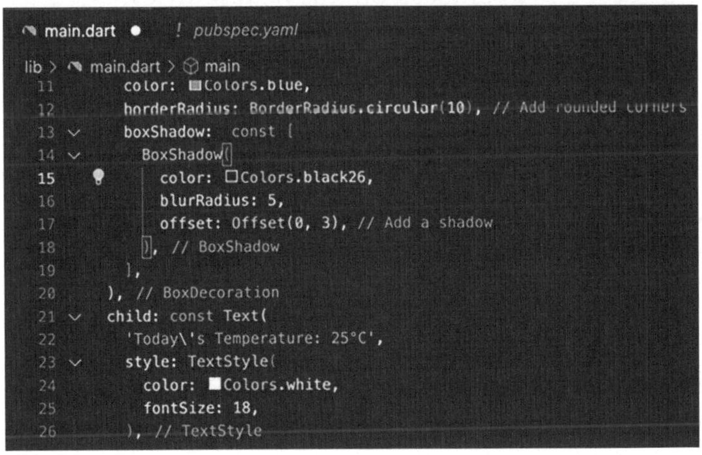

Figure 3.17: VS Code *main.dart*

As you explore Flutter's widgets and build your UI elements, consider using the `` `const` `` keyword where applicable. This practice aligns with Flutter's performance best practices and contributes to a better user experience.

So remember, when you see `const` being used with certain classes, it's not just a minor syntax addition; it's a powerful tool that's helping you build performant and responsive Flutter apps.

Conclusion

As we wrap up this chapter on exploring Flutter widgets and UI elements, you've embarked on a journey through the fundamental building blocks of creating simple and interactive user interfaces. You now possess a toolkit of widgets that enable you to craft beautiful and functional UIs.

We explored the core concepts behind widgets, understanding how they are the key to constructing the visual and interactive elements of your Flutter apps. We looked at various categories of widgets, from the ones responsible for layout and structure to those handling user input and creating delightful animations.

Remember, while we've covered a significant portion of the widget catalog, there are countless more waiting to be explored within the Flutter ecosystem. The Flutter team is continually enhancing this toolkit, introducing new widgets and features that empower developers to build incredible user experiences.

In the next chapter, "*Styling, Theming, and Interactive UI Designs in Flutter*," we'll dive into the art of styling your Flutter app, from creating a visually appealing design to ensuring a seamless and engaging user experience.

So, gear up and get ready to embark on this next journey.

Points to Remember

- Widgets are the foundational building blocks of a Flutter app, responsible for creating the visual and interactive elements of the user interface.
- Accessibility widgets ensure that your app is usable by all users, including those with disabilities.
- The `Container` widget offers structure and styling to your UI elements, acting as your design toolkit.
- The `Row` and `Column` widgets help arrange UI elements horizontally and vertically, respectively, creating flexible layouts.
- The `SizedBox` widget provides spacing and alignment control, contributing to precise UI arrangements.
- The `Text` and `Image` widgets are fundamental for displaying textual content and images in your app.

- User input can be captured using widgets like `ElevatedButton` and `TextField`, enabling interaction between the user and the app.
- `StatelessWidget` represents widgets that don't change over time, while `StatefulWidget` handles dynamic UI updates.
- `setState()` is a crucial function in `StatefulWidget` that triggers UI updates by notifying Flutter's framework.
- Understanding the widget tree, element tree, reconciliation, and hot reload are essential concepts for efficient Flutter development.
- The Flutter Virtual DOM optimizes UI updates, enhancing app performance and responsiveness.
- Keep exploring Flutter's documentation and widget catalog to discover new and exciting widgets that can enhance your app's functionality and appearance.

Assessment

In this assessment, you will put your knowledge of Flutter widgets and UI elements into practice by creating a simple movie list user interface. Follow these steps to complete the task:

See *Figure* 3.18: Simple movie list user interface

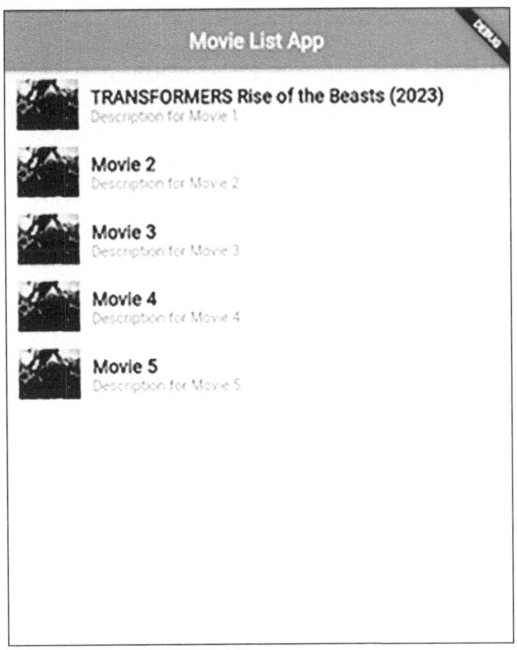

***Figure* 3.18**: *Movie List UI*

1. **Create a New Project:** Open your preferred Flutter development environment and create a new Flutter project.
2. **Design the App Bar:** Use the `AppBar` widget to create a top navigation bar for your app. Customize the title and any relevant icons.
3. **Build the Movie List:** Implement the `ListView.builder` widget to create a scrollable list of movies. For each movie, display its title, an image poster, and a brief description.
4. **Add Images:** Use the `Image.network` widget to display movie poster images. You can use sample URLs from movie databases or any publicly available image URLs.
5. **Use ListTile:** Inside the `ListView.builder`, utilize the `ListTile` widget to display each movie's details neatly. You can display the movie title and description within the `ListTile`.
6. **Styling:** Apply basic styling to the app using the available properties of the widgets. Adjust font sizes, colors, and padding to make the UI visually appealing.
7. **Testing:** Run the app on an emulator or physical device to see your movie list UI in action. Check if the scrolling works correctly and if the movie details are displayed as intended.
8. **Review and Adjust:** Carefully review your app's UI. Ensure that the app bar, movie list, images, and details are properly aligned and styled.
9. **Reflect on the Process:** After completing the assessment, take a moment to reflect on the widgets you used and the structure of the UI you built. Consider how different widgets work together to create a cohesive user experience.
10. **Share Your Achievement:** Take a screenshot of your completed movie list UI and share it on your social media accounts, tagging me and the Flutter community. Celebrate your accomplishments and showcase your progress!

Remember, the goal of this assessment is to practice your understanding of Flutter widgets and their interactions. Don't worry about making the UI too complex; focus on implementing the essential components and creating a clean and functional movie list UI.

Solution

Following is a step-by-step solution to create a simple movie list UI using Flutter widgets:

```
import 'package:flutter/material.dart';

void main() {
  runApp(const MyApp());
}

class MyApp extends StatelessWidget {
  const MyApp({Key? key}) : super(key: key);

  @override
  Widget build(BuildContext context) {
    return MaterialApp(
      home: MovieListScreen(),
    );
  }
}

class MovieListScreen extends StatelessWidget {
// Sample data for movie titles, descriptions, and posters
  final List<String> movieTitles = [
    'TRANSFORMERS Rise of the Beasts (2023)',
    'Movie 2',
    'Movie 3',
    'Movie 4',
    'Movie 5',
  ];

  final List<String> movieDescriptions = [
    'Description for Movie 1',
    'Description for Movie 2',
    'Description for Movie 3',
    'Description for Movie 4',
    'Description for Movie 5',
  ];

  final List<String> moviePosters = [
    'https://i.ebayimg.com/images/g/P7wAAOSwtqFkYoTI/s-l500.jpg',
    'https://i.ebayimg.com/images/g/P7wAAOSwtqFkYoTI/s-l500.jpg',
    'https://i.ebayimg.com/images/g/P7wAAOSwtqFkYoTI/s-l500.jpg',
    'https://i.ebayimg.com/images/g/P7wAAOSwtqFkYoTI/s-l500.jpg',
```

```
    'https://i.ebayimg.com/images/g/P7wAAOSwtqFkYoTI/s-l500.jpg',
  ];

  MovieListScreen({Key? key}) : super(key: key);

  @override
  Widget build(BuildContext context) {
    return Scaffold(
      appBar: AppBar(
        title: const Text('Movie List App'),
      ),
      body: ListView.builder(
        itemCount: movieTitles.length,
        itemBuilder: (context, index) {
         // Leading image for the movie poster
          return ListTile(
            leading: Image.network(
              moviePosters[index],
              width: 60,
              height: 80,
              fit: BoxFit.cover,
            ),
            // Movie title with styling
            title: Text(
              movieTitles[index],
              style: const TextStyle(fontSize: 18, fontWeight: Font-
Weight.bold),
            ),
           // Movie description
            subtitle: Text(
              movieDescriptions[index],
              style: const TextStyle(fontSize: 14),
            ),
          );
        },
      ),
    );
  }
}
```

In this code, we've created a MovieListScreen widget that displays a list of movies using a ListView.builder. Each movie is represented by a ListTile containing an image, title, and description. We've also added basic styling to improve the visual appeal of the UI.

Please replace the placeholder image URLs (https://i.ebayimg.com/images/g/P7wAAOSwtqFkYoTI/s-l500.jpg) with actual URLs of movie posters for accurate display.

Key Terms

- **Widget:** A building block of a Flutter application's user interface, representing a piece of the user interface, such as a button or text.
- **Accessibility Widgets:** Widgets that enhance the accessibility of an app for users with disabilities.
- **UI Element Tree:** A hierarchical representation of the widgets in the widget tree, which Flutter uses to efficiently update the user interface.
- **Reconciliation:** The process by which Flutter updates the UI by comparing the old and new widget trees and making the necessary changes.
- **Hot Reload:** A development feature that allows you to see immediate changes in your app's UI without restarting the app.
- **Flutter Virtual DOM:** An internal representation of the UI used by Flutter to efficiently update and render the user interface.
- **setState():** A method used in a `StatefulWidget` to update the state and trigger a UI update.
- **BuildContext:** An object that represents the location of a widget within the widget tree.
- **State Management:** The management of widget state to ensure accurate UI updates.

SECTION 2

Building Modern UI Designs

CHAPTER 4

Styling, Theming, and Interactive UI Designs in Flutter

Appearances matter just as much as functionality. Just like a property needs to be well-finished and attractive to catch a buyer's eye, an app must be visually appealing to attract users and keep them engaged. Imagine you're trying to sell a property, and it's well built with a solid foundation and quality roofing, but it's unfinished and lacks any aesthetic appeal. Chances are, potential buyers will hesitate, and you might miss out on valuable opportunities.

Similarly, an app's visual design plays a pivotal role in its success. Users are drawn to apps that not only function seamlessly but also provide a delightful and visually pleasing experience. Styling and theming are the tools that allow developers to transform functional code into aesthetically appealing user interfaces.

Structure

In this chapter, we will cover the following topics:

- Colors and themes: Adding life to your app
- Customizing widget appearance
- Using widgets for user interaction
- Animations and motion widgets

Colors and Themes: Adding Life to your App

Imagine you just got a new apartment, and you want to beautify the interior. Your first move is to choose color combinations for the entire apartment, right? Just like how colors can transform the vibe of your living space, they can also create a unique atmosphere in your app.

In Flutter, colors are more than just red, blue, or green. They are your artistic palette, allowing you to infuse life and personality into your app. But how do you choose the right colors and maintain a consistent look? This is where themes come into play.

The Color class

Colors play a fundamental role in designing an attractive and engaging app interface. They are represented using the `Color` class. Think of colors as the paint you used to bring elegance to your app's user interface.

Color representation

Colors are defined using hexadecimal values. A hexadecimal color value is composed of three or four parts: a hash symbol (#), red (R), green (G), blue (B), and sometimes alpha (A) for opacity.

Here's a simple representation of a hexadecimal color value: `#RRGGBB` or `#AARRGGBB` (with alpha).

Using predefined colors

Flutter provides a set of predefined colors that you can directly use. These colors are part of the `Colors` class:

```
Color redColor = Colors.red;
Color blueColor = Colors.blue;
Color greenColor = Colors.green;
```

Creating custom colors

If you need a specific color that's not in the predefined set, you can create a custom color using the `Color` class:

```
Color customColor = Color(0xFFAABBCC);
```

In this example, `0xFF` represents the alpha value (opacity), and `AABBCC` represents the RGB values.

Using colors in widgets

Colors can be applied to various widgets to style your app's UI elements. For instance, you can set the background color of a container:

```
Container(
  color: Colors.blue,
  child: Text('Hello Flutter'),
)
```

Creating a gradient

Colors can also be used to create gradients, which are smooth transitions between two or more colors. Gradients are commonly used for backgrounds or to add depth to UI elements.

Here's how to create a linear gradient:

```
Container(
  decoration: BoxDecoration(
    gradient: LinearGradient(
      colors: [Colors.blue, Colors.green],
      begin: Alignment.topLeft,
      end: Alignment.bottomRight,
    ),
  ),
  child: Text('Gradient Example'),
)
```

In this example, the `LinearGradient` widget creates a smooth transition from blue to green from the top left to the bottom right of the container.

Color opacity (Alpha)

The alpha value of a color determines its opacity. An alpha value of `0xFF` means fully opaque, while an alpha value of `0x00` means fully transparent. This can be useful when you want to create overlays or highlight certain UI elements.

Flutter's `Colors` class also provides predefined colors with different opacities, such as `Colors.red.withOpacity(0.5)`.

Themes: A unified color scheme

Think of a theme as a set of design choices that give your app a coherent appearance. It's like picking the perfect paint colors for your new apartment to create a consistent and pleasing environment. In Flutter, a theme includes colors, typography, and other visual elements that define your app's style.

Creating a consistent app theme with ThemeData

Imagine furnishing a new apartment–selecting paint colors, furniture, and decorations that sync to create a cohesive and appealing ambiance. Similarly, in app development, maintaining a unified visual style enhances the user experience. Flutter offers powerful styling and theming options, allowing you to effortlessly achieve a polished and consistent look across your app's UI elements.

Defining an app-wide theme

To establish a consistent theme throughout your app, provide a `ThemeData` instance to the `MaterialApp` constructor. This encapsulates various stylistic attributes, like colors, typography, and more.

```
void main() {
  runApp(MaterialApp(
    theme: ThemeData(
      brightness: Brightness.dark,
      primaryColor: Colors.lightBlue[800],
      fontFamily: 'Georgia',
      textTheme: const TextTheme(
        displayLarge: TextStyle(fontSize: 70, fontWeight: FontWeight.
bold),
        titleLarge: TextStyle(fontSize: 34, fontStyle: FontStyle.ital-
ic),
        bodyMedium: TextStyle(fontSize: 12, fontFamily: 'Roboto'),
      ),
```

```
    ),
    home: LoginScreen(),
  ));
}
```

In this example, we define a cohesive theme using `ThemeData`. The theme includes brightness, primary color, font preferences, and various text styles tailored for different parts of the app.

Custom themes for specific parts

To further refine your app's style, you can apply unique themes to specific sections using the `Theme` widget.

Unique ThemeData

If you want a distinct theme for a specific widget or section, you can create a new `ThemeData` instance and use it within the `Theme` widget:

```
Theme(
  data: ThemeData(
    splashColor: Colors.green,
  ),
  child: FloatingActionButton(
    onPressed: () {},
    child: const Icon(Icons.add),
  ),
);
```

Extending the Parent Theme

For minor adjustments, it's often practical to extend the parent theme. The `copyWith()` method lets you maintain most attributes from the parent theme while selectively modifying specific properties:

```
Theme(
  data: Theme.of(context).copyWith(splashColor: Colors.yellow),
  child: const FloatingActionButton(
    onPressed: null,
    child: Icon(Icons.add),
  ),
);
```

Applying a theme

After defining a theme, you can easily utilize its attributes within widget `**build()**` methods by invoking `**Theme.of(context)**`. This function searches the widget tree to find the nearest `Theme`.

For example, you can leverage theme colors and text styles as follows:

```
Container(
  color: Theme.of(context).colorScheme.secondary,
  child: Text(
    'Text with a background color',
    style: Theme.of(context).textTheme.headline6,
  ),
);
```

A simple login screen

Now, let's use the theme we initially created in our main function for a simple login screen:

1. **Create a Login Screen Widget:** Inside the `**main.dart**` file, create a new widget named `**LoginScreen**` that extends `**StatelessWidget**`.
2. **Import Required Libraries:** Import the necessary Flutter libraries at the top of your Dart file:

   ```
   import 'package:flutter/material.dart';
   ```

3. **Define the LoginScreen Widget:** Design your login screen using the defined theme. You can use various widgets like **TextField**, **ElevatedButton**, and **Text** to build your UI. Apply the theme's attributes to achieve a consistent style. The final source should look like this:

   ```
   import 'package:flutter/material.dart';
   void main() {
     runApp(MaterialApp(
       theme: ThemeData(
         brightness: Brightness.dark,
         primaryColor: Colors.lightBlue[800],
         fontFamily: 'Georgia',
         textTheme: const TextTheme(
           displayLarge: TextStyle(fontSize: 70, fontWeight:
           FontWeight.bold),
   ```

```
          titleLarge: TextStyle(fontSize: 34, fontStyle: FontStyle.
          italic),
          bodyMedium: TextStyle(fontSize: 12, fontFamily:
          'Roboto'),
        ),
      ),
      home: LoginScreen(),
    ));

  class LoginScreen extends StatelessWidget {
    @override
    Widget build(BuildContext context) {
      return Scaffold(
        appBar: AppBar(title: const Text('Login')),
        body: Center(
          child: Column(
            mainAxisAlignment: MainAxisAlignment.center,
            children: [
              Text(
                'Welcome',
                style: Theme.of(context).textTheme.titleLarge,
              ),
              const TextField(
                decoration: InputDecoration(
                  labelText: 'Username',
                  prefixIcon: Icon(Icons.person),
                ),
              ),
              const SizedBox(height: 16),
              const TextField(
                decoration: InputDecoration(
                  labelText: 'Password',
                  prefixIcon: Icon(Icons.lock),
                ),
                obscureText: true, // Hide password input
              ),
              const SizedBox(height: 24),
              ElevatedButton(
                onPressed: () {},
                child: const Text('Log In'),
              ),
            ],
          ),
        ),
      );
    }
  }
```

4. **Apply the Theme:** Notice how we've used `` `Theme.of(context).textTheme.titleLarge` `` to set the style of our '**`Welcome`**' Text widget. You can also do the same to other widgets as you desire.
5. **Launch the App with LoginScreen:** Inside the `` `main` `` function, launch the app with the `` `MaterialApp` `` widget and the `` `LoginScreen` `` as the home screen: You should see the following output. See *Figure 4.1: Dark mode for Login Screen.*

***Figure 4.1**: Login Screen*

6. **Make changes:** The current theme of the login screen is dark. To make it light, you can change the '**`brightness`**' property of ThemeData in the main function to `` `light` ``.

```
void main() {
  runApp(MaterialApp(
    theme: ThemeData(
      brightness: Brightness.dark,
      primaryColor: Colors.lightBlue[800],
      fontFamily: 'Georgia',
      textTheme: const TextTheme(
        displayLarge: TextStyle(fontSize: 70, fontWeight:
        FontWeight.bold),
        titleLarge: TextStyle(fontSize: 34, fontStyle: FontStyle.
        italic),
        bodyMedium: TextStyle(fontSize: 12, fontFamily: 'Roboto'),
      ),
    ),
```

```
    home: LoginScreen(),
  ));
```

7. **Run the app:** When you run the app again, you should see this new look. See *Figure 4.2: Light mode for Login Screen.*

Figure 4.2: *Login Screen*

As you follow these steps, you're creating a login screen with a consistent color scheme based on the defined theme. This ensures that your app's UI maintains a unified and professional appearance.

At the end of this section, your `main.dart` file should contain the complete code for the login app with a theme. Remember that using themes in Flutter not only helps maintain a consistent look but also simplifies the process of styling your app's UI elements.

Flutter Theme best practices

Styling your Flutter app not only makes it visually appealing but also enhances the user experience. Flutter offers a robust theming system that helps you maintain consistency and customize your app's look and feel.

Here are a few best practices for creating and managing themes.

Create a Theme Class for consistency

To ensure consistent styling throughout your app, consider creating a dedicated theme class. This class will store all your app's colors, text styles, and sizes in one central location. This approach simplifies the maintenance of your app's visual design, making it organized and easy to manage.

Creating a theme class is straightforward. Define a `ThemeData` object with your desired color palette, typography, and other styling attributes. You can then pass this theme to the `MaterialApp` widget when initializing your app. By doing this, you establish a unified design foundation that can be accessed globally.

Utilize `ThemeData` for global styling

`ThemeData` is a powerful inbuilt class that allows you to establish a consistent look and feel for your entire app. It encapsulates colors, fonts, text styles, and more. This means you can define a coherent design language that extends across various screens and widgets.

Leveraging `ThemeData` promotes code organization by centralizing your app's styling setup. Instead of configuring each component individually, you define them collectively within the theme. This makes it easier to maintain and update the app's design. Changes can be applied globally, ensuring a streamlined and cohesive user experience.

Embrace material design widgets

Material Design, Google's design language, offers a set of pre-designed widgets for creating visually consistent user interfaces. These widgets adhere to guidelines for typography, colors, and shapes, resulting in a harmonious experience across platforms. By incorporating Material Design widgets, you can ensure your app's consistency on various devices and operating systems.

Beyond consistency, Material Design widgets offer customization capabilities. You can easily modify color schemes and typography without writing extensive code. This flexibility empowers you to adjust your app's appearance without starting from scratch. Moreover, relying on these built-in widgets accelerates development by leveraging predefined styles.

Leverage `InheritedWidget` for theme access

`InheritedWidget` is a specialized widget that allows descendant widgets to access data from the widget tree. This feature is particularly useful for accessing the current theme throughout your app without having to pass it down explicitly.

To harness InheritedWidget for theme access, create an instance at the root of your widget tree. Wrap descendant widgets with this widget, granting them access to the theme. By invoking the `getTheme()` method on the InheritedWidget, you can retrieve the current theme seamlessly.

This approach ensures that all descendant widgets utilize the same theme while simplifying the process of theme access. It enables efficient theme management across your app's widget hierarchy.

Modularize Theme elements

Break down your theme into separate classes to enhance code organization and readability. By isolating different theme components, such as colors, typography, and sizes, you can locate and modify specific elements more efficiently. This approach simplifies making changes and adding new features while ensuring that adjustments to one element do not inadvertently affect others.

Modularization also fosters maintainability. Separating theme elements into distinct classes promotes independence and isolation. This means that modifications to one aspect of the theme won't impact others, making it easier to manage and update individual components without disrupting the entire theme.

Furthermore, breaking down the theme into smaller components promotes reusability. Colors and styles shared across multiple screens can be stored in dedicated classes and then referenced throughout the app. This prevents redundant code and streamlines maintenance.

Define default values for consistency

Establishing default values for different parts of your theme is crucial for maintaining a uniform look and feel across your app. This becomes especially significant when dealing with multi-screen applications, ensuring design elements remain consistent. By setting defaults for each aspect of your theme, you can effortlessly apply them throughout your app without making manual adjustments.

Default values also enhance future-proofing. If you decide to alter the color palette or font size of your app, you can simply update the default values instead of revisiting every screen. This saves time and effort, allowing you to focus on other essential aspects of your project.

Group-related elements

Grouping related theme elements, such as color palettes and typography, promotes codebase organization and ease of maintenance. It simplifies locating specific styles when making changes or adding features. For example, centralizing all colors in one place streamlines color selection without combing through multiple files.

This grouping approach also facilitates global changes. If typography elements are grouped together, adjusting the font size across the entire app requires only a few lines of code. This method saves time compared to manually updating each individual component.

Flutter provides several mechanisms for grouping related elements. Themes created using `ThemeData` objects, allow developers to define properties like colors and fonts. These properties are then accessible throughout the app via the `ThemeData` object. Additionally, Flutter's `MaterialApp` widget includes a "**theme**" parameter for applying a custom theme to the entire app.

Limit the number of colors

Strive for simplicity and consistency by limiting the number of colors in your theme. An excessive array of colors can overwhelm users and clutter the design. Opting for a clean and focused color scheme prevents confusion and distraction.

A recommended approach is to select a primary color and utilize shades of that color throughout your app. This creates a coherent visual experience while allowing for variation with different hues and tints. Reserve accent colors sparingly to draw attention to specific elements like buttons or links.

Consider the relationships between colors to maintain clarity. If two similar colors are used adjacent to each other, they may be challenging to distinguish. To mitigate this, maximize color contrast wherever possible.

Avoid hardcoded values

Avoid using hardcoded color values or font sizes throughout your codebase. Hardcoding can lead to inconsistencies in your UI, making it difficult for users to navigate your app. By eschewing hardcoded values, you ensure that all components within your app adhere to a consistent design language, enhancing the user experience.

To sidestep hardcoded values, rely on Flutter's `ThemeData` class. `ThemeData` lets you define default colors and fonts used throughout your codebase. This guarantees that all components maintain a cohesive look and feel, regardless of their location. Moreover, this approach simplifies future theme changes, as components will automatically adjust to new settings.

Test across devices

Thoroughly testing your theme on diverse devices with varying screen sizes is essential to ensuring a consistent user experience. This practice guarantees that your theme translates seamlessly across different platforms and screen dimensions. Comprehensive device testing also identifies any potential design or functionality issues before your app goes live.

To facilitate multi-device testing, employ Flutter's Device Preview tool. This tool enables real-time previews of your app on a range of devices, from phones to tablets. It provides invaluable insights into how your theme functions on various screen sizes and device types.

Additionally, automated tests are valuable for assessing your theme's performance on multiple devices simultaneously. Automated tests ensure that your theme delivers the intended experience across different devices, optimizing the testing process.

Customizing widget appearance

In this section, we will embark on a practical journey to create an e-commerce catalog list page. My goal is to guide you through a step-by-step process, allowing you to grasp the concepts of customizing widget appearance using styles and themes. By the end of this challenge, you will have built a modern and simple product catalog screen that's both visually appealing and user-friendly.

Project requirements

Our e-commerce catalog list page will consist of the following components:

1. **App Bar:** A top navigation bar displaying the app's logo and search icon.
2. **Product List:** A grid layout showcasing various products, each with an image, title, and price.
3. **Product Card:** A styled card container for each product, with a shadow effect and proper padding.
4. **Color Scheme:** The app should support both light and dark modes, allowing users to switch between them effortlessly.

See *Figure 4.3: Light and dark mode for Product Catalog screens*

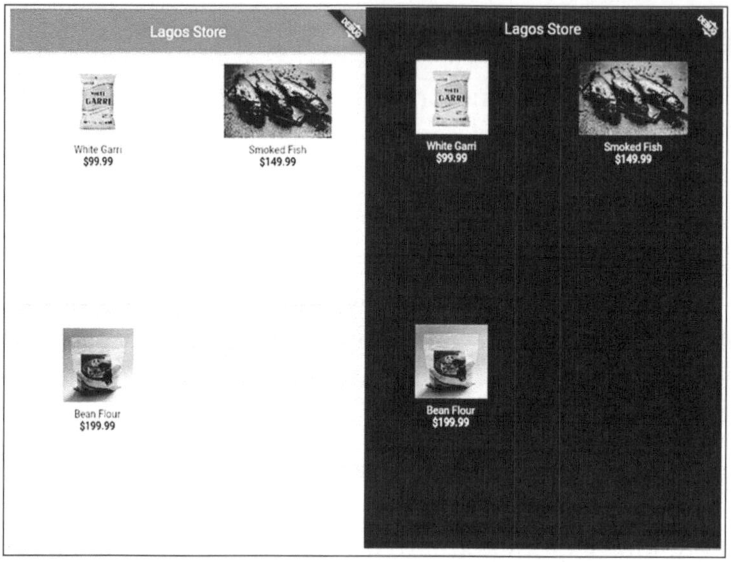

***Figure 4.3**: Product Catalog Screens*

Now let's Dive In!

Step 1: Set Up the Project

Before we begin, create a new Flutter project and structure your folders appropriately.

Step 2: Define the Color Palette

Define the primary and accent colors for your app's theme. For instance, you might choose a shade of blue as your primary color and a contrasting color as your accent.

Step 3: Create a Theme

Inside the `main.dart` file, wrap your `MaterialApp` with a `Theme` widget. Configure the theme with the colors and other properties you've defined.

Step 4: Build the App Bar

Create the app bar with your app's logo and search icon. Use the `AppBar` widget and customize it using your defined theme.

Step 5: Design the Product List

Use the `GridView.builder` widget to create the product list. Each product will be represented by a `ProductCard` widget.

Step 6: Implement the Product Card

Define a custom `ProductCard` widget that represents an individual product. Style it with shadows, borders, and appropriate padding.

Step 7: Implement Light and Dark Modes

Now comes the exciting part. Allow your users to switch between light and dark modes. In your `Theme` widget, set up a `brightness` property that toggles between `Brightness.light` and `Brightness.dark` based on user preference.

As you attempt to create the screen, don't hesitate to experiment with different color palettes, font styles, and element layouts. Change the primary and accent colors to observe how they affect the overall look. Adjust the shadow properties on the product cards to fine-tune their appearance.

Solution

Let's walk through the step-by-step solution for creating the e-commerce catalog list page with custom styles and themes.

Step 1: Define the theme.dart

Create a new file `theme.dart` in your **lib** folder and begin by defining the `AppThemes` and `AppColors` classes to handle theme changes.

```
// theme.dart
import 'package:flutter/material.dart';

class AppColors {
  static const Color primaryColor = Colors.blue;
}

class AppThemes {
  static final lightTheme = ThemeData.light().copyWith(
    primaryColor: AppColors.primaryColor,
  );

  static final darkTheme = ThemeData.dark().copyWith(
    primaryColor: AppColors.primaryColor,
  );
}
```

Step 2: Import Required Packages and Create Theme Manager

In the `main.dart` file, begin by importing the necessary packages and defining the `ThemeManager` class to handle theme changes.

```
import 'package:flutter/material.dart';
import 'package:get/get.dart';
import 'theme.dart'; // Import your theme.dart file here

void main() {
  runApp(MyApp());
}

class ThemeManager {
  static void setThemeMode(ThemeMode mode) {
    Get.changeThemeMode(mode);
  }
}
```

Step 3: Define the Main App Widget

Create the `MyApp` widget which sets up the **MaterialApp** and initializes the app with a light theme.

```
class MyApp extends StatelessWidget {
  const MyApp({Key? key}) : super(key: key);

  @override
  Widget build(BuildContext context) {
    return GetMaterialApp(
      title: 'Lagos Store',
      theme: AppThemes.lightTheme,
      darkTheme: AppThemes.darkTheme,
      home: const CatalogPage(),
    );
  }
}
```

Step 4: Create the Catalog Page

In your **lib** folder, define the `CatalogPage` widget that displays the app bar and the grid of products.

```
class CatalogPage extends StatelessWidget {
  const CatalogPage({Key? key}) : super(key: key);
```

```
  @override
  Widget build(BuildContext context) {
    return Scaffold(
      appBar: AppBar(
        title: const Text('Lagos Store'),
        actions: const [
          ThemeManagerWidget(),
        ],
      ),
      body: GridView.builder(
        gridDelegate: const SliverGridDelegateWithFixedCrossAxisCount(
          crossAxisCount: 2,
          childAspectRatio: 0.7,
        ),
        itemCount: products.length,
        itemBuilder: (context, index) {
          return ProductCard(product: products[index]);
        },
      ),
    );
  }
}
```

Step 5: Define the Product Class

Modify the `**Product**` class to include a price field along with the existing name and **imageUrl** fields.

```
class Product {
  final String name;
  final String imageUrl;
  final double price; // Add the price field

  Product({required this.name, required this.imageUrl, required this.
  price});
}

final List<Product> products = [
  Product(name: 'White Garri', imageUrl: 'assets/product1.jpeg', price:
  99.99),
  Product(name: 'Smoked Fish', imageUrl: 'assets/product2.jpeg', price:
  149.99),
  Product(name: 'Bean Flour', imageUrl: 'assets/product3.jpeg', price:
  199.99),
  // Add more products
];
```

Step 6: Create Product Cards

Adjust the `ProductCard` widget to display the product's name and price.

```
class ProductCard extends StatelessWidget {
  final Product product;

  const ProductCard({Key? key, required this.product}) : super(key: key);

  @override
  Widget build(BuildContext context) {
    return Card(
      margin: const EdgeInsets.all(16),
      child: Column(
        crossAxisAlignment: CrossAxisAlignment.center,
        children: [
          Image.asset(
            product.imageUrl,
            height: 100,
          ),
          const SizedBox(height: 8),
          Text(product.name),
          Text('\$${product.price.toStringAsFixed(2)}',
              style: const TextStyle(fontWeight: FontWeight.bold)),
        ],
      ),
    );
  }
}
```

Step 7: Add Theme Toggle Button

Modify the `ThemeManagerWidget` to include a toggle button for switching between light and dark themes.

```
class ThemeManagerWidget extends StatelessWidget {
  const ThemeManagerWidget({Key? key}) : super(key: key);

  @override
  Widget build(BuildContext context) {
    return IconButton(
      icon: const Icon(Icons.brightness_4),
      onPressed: () {
        if (Get.isDarkMode) {
          ThemeManager.setThemeMode(ThemeMode.light);
        } else {
```

```
          ThemeManager.setThemeMode(ThemeMode.dark);
        }
      },
    );
  }
}
```

And that's it! You've successfully built an e-commerce catalog list page with custom styles and themes using Flutter.

Full source code

theme.dart

```
// theme.dart
import 'package:flutter/material.dart';

class AppColors {
  static const Color primaryColor = Colors.blue;
}

class AppThemes {
  static final lightTheme = ThemeData.light().copyWith(
    primaryColor: AppColors.primaryColor,
  );

  static final darkTheme = ThemeData.dark().copyWith(
    primaryColor: AppColors.primaryColor,
  );
}
```

main.dart

```
import 'package:flutter/material.dart';
import 'package:get/get.dart';
import 'theme.dart';

void main() {
  runApp(MyApp());
}

class ThemeManager {
  static void setThemeMode(ThemeMode mode) {
    Get.changeThemeMode(mode);
  }
}
```

```
class MyApp extends StatelessWidget {
  const MyApp({Key? key}) : super(key: key);

  @override
  Widget build(BuildContext context) {
    return GetMaterialApp(
      title: 'Lagos Store',
      theme: AppThemes.lightTheme,
      darkTheme: AppThemes.darkTheme,
      home: const CatalogPage(),
    );
  }
}

class CatalogPage extends StatelessWidget {
  const CatalogPage({Key? key}) : super(key: key);

  @override
  Widget build(BuildContext context) {
    return Scaffold(
      appBar: AppBar(
        title: const Text('Lagos Store'),
        actions: const [
          ThemeManagerWidget(),
        ],
      ),
      body: GridView.builder(
        gridDelegate: const SliverGridDelegateWithFixedCrossAxisCount(
          crossAxisCount: 2,
          childAspectRatio: 0.7,
        ),
        itemCount: products.length,
        itemBuilder: (context, index) {
          return ProductCard(product: products[index]);
        },
      ),
    );
  }
}

class Product {
  final String name;
  final String imageUrl;
  final double price; // Add the price field
```

```
  Product({required this.name, required this.imageUrl, required this.
  price});
}

final List<Product> products = [
  Product(name: 'White Garri', imageUrl: 'assets/product1.jpeg', price:
  99.99),
  Product(name: 'Smoked Fish', imageUrl: 'assets/product2.jpeg', price:
  149.99),
  Product(name: 'Bean Flour', imageUrl: 'assets/product3.jpeg', price:
  199.99),
  // Add more products
];

class ProductCard extends StatelessWidget {
  final Product product;

  const ProductCard({Key? key, required this.product}) : super(key: key);

  @override
  Widget build(BuildContext context) {
    return Card(
      margin: const EdgeInsets.all(16),
      child: Column(
        crossAxisAlignment: CrossAxisAlignment.center,
        children: [
          Image.asset(
            product.imageUrl,
            height: 100,
          ),
          const SizedBox(height: 8),
          Text(product.name),
          Text('\$${product.price.toStringAsFixed(2)}',
              style: const TextStyle(fontWeight: FontWeight.bold)),
        ],
      ),
    );
  }
}

class ThemeManagerWidget extends StatelessWidget {
  const ThemeManagerWidget({Key? key}) : super(key: key);

  @override
  Widget build(BuildContext context) {
    return IconButton(
      icon: const Icon(Icons.brightness_4),
```

```
      onPressed: () {
        if (Get.isDarkMode) {
          ThemeManager.setThemeMode(ThemeMode.light);
        } else {
          ThemeManager.setThemeMode(ThemeMode.dark);
        }
      },
    );
  }
}
```

Remember, practice makes perfect, so don't hesitate to explore more and apply what you've learned to your own projects. Happy coding!

Using widgets for user interaction

Creating interactive user interfaces is quite straightforward, thanks to widgets like GestureDetector and InkWell. These widgets allow you to capture a wide array of user interactions, from simple taps to complex gestures, making your app not just functional but also delightful to use.

GestureDetector

Think of `GestureDetector` as the gateway to making your Flutter app responsive to user actions like taps, swipes, pinches, and more.

But first, let's set the stage. Imagine you've beautifully designed your e-commerce catalog page with those sleek product cards. It's a visual delight, no doubt. However, at the moment, your users can't do much except stare in awe. They can't interact with the products - can't tap on them to view details or add them to their cart. That's where `GestureDetector` comes in.

What is `GestureDetector`?

The `GestureDetector` widget is your key to adding interactivity to your Flutter app. It listens to gestures made by the user, such as taps, double taps, drags, and more, and triggers actions in response. It's like adding a layer of functionality to your beautiful UI.

Let's break down how you can use `GestureDetector` to enhance our Lagos store catalog page:

1. **Import the GestureDetector Widget:**

First things first, you need to import `**material.dart**`. Make sure to add it to the top of your Dart file where your e-commerce catalog page is located.

```
import 'package:flutter/material.dart';
```

2. **Wrap Your Product Cards:**

   Now, find the part of your code where you've created those sleek product cards using the `**ProductCard**` widget. Wrap each `**ProductCard**` widget with a `**GestureDetector**`.

```
    GestureDetector(
  onTap: () {
    // Define what happens when the product card is tapped.
    // This could be showing product details, adding to cart,
    etc.
  },
  child: ProductCard(product: products[index]),
),
```

Setting the `**onTap**` property allows you to specify what should occur when a user taps on a product card. This could be navigating to a new screen with product details, incrementing a cart count, or taking any action of your choice.

3. **Rinse and Repeat:**

   You can repeat this process for other gestures as well. For instance, you could implement a `onDoubleTap` property to handle double-tap actions.

And that's it! You've now made your e-commerce catalog page interactive using the `**GestureDetector**` widget. Users can tap on products to view details, double-tap to add to favorites, and more, all thanks to the magic of Flutter.

Certainly! Let's dive into the world of the `**InkWell**` widget in Flutter. It's another powerful tool that you can use to handle user interactions and make your app more engaging.

InkWell

The `**InkWell**` widget is a versatile component that's mainly used to add touch interaction to your UI elements. Imagine you want to improve the look of the Lagos store product card custom widget and also want users to interact with it Right now, it's static, and users can only look but not touch. Let's see how `InkWell` can change that:

1. **Import the InkWell Widget:**

   First, make sure you import `material.dart` at the beginning of your Dart file, where your e-commerce catalog page is defined.

   ```
   import 'package:flutter/material.dart';
   ```

2. **Wrap Your Product Cards:**

   Locate the part of your code where you've designed your product cards using the `ProductCard` widget. Now, wrap each `ProductCard` widget with an `InkWell`.

   ```
   InkWell(
     onTap: () {
       // Define what should happen when the product card is tapped.
     },
     child: ProductCard(product: products[index]),
   ),
   ```

Similar to `GestureDetector`, you set the `onTap` property to specify the action to take when a user taps on a product card. This could be navigating to a product details screen, adding it to the cart, or anything else you want.

3. **Additional Features:**

   The `InkWell` widget offers additional features such as `onDoubleTap`, `onLongPress`, and more. You can use these properties to handle other touch interactions, like double-tapping to add to favorites or long-pressing to open a context menu.

4. **Splash Effect:**

   One of the standout features of `InkWell` is its built-in splash effect. When a user taps the card, you get that ripple-like animation around the card, providing visual feedback that the tap was recognized. It's both beautiful and functional!

5. **Rinse and Repeat:**

   You can use the `InkWell` widget for various gestures and UI elements throughout your app. It's a fantastic tool for creating interactive and responsive Flutter apps.

And there you have it! You've just made your Lagos store catalog page interactive using the `InkWell` widget. Users can now tap on products, double-tap to add to favorites, and experience that satisfying ripple animation, making your app more engaging and user-friendly.

So, add `InkWell` to your Flutter app to enhance the user experience further. Happy coding!

Animations and motion widgets

I'm a big fan of football, and beyond the nail-biting action on the pitch, what often captivates me is the presentation of lineups and those captivating goal highlights, beautifully presented on the screen while I'm engrossed in the match. I remember discussing with a friend once about how I adore watching LaLiga games primarily because of the captivating animations and overall immersive experience. They seem to have mastered the art of presenting football, at least in my eyes, better than the Premier League.

But what does football have to do with Flutter, you might wonder? Well, the analogy is striking. Just as captivating animations and fluid transitions enhance the football-watching experience, animations and motion widgets can take your Flutter app from good to stunning.

Imagine this: a user interacts with your app, and elements respond to their touch with smooth transitions, giving it a sense of life. This is the magic of animations and motion widgets in Flutter. They breathe life into your app, making it dynamic, engaging, and visually appealing.

Animations go beyond aesthetics; they convey meaning, guide users' attention, and provide feedback. A well-placed animation can make your app feel intuitive, delightful, and, most importantly, user-friendly.

So let's explore five of the most popular animation widgets in Flutter, each offering a unique way to add movement and life to your app's UI. But remember, Flutter's widget catalog is vast and ever-evolving. The Flutter team constantly introduces new widgets to make your app-building journey even more exciting. So, keep an eye on the official website for the latest updates.

`AnimatedContainer`

The **`AnimatedContainer`** widget in Flutter is a fantastic tool to add a touch of dynamism to your app's interface. It does precisely what its name suggests:

it animates container properties like size, color, padding, and more, creating smooth transitions that can make your app feel more interactive and engaging.

Imagine this scenario: You have a button on your app that, when pressed, expands, drawing attention to its importance. With AnimatedContainer, achieving this effect becomes remarkably straightforward.

Here's a step-by-step guide on how to use **AnimatedContainer** to improve your app's user experience:

Step 1: Import the Flutter Material library

Before you start working with AnimatedContainer, make sure you've imported the Flutter Material library. This library provides a wide range of widgets and tools to enhance the visual appeal and functionality of your app.

```
import 'package:flutter/material.dart';
```

Step 2: Create a StatefulWidget

To make the container's properties change over time, you'll need to work within a StatefulWidget. If you're not familiar with it, feel free to go back to chapter three where stateful and stateless widgets were discussed. Think of a StatefulWidget as a widget that can change its properties or appearance based on interactions or events.

```
class AnimatedContainerExample extends StatefulWidget {
  @override
  _AnimatedContainerExampleState createState() =>
      _AnimatedContainerExampleState();
}
```

Step 3: Define the State

Now, let's define the state for your StatefulWidget. This is where you'll store the properties that will change over time. In this example, we'll use a simple boolean variable to toggle the container's size.

```
class _AnimatedContainerExampleState extends State<AnimatedContainer
Example> {

  bool _isExpanded = false;

}
```

Step 4: Create the AnimatedContainer

Inside your build method, create the **`AnimatedContainer`** widget. Set its properties, such as duration, color, width, height, and any other property you want to animate.

```
@override
Widget build(BuildContext context) {
  return Scaffold(
    appBar: AppBar(
      title: Text('Animated Container Example'),
    ),
    body: Center(
      child: GestureDetector(
        onTap: () {
          setState(() {
            // Toggle the size of the container.
            _isExpanded = !_isExpanded;
          });
        },
        child: AnimatedContainer(
          duration: Duration(seconds: 1), // Animation duration
          width: _isExpanded ? 200.0 : 100.0, // Toggle width
          height: _isExpanded ? 200.0 : 100.0, // Toggle height
          color: _isExpanded ? Colors.blue : Colors.green, // Toggle color
          child: Center(
            child: Text(
              'Tap Me!',
              style: TextStyle(
                color: Colors.white,
                fontSize: 20.0,
              ),
            ),
          ),
        ),
      ),
    ),
  );
}
```

Step 5: Toggle the Animation

In this example, we're using a GestureDetector to trigger the animation when the user taps the container. Inside the onTap function, we use setState to toggle the value of `` `_isExpanded` ``. This triggers the AnimatedContainer to smoothly transition between the defined properties.

And that's it! With just a few lines of code, you've added a delightful animation to your container, making it more interactive and engaging for your users. Experiment with different properties and durations to achieve the perfect animation for your app.

AnimatedCrossFade

User experience is everything. One way to improve it is by making transitions between different UI elements smoother and more visually appealing. This is where the **AnimatedCrossFade** widget comes in handy.

`**AnimatedCrossFade**` is a powerful tool that allows you to transition between two widgets with a cross-fade animation. It's perfect for scenarios where you want to replace one widget with another while maintaining a smooth and visually pleasing transition.

Here's a step-by-step guide on how to use AnimatedCrossFade to enhance your app's user experience:

Step 1: Import the Flutter Material library

Make sure to import the Flutter Material library to access the **AnimatedCrossFade** widget and other essential UI components.

```
import 'package:flutter/material.dart';
```

Step 2: Create a StatefulWidget

To work with **AnimatedCrossFade**, you'll need to use a **StatefulWidget**. This is because you'll be changing the widgets over time, and **StatefulWidget** provides the necessary mechanism to do so.

```
class AnimatedCrossFadeExample extends StatefulWidget {
  @override
  _AnimatedCrossFadeExampleState createState() =>
      _AnimatedCrossFadeExampleState();
}
```

Step 3: Define the State

Define the state for your **StatefulWidget**. In this example, we'll use a boolean variable to toggle between two widgets.

```
class _AnimatedCrossFadeExampleState extends State<AnimatedCrossFade
Example> {
  bool _isFirstWidgetVisible = true;
}
```

Step 4: Create the `AnimatedCrossFade`

Inside your build method, create the **`AnimatedCrossFade`** widget. This widget will smoothly transition between two child widgets based on the value of `_ **isFirstWidgetVisible`**.

```
@override
Widget build(BuildContext context) {
  return Scaffold(
    appBar: AppBar(
      title: Text('Animated CrossFade Example'),
    ),
    body: Center(
      child: Column(
        mainAxisAlignment: MainAxisAlignment.center,
        children: <Widget>[
          AnimatedCrossFade(
            duration: Duration(seconds: 1), // Animation duration
            firstChild: Container(
              width: 200,
              height: 200,
              color: Colors.blue,
              child: Center(
                child: Text(
                  'First Widget',
                  style: TextStyle(
                    color: Colors.white,
                    fontSize: 20,
                  ),
                ),
              ),
            ),
            secondChild: Container(
              width: 200,
              height: 200,
              color: Colors.green,
              child: Center(
                child: Text(
                  'Second Widget',
                  style: TextStyle(
```

```
                  color: Colors.white,
                  fontSize: 20,
                ),
              ),
            ),
          ),
          crossFadeState: _isFirstWidgetVisible
              ? CrossFadeState.showFirst
              : CrossFadeState.showSecond,
        ),
        SizedBox(height: 20),
        ElevatedButton(
          onPressed: () {
            setState(() {
              // Toggle between the two widgets.
              _isFirstWidgetVisible = !_isFirstWidgetVisible;
            });
          },
          child: Text('Toggle Widget'),
        ),
      ],
    ),
  ),
 );
}
```

Step 5: Toggle the Transition

In this example, we have two child widgets inside the **AnimatedCrossFade**: `**firstChild**` and `**secondChild**`. The `**crossFadeState**` property is set based on the value of `**_isFirstWidgetVisible**`. When you tap the "**Toggle Widget**" button, it changes the value of `**_isFirstWidgetVisible**`, triggering the cross-fade animation between the two child widgets.

And that's it! You've added a smooth cross-fade transition between two widgets, making your app's user experience more visually appealing. You can customize the widgets, duration, and transition state to achieve various effects and improve your app's overall look and feel.

AnimatedOpacity

Creating smooth transitions between widget visibility states is essential for a polished user interface. The `**AnimatedOpacity**` widget in Flutter is designed precisely for this purpose. It allows you to gradually change the opacity (transparency) of a widget, making it appear or disappear with a subtle fade-in or fade-out effect.

Here's a step-by-step guide on how to use `**AnimatedOpacity**` to enhance your Flutter app's user experience:

Step 1: Import the Flutter Material library

Ensure that you've imported the Flutter Material library to access the `**AnimatedOpacity**` widget and other essential UI components.

```
import 'package:flutter/material.dart';
```

Step 2: Create a StatefulWidget

To use `**AnimatedOpacity**`, you'll need to work with a **StatefulWidget**. This is because you'll be changing the opacity of a widget over time, and **StatefulWidget** provides the necessary mechanism to do so.

```
class AnimatedOpacityExample extends StatefulWidget {
  @override
  _AnimatedOpacityExampleState createState() => _AnimatedOpacity
ExampleState();
}
```

Step 3: Define the State

Define the state for your **StatefulWidget**. In this example, we'll use a boolean variable to toggle the visibility of the widget.

```
class _AnimatedOpacityExampleState extends State<AnimatedOpacityExample> {
  bool _isVisible = true;
}
```

Step 4: Create the AnimatedOpacity Widget

Inside your build method, create the ****AnimatedOpacity**** widget. This widget will smoothly change the opacity of its child widget based on the value of `_ **isVisible**`.

```
@override
Widget build(BuildContext context) {
  return Scaffold(
    appBar: AppBar(
      title: Text('Animated Opacity Example'),
    ),
    body: Center(
```

```
      child: Column(
        mainAxisAlignment: MainAxisAlignment.center,
        children: <Widget>[
          AnimatedOpacity(
            duration: Duration(seconds: 1), // Animation duration
            opacity: _isVisible ? 1.0 : 0.0, // Change opacity based on
            _isVisible
            child: Container(
              width: 200,
              height: 200,
              color: Colors.blue,
              child: Center(
                child: Text(
                  'Fading Widget',
                  style: TextStyle(
                    color: Colors.white,
                    fontSize: 20,
                  ),
                ),
              ),
            ),
          ),
          SizedBox(height: 20),
          ElevatedButton(
            onPressed: () {
              setState(() {
                // Toggle the visibility of the widget.
                _isVisible = !_isVisible;
              });
            },
            child: Text('Toggle Visibility'),
          ),
        ],
      ),
    ),
  );
}
```

Step 5: Toggle Widget Visibility

In this example, we have an `` `AnimatedOpacity` `` widget wrapping a Container with the text "**Fading Widget**." The opacity of this container is controlled by the `` `_isVisible` `` variable, which changes from 1.0 (fully visible) to 0.0 (completely transparent) when you tap the "**Toggle Visibility**" button. This change in opacity creates a smooth fade-in or fade-out effect.

Flare: Adding stunning 2D animations to flutter

Animations can breathe life into your app, making it more engaging and stunning. While Flutter provides a wide range of built-in animation widgets, sometimes you may need more complex animations. This is where **Flare** comes in. It's a powerful tool that allows you to add beautifully crafted 2D animations to your app.

What is Flare?

Flare is a special tool made by 2Dimensions for crafting cool, smooth animations. These animations are super clear and sharp no matter what device you're using–whether it's a phone or a computer. They're perfect for spicing up mobile apps or websites!

Here's how you can use Flare animations in your app:

Step 1: Install the `flare_flutter` Package

To get started with Flare in Flutter, you'll need to add the **`flare_flutter`** package to your **`pubspec.yaml`** file using this command below:

```
flutter pub add flare_flutter
```

Don't forget to run **`flutter pub get`** to fetch the package.

Here is the link to official documentation for this package

Step 2: Create or Get a Flare Animation

You can create your animations using the Flare design tool, or you can find pre-made Flare animations on websites like [FlareFiles](https://www.2dimensions.com) or [Rive](https://rive.app/). Export the animations in .flr format, which is compatible with the **`flare_flutter`** package.

Step 3: Add the FlareActor Widget

In your Flutter app, use the **`FlareActor`** widget to display the Flare animation. You'll need to provide the path to your **.flr** file and specify the animation you want to play.

```
import 'package:flutter/material.dart';
import 'package:flare_flutter/flare_actor.dart';
```

```
class FlareAnimationExample extends StatelessWidget {
  @override
  Widget build(BuildContext context) {
    return Scaffold(
      appBar: AppBar(
        title: Text('Flare Animation Example'),
      ),
      body: Center(
        child: FlareActor(
          'assets/your_animation.flr', // Path to your .flr file
          animation: 'idle', // Specify the animation to play
        ),
      ),
    );
  }
}
```

Step 4: Customize and Control the Animation

You can customize various aspects of the animation, such as its size, alignment, and position, using the properties of the `FlareActor` widget. Additionally, you can control the animation's playback by changing the `animation` property. For example, to play a different animation when a button is pressed:

```
FlatButton(
  onPressed: () {
    // Change to a different animation
    setState(() {
      _animationName = 'your_animation_name';
    });
  },
  child: Text('Play Animation'),
),
```

Step 5: Run Your Flutter App

Run your Flutter app, and you'll see the Flare animation in action. You can integrate these animations into various parts of your app, such as splash screens, loading indicators, or interactive elements.

Flare opens up a world of possibilities for adding rich animations to your Flutter app without compromising performance. Whether you need subtle transitions or complex character animations, Flare can help you create captivating user experiences. Be sure to explore the [Flare documentation](https://pub.dev/packages/flare_flutter) for more details and advanced usage.

Remember to import the necessary packages:

```
import 'package:flutter/material.dart';
import 'package:flare_flutter/flare_actor.dart';
```

AnimatedPositioned

You often need to move widgets around the screen based on user interactions or changing data. The `**AnimatedPositioned**` widget can help you achieve this by dynamically changing the position and dimensions of child widgets with smooth animations.

Here's how you can use `**AnimatedPositioned**`:

Step 1. Import the Required Package

Ensure you've imported the necessary package:

```
import 'package:flutter/material.dart';
```

Step 2. Create a StatefulWidget

You'll need to create a `**StatefulWidget**` for the widget that you want to animate the position of. For example:

```
class AnimatedPositionedExample extends StatefulWidget {
  @override
  _AnimatedPositionedExampleState createState() =>
      _AnimatedPositionedExampleState();
}
```

Step 3. Create the State Class

In the state class, you can define properties that control the position and other parameters of your widget. For instance:

```
class _AnimatedPositionedExampleState extends State<AnimatedPositioned
Example> {
  bool _isVisible = true;
  double _left = 50.0;
  double _top = 50.0;
}
```

Here, `_isVisible` determines whether the widget is visible, and `_left` and `_top` control its position.

Step 4. Implement the AnimatedPositioned Widget

Now, you can use the `AnimatedPositioned` widget to animate the widget's position based on the properties you defined. For example:

```
AnimatedPositioned(
  duration: const Duration(seconds: 1),
  left: _left,
  top: _top,
  child: _isVisible
      ? Container(
          width: 100,
          height: 100,
          color: Colors.blue,
          child: Center(
            child: Text(
              'Animated Widget',
              style: TextStyle(color: Colors.white),
            ),
          ),
        )
      : null,
)
```

- `duration` determines how long the animation will take.
- `left` and `top` specify the position.
- `child` is the widget that you want to animate. It will appear and disappear based on `_isVisible`.

Step 5. Control the Animation

You can control the animation by updating the properties in response to user interactions or changes in your app's data. For example, to move the widget to a new position when a button is pressed:

```
FlatButton(
  onPressed: () {
    setState(() {
      _left = 200.0;
      _top = 200.0;
    });
  },
```

```
  child: Text('Move Widget'),
)
```

Step 6. Toggle Visibility

You can also toggle the visibility of the widget by updating `_isVisible`:

```
FlatButton(
  onPressed: () {
    setState(() {
      _isVisible = !_isVisible;
    });
  },
  child: Text('Toggle Visibility'),
)
```

Now, when you tap the buttons, the widget will smoothly animate to the new position or toggle its visibility.

`AnimatedPositioned` is a versatile widget that enables you to create dynamic and engaging user interfaces by animating the position and visibility of widgets. Whether you're building interactive elements or creating custom animations, this widget can add a layer of polish to your Flutter app.

Conclusion

In this chapter, we embarked on an exciting journey through styling, theming, and crafting interactive UI designs in Flutter. We dug deep into the art of making your Flutter apps not just functional but also visually appealing and user-friendly.

We began our exploration by understanding the significance of styling and theming in app development and drawing parallels with practical scenarios. Just as a well-decorated apartment can charm its inhabitants, a well-styled app can captivate its users. We uncovered how to create and manage themes, and we explored best practices to maintain a consistent and eye-catching design.

With this foundation in place, we went on to explore user interaction. We introduced the `GestureDetector` and `InkWell` widgets, powerful tools that enable you to capture and respond to user gestures effectively. We illustrated their usage with practical examples, making your apps not just responsive but delightful to use.

But we didn't stop there. Flutter is a world in motion. We expounded on animations and transitions, highlighting ten popular animation widgets to make your apps come alive.

As we conclude this chapter, remember that styling, theming, and interactivity are essential aspects of app development. A well-crafted user interface can make your app look exquisite, while thoughtful animations can create a memorable user experience.

So, what's next? In the next chapter, we'll explore images, media, and effects. Get ready to bring your apps to life with stunning visuals and engaging multimedia. Keep your creativity flowing as we consider another exciting dimension of Flutter development.

Points to Remember

- Just as a well-decorated space is inviting, a well-styled app can captivate users. Pay attention to styling and theming to make your app visually appealing.
- Use themes to maintain a consistent look and feel throughout your app. Define default colors, fonts, and text styles in one place for easy management.
- Leveraging Flutter's built-in Material Design widgets helps ensure a consistent and attractive user interface, especially across different devices and platforms.
- Utilize InheritedWidget to efficiently share theme data throughout your widget tree, making it easy to access the theme without passing it down manually.
- Separate different parts of your theme into their own classes for better code organization, maintainability, and reusability.
- Define default values for each part of your theme to maintain a consistent look and feel across your app.
- Group related pieces of your theme together, such as colors or typography, to make it easier to manage and update.
- Keep the number of colors used in your theme to a minimum to maintain a clean and uncluttered design.
- Avoid hardcoded colors or font sizes in your code. Instead, use Flutter's ThemeData class to define default styles for your app.
- Test your theme on various devices with different screen sizes to ensure a consistent and appealing user experience across the board.

Assessment

Objective: Implement styling, theming, and interactive UI elements in a Flutter app.

Instructions:

1. Create a new Flutter project if you haven't already.
2. In the project's `lib` directory, create a new Dart file named `theme.dart`.
3. In `theme.dart`, define a theme class with the following:
   - A primary color.
   - Two themes: light and dark, each with primary colors.
4. In your project's `main.dart` file:
   - Import the `theme.dart` file.
   - Create a simple Flutter app using `GetMaterialApp`.
   - Use the light theme as the default theme for your app.
   - Implement a toggle button in the `AppBar` to switch between light and dark themes.
5. Create a new Dart file named `product.dart` in the `lib` directory.
   - Define a `Product` class with properties like `name`, `imageUrl`, and `price`.
6. In your project's `main.dart` file:
   - Import the `product.dart` file.
   - Create a list of `Product` objects with various products, including names, image URLs, and prices.
7. Implement a `CatalogPage` widget:
   - Display an `AppBar` with the title "`Flutter Store`" and the theme toggle button.
   - Use a `GridView` or `ListView.builder` to display the list of products.
   - Each product should be shown as a card with its name, image, and price.
8. Make use of either `GestureDetector` or `InkWell` to make the product cards interactive:
   - When a user taps a card, display a simple dialog or toast with the product's name.

9. Test your app on both Android and iOS simulators/emulators or physical devices to ensure it works correctly.
10. Bonus (Optional): Implement an animation of your choice (e.g., `AnimatedContainer`, `AnimatedOpacity`) to add a subtle visual effect to your app.

Remember to add comments in your code to explain each section's purpose and functionality.

Assessment Feedback:

- Did you successfully create a theme class with light and dark themes?
- Does your app have a `toggle` button to switch between light and dark themes?
- Are you displaying a list of products with their names, images, and prices?
- Did you implement interactivity using `GestureDetector` or `InkWell` for the product cards?
- Have you added comments to explain your code?
- Did you consider using animations for added visual appeal?

Feel free to refer to the concepts and code examples from this chapter to complete this assessment. Good luck!

Key Terms

- **Styling:** The process of defining the visual appearance of widgets, including colors, fonts, and spacing, to create an aesthetically pleasing user interface.
- **Theming:** The practice of applying a consistent set of styles and colors to an entire Flutter app to create a unified and cohesive look and feel.
- **Themes:** They are used to define and manage the visual aspects of an app, such as colors, typography, and text styles.
- **Material Design:** A design language developed by Google that provides guidelines for creating user interfaces with a focus on consistency, usability, and a modern look.
- **InheritedWidget:** A special type of widget in Flutter that allows data to be passed down the widget tree without explicitly passing it as parameters to each widget.
- **Global Themes:** Themes that are applied to the entire app, ensuring a consistent design across all screens and widgets.

- **Local Themes:** Themes that are applied to specific parts of an app, overriding global themes for those specific components.
- **Color Palette:** A set of predefined colors used consistently throughout an app to maintain a harmonious color scheme.
- **Hardcoded Values:** Static values (such as specific colors or font sizes) that are directly embedded into the code and are not dynamically adjustable.
- **User Interaction Widgets:** Widgets like `GestureDetector` and `InkWell` enable users to interact with the app through various gestures, such as tapping or swiping.

CHAPTER 5

Working with Images, Media, and Effects in Flutter

Have you ever sat through a technical presentation where the speaker droned on with slide after slide filled with dense text, leaving you and the audience in a state of collective boredom? It's a familiar scenario. People start checking their phones or, worse, give in to a brief nap.

I once attended a technical conference where various speakers took the stage to present their respective topics. During the first speaker's presentation, something became painfully clear—the room was slowly succumbing to boredom. Slide after slide, filled with an overwhelming amount of text, left the audience disengaged. Some resorted to their phones, seeking distraction, while others fought the battle against drowsiness.

However, the atmosphere took a dramatic turn when the second speaker stepped up. From the moment he uttered his first words and displayed the initial slide, a palpable shift occurred. He had the audience's attention in the palm of his hand. Throughout his presentation, he relied less on text and more on striking visuals. The impact was profound; people were attentive, engaged, and even excited.

As humans, we are naturally drawn to images. You hold the key to creating an engaging and immersive user experiences by leveraging the right assets—images, videos, and effects. In the previous chapter, we discussed the art of styling, theming, and interactive UI design. However, without the judicious use of relevant visuals, all your hard work may go unnoticed.

Your ultimate goal is to ensure that users not only interact with your app but become genuinely hooked on the experience. In this chapter, we'll explore the art of working with images, media, and effects. These elements are your tools to craft an immersive and visually appealing app that keeps users actively engaged.

So, prepare to unlock the potential of visual storytelling in Flutter as we journey through the world of images, media, and effects.

Structure

In this chapter, we will cover the following topics:

- Loading and Displaying Images in Flutter
- Working with Icons and Fonts
- Incorporating Media Elements (audio, video) into Flutter Apps
- Applying Visual Effects to UI Elements
- Implementing Custom Painting and Shaders

Loading and Displaying Images

In the digital age, images are the lifeblood of engaging user experiences. They evoke emotions, convey information, and transform a mundane interface into a captivating one. In *Chapter 3: Exploring Flutter Widgets and UI Elements*, we took a closer look at the fundamental Image widget and its workings. If you still find yourself navigating the world of images in Flutter, don't worry; this section is here to provide you with clarity and hands-on experience.

Imagine you're using a news app to stay informed about the latest trends. What draws your attention first? It's those eye-catching images accompanying each news article, right? In this section, we are creating a news page that loads and displays images, headlines, and concise descriptions in a well-organized list.

Introducing the `http` Package

Before we create a news list screen that loads and displays images from URL sources, let's get acquainted with the `http` package. The `http` package is a popular Flutter package that allows you to make HTTP requests to fetch data from the web, including data from APIs. In this section, we'll provide an overview of the package and its basic usage.

Adding the `http` Package to Your Project

To use the `http` package in your Flutter project, you need to add it as a dependency. Here's how to do it:

1. Open your project's `**pubspec.yaml**` file.
2. Under the `dependencies` section, add the `http` package with the desired version.

```
dependencies:
  flutter:
    sdk: flutter
  http: ^0.13.3
```

3. Save the file, and run **`flutter pub get`** to fetch and install the package.

Making HTTP Requests

The `http` package provides functions for making various types of HTTP requests, such as GET, POST, PUT, and DELETE. Here's an example of how to make a simple GET request:

```
import 'package:http/http.dart' as http;

Future<void> fetchData() async {
  final response = await http.get(Uri.parse('https://api.example.com/
  data'));

  if (response.statusCode == 200) {
    // The request was successful, and you can process the response data
    here.
    print('Response data: ${response.body}');
  } else {
    // The request failed.
    print('Request failed with status: ${response.statusCode}');
  }
}
```

In the preceding example, we imported the `http` package with the alias `http` to avoid naming conflicts. We used the `http.get` function to make a GET request to a URL and processed the response accordingly.

Security Considerations

When making HTTP requests to external servers, security is a crucial concern. Always ensure that you are making requests to secure and trusted sources, especially when handling sensitive data.

With this introduction to the `**http**` package, you'll be better prepared to fetch data from external sources in the upcoming challenge.

Now, you can proceed with the challenge of creating the news list screen that loads and displays images from URL sources, with the added knowledge of how to use the `http` package to fetch data.

Understanding `ListView.builder` and `FutureBuilder` Widget

`**ListView.builder**` and `**FutureBuilder**` are awesome tools to display lists in your app. Imagine you have a long list of items, and you don't want to load them all at once. That's where ListView.builder comes in! It dynamically loads only the items you see on your screen, making your app super efficient.

Now, let's talk about `**FutureBuilder**`. Sometimes, you need to fetch data from the internet or a database. It might take a bit of time, and you don't want your app to freeze while waiting. Here's where `**FutureBuilder**` helps. It lets you display a loading spinner or an error message while your data is being fetched. Once the data is ready, it smoothly updates your app.

Defining `FutureBuilder`

FutureBuilder is a widget provided by Flutter that helps you work with `Future` objects, which represent values that may not be available yet. It's a fundamental widget for managing asynchronous operations and updating your UI when the operation completes.

How does `FutureBuilder` work?

The core idea behind `**FutureBuilder**` is to define a `**Future**` that represents the asynchronous operation you want to perform, and then use **FutureBuilder** to manage the UI based on the state of that `**Future**`. Here's how it works:

1. **Define a `Future`**: You create a `**Future**` object that represents the asynchronous operation you want to perform. In many cases, this involves fetching data from an API or a web service.

2. **Use `FutureBuilder`:** Within your Flutter widget tree, you place a **FutureBuilder** widget and provide it with the **Future** you want to monitor.
3. **Handle different states:**
    a. While the `Future` is in progress, **FutureBuilder** displays a loading indicator or placeholder.
    b. If the `Future` completes successfully, **FutureBuilder** rebuilds with the data, allowing you to display it in your UI.
    c. If there's an error during the operation, **FutureBuilder** handles that too, allowing you to show an error message or take appropriate action.

Example Usage

Here's a simplified example of how you might use **FutureBuilder**:

```
Future<String> fetchData() async {
  // Simulate fetching data from an API
  await Future.delayed(Duration(seconds: 2));
  return 'Data from the API';
}

// Inside your widget tree
FutureBuilder<String>(
  future: fetchData(),
  builder: (context, snapshot) {
    if (snapshot.connectionState == ConnectionState.waiting) {
      return CircularProgressIndicator(); // Display a loading indicator.
    } else if (snapshot.hasError) {
      return Text('Error: ${snapshot.error}');
    } else {
      return Text('Data: ${snapshot.data}');
    }
  },
)
```

In this example, **FutureBuilder** monitors the `fetchData` function, and based on the `snapshot` provided in the builder, it displays a loading indicator, an error message, or the fetched data.

Using `FutureBuilder` in the Challenge

In the upcoming challenge, you'll be using the `FutureBuilder` widget to load and display news data from URL sources. It's a valuable tool for handling asynchronous operations in Flutter, and this hands-on experience will help you become proficient in its usage.

Challenge: Creating a News List Page

In this challenge, we will create a news list page in Flutter. This page will display a list of news articles with their titles, short descriptions, and images. The images will be loaded from URL sources. This is a practical exercise to help you become more comfortable with working with images and fetching data in Flutter (See *Figure 5.1*).

Prerequisites:

- Basic knowledge of Flutter widgets.
- Understanding of the `FutureBuilder` widget (explained in the previous section).

Figure 5.1: *News Light and Dark Screen*

OpenSource NewsApi Data

To use the News API (https://newsapi.org/) in the challenge to fetch news articles from the internet, follow these steps:

1. **Sign Up for an API Key:**
    - Go to https://newsapi.org/register.
    - Sign up for an account if you don't have one.
    - After signing up, you will receive an API key. Keep this key safe.
2. **Include the HTTP Package:**
    - In your Flutter project, make sure you have the `**http**` package added to your `**pubspec.yaml**` file:

    ```
    dependencies:
      flutter:
        sdk: flutter
      http: ^0.13.3 // Use the latest version
    ```

    - Run `**flutter pub get**` to install the package.
3. **Use the API Key:**
    - In your Dart code where you want to fetch news articles, you'll need to use the API key you obtained.
    - You can set it as a constant or variable in your code. For example:

    ```
    final apiKey = 'YOUR_API_KEY_HERE';
    ```

    Replace `**'YOUR_API_KEY_HERE'**` with the actual API key you received from News API.
4. **Make API Requests:**
    - You can now use the `http` package to make HTTP GET requests to the News API's endpoints.
    - Use the `**Uri.parse()**` method to construct the API URL with your API key. For example:

    ```
    final apiUrl = 'https://newsapi.org/v2/top-headlines?
    country=us&apiKey=$apiKey';
    final response = await http.get(Uri.parse(apiUrl));
    ```

Adjust the API endpoint and query parameters (for example, `country`, `category`, and so on) as needed for your specific use case.

5. **Handle API Responses:**
   - After making the request, you can handle the API response, including parsing the JSON data into Dart objects. Use the `json` package for JSON parsing.

```
if (response.statusCode == 200) {
  final Map<String, dynamic> data = json.decode(response.body);
  final List<dynamic> articlesData = data['articles'];

  // Parse the articlesData into Dart objects (e.g., Article
  models).
  // Your parsing logic goes here.
} else {
  throw Exception('Failed to load news');
}
```

6. **Implement Error Handling:**
   - Always implement error handling to deal with cases where the API request fails. In the preceding example, an exception is thrown when the request fails.
7. **Display News Data:**
   - Once you've parsed the data into Dart objects (for example, `Article` models), you can display the news articles in your Flutter app's UI as desired.

Remember to check the News API documentation for available endpoints, query parameters, and usage limits. Ensure you comply with their terms of service and rate limits while making API requests.

Step-by-Step Instructions

Step 1: Set Up a New Flutter Project

1. Open your preferred Flutter development environment (for example, Android Studio, Visual Studio Code).
2. Create a new Flutter project using the following command in your terminal:

```
flutter create news_app
```

3. Navigate to the project directory:

```
cd news_app
```

Step 2: Add Dependencies

1. Open the **pubspec.yaml** file in your project.
2. Add the following dependencies under `` `dependencies` ``:

```
dependencies:
 flutter:
   sdk: flutter
 http: ^0.13.3
 cached_network_image: ^3.0.0
```

3. Save the `**pubspec.yaml**` file, and run `` `flutter pub get` `` to fetch the new dependencies:

```
flutter pub get
```

Step 3: Create a News Model Class

1. Inside your project's `lib` directory, create a new Dart file named `news.dart`.
2. Define a Dart class to represent a news article. It should include fields for *title*, `description`, and `imageUrl`.

Step 4: Create a News List Widget

1. Create a new Dart file named `news_list.dart` in your `lib` directory.
2. Define a `StatelessWidget` named `NewsList`.
3. In the `` `build` `` method of `` `NewsList` ``, create a `` `ListView.builder` `` that displays a list of news articles. You can use the `` `CachedNetworkImage` `` widget from the `` `cached_network_image` `` package to load images from URLs.

Step 5: Fetch News Data

1. Import the `` `http` `` package in your `` `news_list.dart` `` file.
2. Create a function to fetch news data from a URL. You can use the `` `http` `` package to make a GET request to the news API.

3. Use the `FutureBuilder` widget to fetch and display news data. Display a loading indicator while fetching data, and handle errors gracefully.

Step 6: Display the News List

1. In your app's main Dart file (**main.dart**), use the **NewsList** widget as the home screen of your app.
2. Run your Flutter app to see the news list in action.

Step 7: Test Your App

1. Test your app by running it on an emulator or physical device.
2. Ensure that the news list is displayed correctly and that images are loaded from the provided URLs.
3. Test the app's behavior when there are network issues or errors while fetching data.

Congratulations! You've successfully created a news list page in Flutter that fetches and displays news articles with images loaded from URL sources. This exercise has given you practical experience in working with images, making HTTP requests, and using the **FutureBuilder** widget to handle asynchronous operations.

Feel free to explore further by adding more features, such as tapping on a news article to view its details or implementing a pull-to-refresh mechanism to update the news list.

Solution

First, let's create the `news.dart` file to define the `News` model class:

1. **news.dart**: This file defines the `News` model class. It represents a news article and contains properties such as `title`, `description`, and `imageUrl`.

```
// news.dart

class Article {
  final String sourceName;
  final String author;
  final String title;
  final String description;
  final String url;
```

```
    final String imageUrl;
    final String publishedAt;
    final String content;

    Article({
      required this.sourceName,
      required this.author,
      required this.title,
      required this.description,
      required this.url,
      required this.imageUrl,
      required this.publishedAt,
      required this.content,
    });

    factory Article.fromJson(Map<String, dynamic> json) {
      return Article(
        sourceName: json['source']['name'],
        author: json['author'] ?? '',
        title: json['title'] ?? '',
        description: json['description'] ?? '',
        url: json['url'] ?? '',
        imageUrl: json['urlToImage'] ?? '',
        publishedAt: json['publishedAt'] ?? '',
        content: json['content'] ?? '',
      );
    }
  }
```

2. **`news_list.dart`:** In this file, we implement the `NewsList` widget, which displays a list of news articles fetched from an API.
   - **`fetchNews()` function:** This function is responsible for fetching news data from an API using the `http` package. It sends an HTTP GET request to the API URL and processes the response.
   - **`FutureBuilder` widget:** This widget allows us to asynchronously load news data and display different UI components based on the current state (loading, error, or data available).
   - **`CircularProgressIndicator`:** This is a loading indicator widget shown while waiting for the news data to be fetched.
   - **`ListView.builder`:** This widget displays the list of news articles using a `ListView`. It builds a list of `ListTile` widgets, each representing a news article.

- **`CachedNetworkImage`**: This widget is used to load and cache images from network URLs. It displays a loading indicator while the image is being fetched and handles errors gracefully.

```
// news_list.dart

import 'dart:developer';

import 'package:flutter/material.dart';
import 'package:http/http.dart' as http;
import 'dart:convert';

import 'lagosstore.dart';
import 'news.dart';
import 'package:cached_network_image/cached_network_image.dart';

class NewsList extends StatelessWidget {
  const NewsList({Key? key}) : super(key: key);

  Future<List<Article>> fetchNews() async {
    final apiKey = 'YOUR_API_KEY_HERE';
      //Replace `'YOUR_API_KEY_HERE'` with the actual API key
      you received from News API.

    final apiUrl = 'https://newsapi.org/v2/top-headlines?coun-
    try=us&apiKey=$apiKey';
    final response = await http.get(
      Uri.parse(apiUrl), // Replace with your API URL
    );

    if (response.statusCode == 200) {
      final Map<String, dynamic> data = json.decode(response.body);
      final List<dynamic> articlesData = data['articles'];

      List<Article> articles = articlesData.map((articleData) {
        return Article.fromJson(articleData);
      }).toList();

      return articles;
    } else {
      throw Exception('Failed to load news');
    }
  }

  @override
  Widget build(BuildContext context) {
```

```
    return Scaffold(
      appBar: AppBar(
        title: const Text('News App'),
        actions: const [
          ThemeManagerWidget(), //Implement the light and dark
          theme created in the previous chapter
        ],
      ),
      body: FutureBuilder<List<Article>>(
        future: fetchNews(),
        builder: (context, snapshot) {
          if (snapshot.connectionState == ConnectionState.waiting) {
            return const Center(
              child: CircularProgressIndicator(),
            );
          } else if (snapshot.hasError) {
            return Center(
              child: Text('Error: ${snapshot.error}'),
            );
          } else {
            final newsList = snapshot.data;

            return ListView.builder(
              itemCount: newsList?.length,
              itemBuilder: (context, index) {
                final news = newsList?[index];
                log(news!.imageUrl);
                return ListTile(
                  leading: CachedNetworkImage(
                    imageUrl: news.imageUrl,
                    placeholder: (context, url) =>
                        const CircularProgressIndicator(),
                    errorWidget: (context, url, error) =>
                        const Icon(Icons.error),
                  ),
                  title: Text(news.title),
                  subtitle: Text(news.description),
                );
              },
            );
          }
        },
      ),
    );
  }
}
```

3. **main.dart:** In the main file, we define the entry point of our Flutter app and configure the app's theme. We use the `**NewsList**` widget as the home screen of the app.
   - **`MyApp` widget:** This is the root widget of the app. It defines the app's title, theme, and home screen, which is set to `**NewsList()**`.
   - `**MaterialApp**`: This widget provides the basic structure for a Material Design app, including the app's theme and navigation.
   - `**Scaffold**`: This widget defines the app's basic layout structure, including an `AppBar` and the `body` of the app.
   - `**AppBar**`: The app bar at the top of the screen contains the app's title.
   - `**NewsList()**`: This is the custom widget we defined earlier, responsible for displaying the list of news articles.

```
// main.dart

import 'package:flutter/material.dart';
import 'news_list.dart';

void main() {
  runApp(MyApp());
}

class ThemeManager {
  static void setThemeMode(ThemeMode mode) {
    Get.changeThemeMode(mode);
  }
}

class MyApp extends StatelessWidget {
  const MyApp({Key? key}) : super(key: key);

  @override
  Widget build(BuildContext context) {
    return GetMaterialApp(
      title: 'News App,
      theme: AppThemes.lightTheme,
      darkTheme: AppThemes.darkTheme,
      home: const NewsList(),
    );
  }
}
```

With this source code, you can run your Flutter app, and it should display a news list page with images loaded from URL sources.

Working with Icons and Fonts

Icons and fonts are essential elements in app design that help convey information, aesthetics, and branding. In Flutter, working with icons and custom fonts is a seamless process, and it greatly enhances the visual appeal of your application. Here, we'll explore how to integrate icons and custom fonts into your Flutter project.

Icons for Visual Communication

Icons are a universal language in app design. They provide users with quick visual cues, making it easier to navigate and understand your app's functionality. Flutter offers a wide range of built-in icons that you can use out of the box, including Material Design icons and Cupertino icons.

- **Material Design Icons:** Flutter provides Material Design icons, which are ready to use in your app. These icons adhere to the Material Design guidelines and are commonly used in Android apps. You can easily add them to your app's interface.
- **Cupertino Icons:** If you're developing an iOS app, Flutter also includes Cupertino icons that match the iOS design language. These icons help maintain a consistent and native look for iOS users.

Adding icons is straightforward. You can use the `Icon` widget and specify the icon you want to display. Here's an example of adding a Material Design icon:

```
Icon(
  Icons.star,
  color: Colors.yellow,
  size: 24.0,
)
```

Custom Fonts for Unique Typography

Custom fonts are another powerful tool for giving your app a unique identity. Whether you want to match your brand's font or create a distinct visual style, Flutter allows you to use custom fonts effortlessly.

To use custom fonts:

1. **Include the Font Files:** Add your custom font files (typically in `.ttf` or `.otf` format) to your Flutter project, typically in a folder like `` `fonts/` `` in the project directory.
2. **Declare the Font in `` `pubspec.yaml` ``:** In your project's `pubspec.yaml` file, declare the custom font and specify its location. Here's an example:

```
flutter:
  fonts:
    - family: MyCustomFont
      fonts:
        - asset: fonts/MyCustomFont-Regular.ttf
```

3. **Load the Font:** To load and use the custom font in your app, use the `` `TextStyle` `` class along with the `` `fontFamily` `` property. For instance:

```
Text(
  'Custom Font Text',
  style: TextStyle(
    fontFamily: 'MyCustomFont',
    fontSize: 18.0,
    fontWeight: FontWeight.bold,
  ),
)
```

This setup allows you to apply your custom font to various text widgets throughout your app.

Customizing the News App

Let's take your News app to the next level by adding a touch of uniqueness and style. In this task, we'll guide you through the process of incorporating custom fonts into your app. Fonts play a pivotal role in design and readability, and by the end of this task, you'll be able to give your news articles a distinctive look and feel. We'll go step-by-step, ensuring that even if you're new to working with fonts in Flutter, you'll find it straightforward and rewarding.

Step 1: Choose a Custom Font

Start by selecting a custom font for your news app. There are many websites where you can find free fonts, such as Google Fonts (https://fonts.google.com/) or fontsquirrel.com. For this example, let's assume you've chosen a font called **OpenSans**.

Step 2: Download the Font Files

Download the font files in .ttf or .otf format from the source you've selected. In our case, we'll download **OpenSans-Regular.ttf**.

Step 3: Add Font Files to Your Flutter Project

1. Create a folder named "**fonts**" in the root directory of your Flutter project (if it doesn't already exist).

2. Place the downloaded font file, for example, "**OpenSans-Regular.ttf**," into the "**fonts**" folder.

Step 4: Declare the Font in `pubspec.yaml`

1. Open your project's **`pubspec.yaml`** file.

2. Inside the **`flutter`** section, declare the custom font by specifying its family name and the path to the font file:

```
flutter:
  fonts:
    - family: OpenSans
      fonts:
        - asset: fonts/OpenSans-Regular.ttf
```

Make sure the indentation is correct in your YAML file.

Step 5: Load and Use the Custom Font in Your App

1. Open the Dart file where you want to use the custom font. In our case, it's the "**news_list.dart**" file.

2. Import the **`package:flutter/material.dart`** library if it's not already imported.

3. To apply the custom font to a **Text** widget, use the **TextStyle** class and specify the **`fontFamily`** property. Here's an example:

```
ListTile(
                  leading: CachedNetworkImage(
                    imageUrl: news.imageUrl,
                    placeholder: (context, url) =>
                        const CircularProgressIndicator(),
                    errorWidget: (context, url, error) =>
                        const Icon(Icons.error),
                  ),
```

```
                  title: Text(news.title,   style: TextStyle(
    fontFamily: 'OpenSans', // Use the fontFamily you declared
    fontSize: 18.0,
    fontWeight: FontWeight.bold,
  ),),
                  subtitle: Text(news.description,   style:
                  TextStyle(
    fontFamily: 'OpenSans', // Use the fontFamily you declared
    fontSize: 18.0,
    fontWeight: FontWeight.bold,
  ),),
                );
```

Now, the "`title`" and "`description`" will be displayed in the "**OpenSans**" font.

Step 6: Update Your News List

1. Search for the places in your "**news_list.dart**" file where you want to apply the custom font.
2. For each `` `Text` `` widget that displays text related to news articles, apply the custom font using the `` `TextStyle` `` class as shown in Step 5.

Step 7: Test Your App

1. Save your changes and run your Flutter app on a simulator or a physical device.
2. Navigate to the news list page to see your custom font in action. The article titles or descriptions should now use the "**OpenSans**" font.

Incorporating Media Elements

Adding multimedia capabilities can significantly enhance the user experience, whether you're building a music player, a video streaming app, or any other application that involves audio and video content.

Users expect more than just text and images; they crave rich media experiences. Flutter provides a robust set of tools and plugins to help you deliver just that. Throughout this section, we'll walk you through the process, step-by-step, so that even if you're new to multimedia integration, you'll be able to master it with ease.

Audio Player

Here are step-by-step instructions on incorporating audio elements into your Flutter app:

Step 1: Import Dependencies

- Open your `**pubspec.yaml**` file.
- Under `**dependencies**`, add the `**audioplayers**` package:

```
dependencies:
  flutter:
    sdk: flutter
  audioplayers: ^5.1.0 # Use the latest version
```

- Save the file and run `**flutter pub get**` to fetch the package.

Step 2: Create an Audio Player Instance

- In your Dart code, import the necessary packages:

```
import 'package:flutter/material.dart';
import 'package:audioplayers/audioplayers.dart';
```

- Create an instance of the `AudioPlayer`:

```
AudioPlayer audioPlayer = AudioPlayer();
```

Step 3: Play an Audio File

- Place your audio file (for example, '**audio.mp3**') in your project directory (commonly in a folder named **'assets'**).
- Load and play the audio file when an action, like tapping a button, is triggered:

```
ElevatedButton(
  onPressed: () async {
    int result = await audioPlayer.play('assets/audio.mp3',
    isLocal: true);
    if (result == 1) {
      // Success
      print('Audio played successfully.');
    } else {
      // Handle errors
      print('Error playing audio.');
    }
  },
  child: Text('Play Audio'),
)
```

Step 4: Pause and Stop Audio

- You can also pause and stop the audio using the `**pause()**` and `**stop()**` methods of the `**audioPlayer**` instance.

```
ElevatedButton(
  onPressed: () {
    audioPlayer.pause();
  },
  child: Text('Pause'),
)

ElevatedButton(
  onPressed: () {
    audioPlayer.stop();
  },
  child: Text('Stop'),
)
```

Step 5: Handle Audio Completion

- If you want to perform an action when the audio playback completes, you can listen for the completion event:

```
audioPlayer.onPlayerCompletion.listen((event) {
  // Perform your action here
  print('Audio playback completed.');
});
```

Step 6: Dispose of the Audio Player

- Don't forget to dispose of the `**audioPlayer**` when you're done with it to release resources:

```
@override
void dispose() {
  audioPlayer.dispose();
  super.dispose();
}
```

Solution

Here's a full source code example for incorporating audio elements.

```
import 'package:flutter/material.dart';
import 'package:audioplayers/audioplayers.dart';
```

```
void main() {
  runApp(const MyApp());
}

class MyApp extends StatelessWidget {
  const MyApp({Key? key}) : super(key: key);

  @override
  Widget build(BuildContext context) {
    return const MaterialApp(
      home: AudioPlayerApp(),
    );
  }
}

class AudioPlayerApp extends StatefulWidget {
  const AudioPlayerApp({Key? key}) : super(key: key);

  @override
  _AudioPlayerAppState createState() => _AudioPlayerAppState();
}

class _AudioPlayerAppState extends State<AudioPlayerApp> {
  AudioPlayer audioPlayer = AudioPlayer();

  @override
  void dispose() {
    audioPlayer.dispose();
    super.dispose();
  }

  @override
  Widget build(BuildContext context) {
    return Scaffold(
      appBar: AppBar(
        title: const Text('Audio Player App'),
      ),
      body: Center(
        child: Column(
          mainAxisAlignment: MainAxisAlignment.center,
          children: <Widget>[
            ElevatedButton(
              onPressed: () async {
                int result = await audioPlayer.play(
                  'assets/audio.mp3',
                  isLocal: true,
```

```
                );
                if (result == 1) {
                  print('Audio played successfully.');
                } else {
                  print('Error playing audio.');
                }
              },
              child: const Text('Play Audio'),
            ),
            ElevatedButton(
              onPressed: () {
                audioPlayer.pause();
              },
              child: const Text('Pause'),
            ),
            ElevatedButton(
              onPressed: () {
                audioPlayer.stop();
              },
              child: const Text('Stop'),
            ),
          ],
        ),
      ),
    );
  }
}
```

In this code, we've created a simple Flutter app with an audio player that can play, pause, and stop audio using buttons. Make sure you have an 'audio.mp3' file in your project's 'assets' folder. You'll also need to include the necessary dependencies for the audioplayers package in your **pubspec.yaml** file.

Remember to add any necessary assets and dependencies to your project before running the code.

Video Player

We'll use the `video_player` package to display a video. Make sure to add the `video_player` dependency to your `pubspec.yaml` file:

```
dependencies:
  flutter:
```

```
      sdk: flutter
    video_player: ^2.7.1 # Use the latest version
```

Now, let's create a Flutter app:

1. **Import Required Packages:**

Import the necessary packages at the top of your Dart file:

```
import 'package:flutter/material.dart';
import 'package:video_player/video_player.dart';
```

2. **Create a `StatefulWidget`:**

Create a **`StatefulWidget`** class to manage the video player state. We'll call it `**VideoPlayerApp**`:

```
class VideoPlayerApp extends StatefulWidget {
  @override
  _VideoPlayerAppState createState() => _VideoPlayerAppState();
}
```

3. **Define the Video Player Controller:**

In the `**_VideoPlayerAppState**` class, define a `**VideoPlayerController**` to control the video playback. Initialize it in the `**initState**` method:

```
class _VideoPlayerAppState extends State<VideoPlayerApp> {
  late VideoPlayerController _controller;

  @override
  void initState() {
    super.initState();
    _controller = VideoPlayerController.asset('assets/sample_video.mp4')
      ..initialize().then((_) {
        setState(() {});
      });
  }

  @override
  void dispose() {
    super.dispose();
    _controller.dispose();
  }
}
```

In this example, we're using an asset video, so make sure you have a video file named '**sample_video.mp4**' in your project's '**assets**' folder.

4. **Build the UI:**

In the `**_VideoPlayerAppState**` class, implement the `build` method to create the app's UI:

```
@override
Widget build(BuildContext context) {
  return Scaffold(
    appBar: AppBar(
      title: Text('Video Player App'),
    ),
    body: Center(
      child: _controller.value.isInitialized
          ? AspectRatio(
              aspectRatio: _controller.value.aspectRatio,
              child: VideoPlayer(_controller),
            )
          : CircularProgressIndicator(),
    ),
    floatingActionButton: FloatingActionButton(
      onPressed: () {
        setState(() {
          if (_controller.value.isPlaying) {
            _controller.pause();
          } else {
            _controller.play();
          }
        });
      },
      child: Icon(
        _controller.value.isPlaying ? Icons.pause : Icons.play_arrow,
      ),
    ),
  );
}
```

Here, we check if the video is initialized before displaying it. If it's not initialized yet, we show a `**CircularProgressIndicator**`. We also add a `**floatingActionButton**` to play/pause the video.

5. **Run the App:**

In your `**main.dart**` file, run the `**VideoPlayerApp**` within a `**MaterialApp**`:

```
void main() {
  runApp(MaterialApp(
    home: VideoPlayerApp(),
  ));
}
```

6. **Test the App:**

Run your Flutter app, and you should see the video player interface with the ability to play and pause the video.

As a note, ensure that the video file (**'sample_video.mp4**' in this example) is correctly placed in the **'assets'** folder and listed in your `**pubspec.yaml**` file under 'assets.'

Solution

Here's the full source code for the Flutter app that incorporates video elements using the `**video_player**` package:

```
import 'package:flutter/material.dart';
import 'package:video_player/video_player.dart';

void main() {
  runApp(MaterialApp(
    home: VideoPlayerApp(),
  ));
}

class VideoPlayerApp extends StatefulWidget {
  @override
  _VideoPlayerAppState createState() => _VideoPlayerAppState();
}

class _VideoPlayerAppState extends State<VideoPlayerApp> {
  late VideoPlayerController _controller;

  @override
  void initState() {
    super.initState();
    _controller = VideoPlayerController.asset('assets/sample_video.mp4')
```

```
      ..initialize().then((_) {
        setState(() {});
      });
  }
  @override
  void dispose() {
    super.dispose();
    _controller.dispose();
  }

  @override
  Widget build(BuildContext context) {
    return Scaffold(
      appBar: AppBar(
        title: const Text('Video Player App'),
      ),
      body: Center(
        child: _controller.value.isInitialized
            ? AspectRatio(
                aspectRatio: _controller.value.aspectRatio,
                child: VideoPlayer(_controller),
              )
            : CircularProgressIndicator(),
      ),
      floatingActionButton: FloatingActionButton(
        onPressed: () {
          setState(() {
            if (_controller.value.isPlaying) {
              _controller.pause();
            } else {
              _controller.play();
            }
          });
        },
        child: Icon(
          _controller.value.isPlaying ? Icons.pause : Icons.play_arrow,
        ),
      ),
    );
  }
}
```

To use this code:

1. Make sure you have the `**video_player**` package added to your `**pubspec.yaml**` file as mentioned in the previous instructions.

2. Place your video file (for example, '**sample_video.mp4**') in the 'assets' folder of your Flutter project.

3. Update the video path in the `VideoPlayerController.asset` method if your video file has a different name or path.

4. Run the app, and you should see the video player interface with the ability to play and pause the video.

As a note, remember to adjust the video file path and customize the app's appearance and functionality as needed for your specific project.

Applying Visual Effects to UI Elements

As developers, we understand that creating eye catching and dynamic user interfaces is essential for capturing and retaining users' attention. In this digital age, users have come to expect more than static screens; they crave engaging visual experiences. Flutter empowers us to meet these expectations by providing an array of tools and widgets to apply captivating visual effects to our UI elements.

Let's explore how Flutter enables us to create a stunning and fluid user experience using some of the top visual effects.

Implementing the BackdropFilter Effect

The `BackdropFilter` is a powerful tool that allows you to blur the content behind a widget, creating various visually appealing effects, such as frosted glass, a soft focus, or a dreamy atmosphere. Let's dive in and learn how to implement this effect step-by-step.

Step 1: Import the Necessary Package

Before we can use the `BackdropFilter` widget, we need to import the required package. Add the following import statement to your Dart file:

```
import 'package:flutter/material.dart';
import 'dart:ui';
```

Step 2: Create a Flutter App

If you don't already have a Flutter app set up, create one using the `flutter create` command in your terminal. You can replace "`my_app`" with your preferred app name.

```
flutter create my_app
```

Step 3: Create a Flutter Widget

Inside your app's Dart file, define a Flutter widget where you want to apply the `**BackdropFilter**` effect. For example, let's create a simple container with an image background:

```
class MyBackdropFilterApp extends StatelessWidget {
  @override
  Widget build(BuildContext context) {
    return MaterialApp(
      home: Scaffold(
        appBar: AppBar(
          title: Text('BackdropFilter Example'),
        ),
        body: Center(
          child: MyBackdropFilterWidget(),
        ),
      ),
    );
  }
}
```

Step 4: Create the Widget with BackdropFilter

Now, let's create the `**MyBackdropFilterWidget**` widget, which will contain the `**BackdropFilter**` effect. In this example, we'll use a `**Stack**` to layer the content and the filter.

```
class MyBackdropFilterWidget extends StatelessWidget {
  const MyBackdropFilterWidget({Key? key}) : super(key: key);
  @override
  Widget build(BuildContext context) {
    return Stack(
      children: [
        // Background image or content
        Image.asset(
          'leather.png', // Replace with your image path
          fit: BoxFit.cover,
          width: double.infinity,
          height: double.infinity,
        ),
        // Apply BackdropFilter
        BackdropFilter(
          filter:
              ImageFilter.blur(sigmaX: 5, sigmaY: 5), // Adjust blur
```

```
              intensity
            child: Container(
              color: Colors.black
                  .withOpacity(0.2), // Adjust overlay color and opacity
              width: double.infinity,
              height: double.infinity,
            ),
          ),
          // Your content goes here
          const Center(
            child: Text(
              'Hello, BackdropFilter!',
              style: TextStyle(fontSize: 24, color: Colors.white),
            ),
          ),
        ],
      );
    }
}
```

In this code:

- We use a `Stack` to layer the background image, the `BackdropFilter` effect, and the content.
- The `Image.asset` widget displays your background image. Replace `leather.png` with the path to your image.
- The `BackdropFilter` widget applies the blur effect with adjustable intensity using `sigmaX` and `sigmaY` properties. You can tweak these values to control the blur level.
- The `Container` within the `BackdropFilter` defines the overlay color and opacity. In this example, we use a semi-transparent black color.

Step 5: Run Your Flutter App

Save your changes and run your Flutter app using the `flutter run` command in your terminal:

```
flutter run
```

You should now see your Flutter app with the stunning `BackdropFilter` effect applied to your chosen UI element. Feel free to experiment with different background images, blur intensities, and overlay colors to achieve the desired visual effect (Refer to *Figure* 5.2)

***Figure* 5.2**: *Opacity Effect Screen*

Implementing the Opacity Effect in Flutter

The `Opacity` widget allows you to adjust the visibility of a widget by changing its opacity level. Whether you want to create fade-in/fade-out effects or simply make a widget partially transparent, Flutter's `Opacity` widget makes it easy. Let's follow the step-by-step implementation of this effect.

Step 1: Import the Necessary Package

Before we can use the `Opacity` widget, we need to import the required package. Add the following import statement to your Dart file:

```
import 'package:flutter/material.dart';
import 'dart:ui';
```

Step 2: Create a Flutter App

If you haven't already set up a Flutter app, create one using the `flutter create` command:

```
flutter create my_app
```

Replace "**my_app**" with your preferred app name.

Step 3: Create a Flutter Widget

Inside your app's Dart file, define a Flutter widget where you want to apply the `Opacity` effect. For this example, we'll create a simple container with an image:

```
class MyOpacityApp extends StatelessWidget {
  @override
  Widget build(BuildContext context) {
    return MaterialApp(
      home: Scaffold(
        appBar: AppBar(
          title: Text('Opacity Example'),
        ),
        body: Center(
          child: MyOpacityWidget(),
        ),
      ),
    );
  }
}
```

Step 4: Create the Widget with Opacity

Now, let's create the `MyOpacityWidget` widget, which will contain the `Opacity` effect. In this example, we'll use an `Opacity` widget to make a text widget partially transparent:

```
class MyOpacityWidget extends StatelessWidget {
  const MyOpacityWidget({Key? key}) : super(key: key);

  @override
  Widget build(BuildContext context) {
    return Opacity(
      opacity: 0.5, // Adjust the opacity level (0.0 - 1.0)
      child: Container(
        color: Colors.blue,
        width: 200,
        height: 200,
        child: const Center(
          child: Text(
            'This is partially transparent text',
            style: TextStyle(fontSize: 20, color: Colors.white),
          ),
        ),
      ),
```

```
    );
  }
}
```

In this code:

- We use the `Opacity` widget to wrap the `Container`, which contains a text widget.
- The `opacity` property inside the `Opacity` widget controls the transparency level. You can set it to a value between 0.0 (completely transparent) and 1.0 (fully opaque) to achieve the desired transparency.

Step 5: Run Your Flutter App

Save your changes and run your Flutter app using the `flutter run` command:

```
flutter run
```

You should now see your Flutter app with the `Opacity` effect applied to the text widget, making it partially transparent. Feel free to adjust the opacity level to create the desired visual effect.

Implementing the RotatedBox Widget in Flutter

The `RotatedBox` widget allows you to apply rotations to widgets, which can be handy for various scenarios like creating angled text or rotating images. Let's dive into the step-by-step implementation of this effect.

Step 1: Import the Necessary Package

Before we can use the `RotatedBox` widget, we need to import the required package. Add the following import statement to your Dart file:

```
import 'package:flutter/material.dart';
import 'dart:ui';
```

Step 2: Create a Flutter App

If you haven't already set up a Flutter app, create one using the `flutter create` command:

```
flutter create my_app
```

Replace "**my_app**" with your preferred app name.

Step 3: Create a Flutter Widget

Inside your app's Dart file, define a Flutter widget where you want to apply the `**RotatedBox**` effect. For this example, we'll create a rotated text widget:

```
class MyRotatedBoxApp extends StatelessWidget {
  @override
  Widget build(BuildContext context) {
    return MaterialApp(
      home: Scaffold(
        appBar: AppBar(
          title: Text('RotatedBox Example'),
        ),
        body: Center(
          child: MyRotatedBoxWidget(),
        ),
      ),
    );
  }
}
```

Step 4: Create the Widget with RotatedBox

Now, let's create the **MyRotatedBoxWidget** widget, which will contain the `**RotatedBox**` effect. In this example, we'll use a **RotatedBox** widget to rotate a text widget:

```
class MyRotatedBoxWidget extends StatelessWidget {
  const MyRotatedBoxWidget({Key? key}) : super(key: key);

  @override
  Widget build(BuildContext context) {
    return RotatedBox(
      quarterTurns: 1, // Number of clockwise quarter turns (90 degrees
      each)
      child: Container(
        color: Colors.blue,
        width: 200,
        height: 200,
        child: const Center(
          child: Text(
            'Rotated Text',
            style: TextStyle(fontSize: 20, color: Colors.white),
          ),
```

```
        ),
      ),
    );
  }
}
```

In this code:

- We use the **RotatedBox** widget to wrap the `` `Container` ``, which contains a rotated text widget.
- The `` `quarterTurns` `` property inside the `` `RotatedBox` `` widget specifies the number of clockwise quarter turns to apply. In this case, we've set it to `` `1` ``, which represents a 90-degree clockwise rotation. You can adjust this value to achieve different rotations.

Step 5: Run Your Flutter App

Save your changes and run your Flutter app using the `` `flutter run` `` command:

```
flutter run
```

You should now see your Flutter app with the **RotatedBox** effect applied to the text widget, rotating it by 90 degrees clockwise.

Remember that the widget catalog is vast and continually evolving. The Flutter team is dedicated to enhancing the framework by introducing new widgets and features regularly. This means that there's always something new and exciting to discover.

Implementing Custom Painting and Shaders

There's a powerful and artistic side to creating user interfaces, and it's known as custom painting and shaders. These techniques allow you to craft stunning visuals and graphics that go beyond the capabilities of standard widgets.

Imagine being able to draw shapes, patterns, or even entirely unique designs on your app's canvas. With custom painting, you have the creative freedom to bring your imagination to life.

But what about shaders? Shaders take your visual artistry to the next level by adding dynamic effects like gradients, distortions, and animations. They can make your app's visuals not just beautiful but also interactive and engaging.

We'll provide a guide on how to implement custom painting and shaders step-by-step.

Step 1: Create a New Flutter Project

Begin by creating a new Flutter project or using an existing one. Open your favorite code editor and ensure you have the Flutter SDK installed.

Step 2: Import the Necessary Libraries

In your Dart file, import the required libraries for custom painting:

```
import 'package:flutter/material.dart';
```

Step 3: Create a Custom Painter Class

To perform custom painting, you need to create a custom painter class that extends the `CustomPainter` class. This class will define how your custom graphics should be drawn. Here's a basic example:

```
class MyPainter extends CustomPainter {
  @override
  void paint(Canvas canvas, Size size) {
    // Define your custom painting logic here
    final paint = Paint()
      ..color = Colors.blue
      ..strokeWidth = 5;

    canvas.drawLine(Offset(0, 0), Offset(size.width, size.height), paint);
  }

  @override
  bool shouldRepaint(CustomPainter oldDelegate) {
    return false; // Return true if your painting should be updated
  }
}
```

Step 4: Use a CustomPaint Widget

Now, you'll use the `CustomPaint` widget to display your custom painting within your Flutter app's UI. Place it within your widget tree, usually inside a `Container` or `SizedBox`:

```
CustomPaint(
  painter: MyPainter(),
  child: Container(
    // Your other widgets can go here
  ),
)
```

Step 5: Create Shader Effects (Optional)

If you want to add shader effects, like gradients or patterns, you can use the **ShaderMask** widget. For example, to create a linear gradient, you can do the following:

```
ShaderMask(
  shaderCallback: (Rect bounds) {
    return LinearGradient(
      begin: Alignment.topLeft,
      end: Alignment.bottomRight,
      colors: [Colors.blue, Colors.green],
    ).createShader(bounds);
  },
  child: YourWidget(),
)
```

Step 6: Run Your App

With your custom painting and shaders in place, you can run your Flutter app using the `flutter run` command. You should see your custom graphics and effects displayed on the screen.

Step 7: Experiment and Explore

Custom painting and shaders offer endless possibilities for creative expression. Feel free to experiment with different shapes, colors, gradients, and effects to achieve your desired visual style.

Conclusion

In this chapter, we dived into working with images, media, and visual effects in Flutter. We began by recognizing the importance of visual content in engaging users and learning how to incorporate images into our apps. We explored the usage of asset images and network images, adding vibrancy to our user interfaces.

Custom fonts were our next focus, and we learned how to choose, integrate, and apply custom fonts for text elements. Typography plays a significant role in app design, and by mastering fonts, we enhanced the visual appeal of our Flutter apps.

We didn't stop at images and fonts; we ventured into media elements. We discovered how to implement audio playback, allowing users to listen to their favorite tunes or audio content seamlessly. Moreover, we explored video playback, enabling users to watch videos within our Flutter apps.

Visual effects are essential to creating modern and appealing user interfaces. We delved into various widgets like `BackdropFilter`, `Opacity`, and `RotatedBox`, understanding how to apply these effects to enhance the aesthetics of our UI elements.

Lastly, we explored custom painting and shaders, empowering ourselves to create unique and custom visual elements within our apps.

As we wrap up this chapter, remember that visuals, media, and effects can greatly impact the user experience. Mastering these techniques allows us to create engaging, attractive, and functional Flutter apps. In the next chapter, *Chapter 6: Typography, Slivers, and Advanced UI Techniques in Flutter*, we'll explore advanced techniques and design principles that will elevate your app to the next level.

Points to Remember

- Incorporating images and visual content into your Flutter app is crucial for creating an engaging and attractive user interface.
- Use asset images for static content bundled with your app. Declare them in the pubspec.yaml file and access them using `AssetImage`.
- For dynamic content from the internet, employ network images by using the `NetworkImage` widget. Ensure a reliable internet connection for these images to load.
- Improve your app's typography by adding custom fonts. Download font files, declare them in the **pubspec.yaml** file, and apply them to text elements using the `TextStyle` widget.
- Utilize audio player packages to implement audio playback in your Flutter app. Consider factors like compatibility and audio formats when choosing a package.
- For video content, select a suitable video player package and implement video playback. Ensure your app supports common video formats and codecs.

- Apply visual effects to UI elements to enhance aesthetics. Flutter provides widgets like `BackdropFilter`, `Opacity`, and `RotatedBox` for this purpose.
- If you need to create custom drawings or shapes, use the custom painting feature with the `` `CustomPaint` `` widget. Implement custom painting logic in a custom painter class.
- Shaders allow you to create advanced visual effects. Use them to apply gradients, blurs, or filters to shapes and images within your app.
- Flutter's widget catalog is continuously expanding. Stay updated by exploring new widgets and features added by the Flutter team to keep your app modern and competitive.

Assessment

Project Title: Flutter Portfolio Showcase

Objective: Build a Flutter app that showcases your skills, experiences, and projects in a visually appealing way. You'll utilize images, fonts, audio, and custom painting to create an engaging portfolio.

Step 1: Create a New Flutter Project

Start by creating a new Flutter project using your preferred development environment (Android Studio, Visual Studio Code, or others).

Step 2: Design Your Portfolio Home Screen

Design a home screen that will serve as the landing page for your portfolio. You can use a `` `Column` `` or `` `ListView` `` to organize the content. Include:

- A profile picture
- Your name and a brief bio
- Links to your social media profiles or contact information
- A button to navigate to project showcases

Step 3: Incorporate Fonts

Choose a custom font to enhance the typography of your app. You can download free fonts from websites like Google Fonts. Explain in your project how to integrate the chosen font into your Flutter app.

Step 4: Add Audio

Include an audio section where you introduce yourself or provide additional details about your projects. Use the Flutter audio plugins you learned about to play this audio.

Step 5: Implement Custom Painting

Create a custom-painted section that adds a unique visual element to your portfolio. You could use custom shapes, patterns, or even an animated background to make your portfolio stand out.

Step 6: Polish Your App

- Apply themes and styles to make your app visually appealing.
- Add any additional features or personalization you'd like to include.

Step 7: Test Your App

Test your app thoroughly on different devices and screen sizes to ensure its responsive and looks great.

Step 8: Publish or Share Your Portfolio

You can either publish your portfolio on platforms like GitHub, or share it with potential employers and clients as a showcase of your Flutter skills.

Step 9: Reflect and Improve

After completing your portfolio, take some time to reflect on what you've learned during this project. Think about ways to improve it or add more features.

Key Terms

- **Image Widget:** A Flutter widget used for displaying images, often loaded from various sources like assets or network URLs.
- **Asset Image:** An image loaded from the app's assets, typically used for static images bundled with the app.
- **Network Image:** An image loaded from a network URL, used for dynamic content fetched from the internet.
- **Font Family:** A collection of font styles that can be applied to text elements in the app, allowing for custom typography.
- **Audio Player:** A Flutter package or library used to play audio files within a Flutter app.
- **Custom Painter:** A Flutter feature that allows you to create custom drawings and shapes within a widget by implementing a custom painting class.
- **Shader**: A graphics program used to apply visual effects, like gradients or filters, to shapes and images in Flutter.

- **Backdrop Filter:** A Flutter widget used to apply visual effects to the background of a widget, such as blurring or changing the backdrop's appearance.
- **Opacity:** A Flutter widget for adjusting the transparency or visibility of a child widget.
- **Video Player:** A Flutter package or library for playing video files within a Flutter app, providing video playback functionality.

CHAPTER 6

Typography, Slivers, and Advanced UI Techniques in Flutter

Introduction

A few weeks ago, in the midst of juggling the many hats of a conference planner, I unexpectedly found myself in design. It wasn't planned, but as the founder of the tech conference, multitasking is more of a necessity than a choice. The task at hand? Creating eye-catching designs for our social media promotions Why? In the digital age, attention spans are fleeting, and grabbing the audience's focus is an art in itself.

This made me realize a fundamental truth: whether you're crafting social media graphics or Flutter UIs, aesthetics matter. In fact, they matter significantly. The look and feel of your app can be the difference between a one-time download and a loyal, engaged user base. It's the visual appeal that keeps users scrolling, tapping, and interacting beyond the first glance.

This chapter explores the art of creating visually compelling Flutter interfaces. We'll look at typography, slivers, and advanced UI techniques that not only make your app functional but also irresistibly beautiful. It's not just about lines of code; it's about crafting experiences that captivate and retain your audience.

Structure

In this chapter, we will cover the following topics:

- Exploring advanced typography and text styling options
- Creating scrollable and responsive UIs with slivers
- Implementing complex UI layouts (Stack, Positioned)
- Understanding advanced UI techniques (Hero animations, ClipRRect)
- Optimizing performance in UI design

Exploring advanced typography and text styling options

Text isn't just information; it's an experience. How your words are presented can profoundly influence how users engage with your app. Flutter, being a versatile and expressive framework, offers a rich palette of tools to craft text in ways that are not only readable but also visually captivating.

Mastering the Art of Typography

Typography is more than just selecting pretty fonts; it's the art of making text not only legible but also visually engaging. In the world of app design, typography plays a fundamental role in conveying your app's personality and enhancing the overall user experience. Think of it as the voice of your app - the way it communicates with your users.

Choosing the Right Typeface

Choosing a typeface (or font) can be a daunting task, with thousands of options available. But fear not; we're here to guide you. Begin by considering the tone of your app. Is it formal and professional, playful and casual, or somewhere in between? Your typeface should align with this tone.

For instance, if you're developing a finance app, you'd lean towards a clean and straightforward sans-serif font like 'Roboto' to convey reliability. Conversely, a gaming app might opt for a more playful font like 'Comic Sans' to reflect its fun nature. Remember, there's no one-size-fits-all, and experimentation can lead to great discoveries.

The Hierarchy of Text

Hierarchy is all about organizing your text to guide users through your app effortlessly. Here's a common hierarchy you might recognize: headers, subheaders, body text, and captions. Each serves a specific purpose, as explained here:

- **Headers**: These are your attention grabbers, usually large and bold, used for titles and major sections.
- **Subheaders**: Slightly smaller than headers, subheaders indicate subsections or categories.
- **Body Text**: The main content of your app, presented in a legible and consistent font size.
- **Captions**: Tiny but vital, captions label images or provide context.

Maintaining consistent font sizes, weights, and styles across your app ensures a beautiful user experience.

Spacing and Line Height

Typography isn't just about fonts; it's also about how you space and align your text. Flutter makes it easy to control text spacing and line height. Adequate spacing between lines (line height) and around text elements (letter spacing) enhances readability.

Spacing between Letters (Letter Spacing)

Flutter's **`letterSpacing`** property lets you control the space between letters in your text. This subtle adjustment can significantly enhance readability and add a touch of elegance to your text.

```
Text(
  'Flutter',
  style: TextStyle(
    letterSpacing: 2.0, // Experiment with different values
  ),
)
```

In the preceding example, the letters in "Flutter" will be spaced 2 logical pixels apart. Experiment with different values until you find the perfect balance between letters, ensuring clarity without compromising aesthetics.

Line Height (Leading)

Leading, pronounced as ledding, refers to the vertical space between lines of text. An optimal line height prevents lines from crowding together, making it easier for readers to follow along. In Flutter, you can achieve this with the height property.

```
Text(
  'Flutter Typography',
  style: TextStyle(
    height: 1.5, // This multiplies with the font size
  ),
)
```

In this instance, the line height is set to 1.5 times the font size. This extra breathing room ensures that lines don't feel cramped, particularly in paragraphs of text.

Whitespace and Padding

Whitespace and padding are essential for comfortable reading. When arranging text elements, use `SizedBox` or `Padding` widgets generously. These widgets provide the necessary space around your text, preventing it from feeling cramped against other UI elements.

```
SizedBox(height: 20.0), // Adds vertical space of 20 logical pixels
```

Text Shadows and Effects

Text can pop off the screen with subtle effects like shadows and outlines. A well-placed shadow can add depth, while an outline can make text stand out. But remember, moderation is key. Overdoing it can lead to a cluttered and distracting interface.

Text Shadows:

Adding shadows to your text can instantly elevate its presence on the screen. The `shadows` property in the **`TextStyle`** widget allows you to experiment with various shadow configurations.

```
Text(
  'Flutter',
  style: TextStyle(
    shadows: [
      Shadow(
```

```
        offset: Offset(2.0, 2.0), // Specifies the shadow's offset
        color: Colors.black, // Shadow color
        blurRadius: 3.0, // Radius of the shadow blur
      ),
    ],
  ),
)
```

In this example, the text **Flutter** will have a subtle black shadow, creating a sense of elevation. Adjust the `offset`, `color`, and `blurRadius` values to fine-tune the shadow effect to match your design aesthetics.

Text Effects:

Adding effects to your text can inject personality and style. Flutter allows you to combine multiple text styles using the `RichText` widget, enabling you to create eye-catching effects within a single text element.

```
RichText(
  text: TextSpan(
    text: 'Flutter',
    style: TextStyle(
      color: Colors.blue,
      fontSize: 24.0,
      fontWeight: FontWeight.bold,
    ),
    children: <TextSpan>[
      TextSpan(
        text: ' Rocks!',
        style: TextStyle(
          color: Colors.green,
          decoration: TextDecoration.underline,
          decorationColor: Colors.red,
          decorationThickness: 2.0,
        ),
      ),
    ],
  ),
)
```

In this example, the word "`Rocks!`" appears in green, underlined with a red dashed line. Play around with ****`TextDecoration`**** properties like `underline`, `overline`, and `lineThrough` to create varied effects. Combine these with different colors and font styles for visually stunning results.

Glow Effect:

The glow effect can make your text appear as if it's illuminated from within. Flutter's **`GlowingOverscrollIndicator`** can be utilized to create this effect on scrollable widgets.

```
ListView(
  children: <Widget>[
    GlowingOverscrollIndicator(
      axisDirection: AxisDirection.down,
      color: Colors.blue, // Glow color
      child: ListTile(title: Text('Item 1')),
    ),
    // Add more list items as needed
  ],
)
```

Custom Fonts

Flutter allows you to use custom fonts, so you're not limited to system fonts. If you have a specific font in mind that aligns perfectly with your app's branding, you can easily integrate it.

Font Integration

Integrating a custom font into your Flutter project is surprisingly simple. First, add your font file (TTF or OTF) to your project's assets. You can download from internet, there are thousands of them available on a simple google search Then, in your `pubspec.yaml`, specify the font file under flutter:

```
flutter:
  fonts:
    - family: YourCustomFont
      fonts:
        - asset: assets/YourCustomFont.ttf
```

This configuration makes your custom font accessible throughout your project.

Applying Custom Fonts

To apply your custom font to a text widget, use the `fontFamily` property within the `TextStyle` widget:

```
Text(
  'Hello, Flutter!',
  style: TextStyle(
    fontFamily: 'YourCustomFont',
    fontSize: 18.0,
    fontWeight: FontWeight.bold,
  ),
)
```

Now, your text is no longer confined to the default fonts; it aligns with your custom typeface.

Font Packages

If you prefer a more diverse font selection, explore packages like `google_fonts`. Add the package to your `pubspec.yaml`:

```
dependencies:
  google_fonts: ^6.1.0 # Check for the latest version on pub.dev
```

Then, import and use it in your project:

```
import 'package:google_fonts/google_fonts.dart';

Text(
  'Hello, Flutter!',
  style: GoogleFonts.yourChosenFont(
    textStyle: TextStyle(fontSize: 18.0, fontWeight: FontWeight.bold),
  ),
)
```

`google_fonts` provides access to a myriad of Google Fonts, granting you a vast palette to paint your textual masterpiece.

Custom Font Best Practices

- **File Formats:** Ensure your custom font files are in TTF or OTF formats for optimal compatibility.
- **Font Weights and Styles:** Custom fonts often come in various weights (like bold, regular, light) and styles (italic). Leverage these variations to add emphasis and hierarchy to your text.

- **Performance Considerations:** Custom fonts can slightly impact your app's performance due to the additional file size. Balance aesthetics with performance for an optimal user experience.

Creating scrollable and responsive UIs with slivers

Crafting interfaces that seamlessly respond to user gestures is an art. Flutter, with its sliver widgets, offers a canvas where your creativity can unfurl, making scrollable and responsive UIs intuitive and delightful.

Understanding CustomScrollView

`CustomScrollView` is a powerful widget in Flutter that allows you to create custom scrolling effects and layouts. It's a versatile tool for building complex scrollable views that go beyond the capabilities of simpler scrollable widgets like ListView or GridView. With CustomScrollView, you can create scrollable layouts with multiple sections, parallax effects, and custom scrolling behaviors.

Working of CustomScrollView

At its core, CustomScrollView works by assembling a list of slivers. Slivers are portions of a scrollable area in your app. Each sliver can represent different content or effects, and they can be stacked vertically or horizontally within the CustomScrollView.

Slivers

Imagine slivers as flexible, interactive portions of your UI. Unlike traditional widgets, slivers can shrink, expand, float, and collide, adapting to diverse screen sizes and user interactions.

AppBar and `SliverAppBar`

The `AppBar` widget provides app-specific functionalities, but when wrapped in a `SliverAppBar`, it seamlessly integrates into scrollable views. Users can smoothly pull down to reveal the app bar, ensuring content is never obstructed.

Creating Dynamic App Bars with AppBar and SliverAppBar

App bars are fundamental components for building beautiful and functional UIs. They provide navigation, titles, and actions, enhancing user experience. `AppBar` and `SliverAppBar` are widgets that enable us to create dynamic, responsive app bars that adapt to scrolling behavior.

Using AppBar for Basic Static App Bars:

The **Scaffold** widget's `appBar` property typically accepts an instance of the **AppBar** widget. This **AppBar** provides a fixed app bar that remains unchanged as users scroll through the content. However, it's essential to note that the `appBar` property doesn't directly accept any custom widgets. This limitation might be challenging for those who want to create a custom app bar using regular widgets.

To overcome this, Flutter provides the **PreferredSizeWidget** class. By implementing this class, you can create a custom widget that specifies its preferred size. This opens up the possibility of using any widget as an app bar within the **Scaffold**. Simply create a widget that extends **PreferredSize** and set its preferred size accordingly. Then, you can use this custom widget as an app bar, allowing for more flexibility and creativity in designing your app's user interface.

To use an AppBar widget

```
Scaffold(
  appBar: AppBar(
    title: Text('Static App Bar'),
    actions: [
      IconButton(
        icon: Icon(Icons.search),
        onPressed: () {
          // Implement your search action here
        },
      ),
    ],
  ),
  body: YourContentWidget(),
)
```

In this example, the **`AppBar`** remains fixed at the top of the screen, regardless of scrolling. You can customize it with titles, icons, and actions according to your app's needs.

If you want to use a custom widget, here is how you can achieve it:

```
import 'package:flutter/material.dart';

class CustomAppBar extends StatelessWidget implements PreferredSizeWidget {
```

```
  @override
  Size get preferredSize => Size.fromHeight(56.0);

  @override
  Widget build(BuildContext context) {
    return AppBar(
      title: Text(
        'Custom App Bar',
        style: TextStyle(color: Colors.white),
      ),
      backgroundColor: Colors.blue,
    );
  }
}

void main() {
  runApp(MyApp());
}

class MyApp extends StatelessWidget {
  @override
  Widget build(BuildContext context) {
    return MaterialApp(
      home: Scaffold(
        appBar: CustomAppBar(), // Use the custom app bar here
        body: Center(
          child: Text('Your App Content Goes Here'),
        ),
      ),
    );
  }
}
```

Using SliverAppBar for Dynamic Scroll Effects:

`SliverAppBar` is a more versatile version of the app bar that can change its appearance as users scroll. Here's how you can create a `SliverAppBar` within a **`CustomScrollView`**:

```
CustomScrollView(
  slivers: <Widget>[
    SliverAppBar(
      expandedHeight: 200, // Height when fully expanded
      floating: false, // App bar will not float as users scroll
      pinned: true, // App bar will remain pinned at the top
      flexibleSpace: FlexibleSpaceBar(
```

```
        title: Text('Dynamic App Bar'),
        background: Image.network(
          'https://example.com/your_image.jpg',
          fit: BoxFit.cover,
        ),
      ),
    ),
    // Add more slivers as needed, like SliverList or SliverGrid
  ],
)
```

In this example, the **SliverAppBar** collapses and becomes pinned to the top as users scroll. The expandedHeight defines the height when the app bar is fully expanded. You can customize the **FlexibleSpaceBar** with titles, background images, or any other widgets.

Adding Scroll Effects:

SliverAppBar allows for creative scroll effects. For instance, you can make it collapse smoothly, reveal additional content, or change colors as users scroll. These effects can be achieved by adjusting properties like **snap**, **floating**, and **stretch**.

```
SliverAppBar(
  expandedHeight: 200,
  floating: false,
  pinned: true,
  snap: true, // App bar snaps into place when scrolled up partially
  stretch: true, // Background image stretches as users scroll
  flexibleSpace: FlexibleSpaceBar(
    title: Text('Dynamic App Bar'),
    background: Image.network(
      'https://example.com/your_image.jpg',
      fit: BoxFit.cover,
    ),
  ),
)
```

In this example, *snap* ensures a smooth snap effect, and *stretch* stretches the background image as users scroll. Tweak these properties to achieve your desired scroll behavior.

SliverList and SliverGrid

`SliverList` and `SliverGrid` provide powerful ways to create dynamic, scrollable lists and grids within a `CustomScrollView`. They allow you to efficiently handle large datasets, providing a smooth user experience. Here's how you can utilize them in your applications:

Using SliverList for Dynamic Lists:

`SliverList` is perfect when you need to display a dynamic list that can scroll smoothly. Here's how you can use it:

```
CustomScrollView(
  slivers: <Widget>[
    SliverAppBar(
      // Your SliverAppBar configuration here
    ),
    SliverList(
      delegate: SliverChildBuilderDelegate(
        (BuildContext context, int index) {
          // Build your list item here using the index
          return ListTile(
            title: Text('Item $index'),
          );
        },
        childCount: yourItemList.length, // Replace with your actual
        list length
      ),
    ),
  ],
)
```

In this example, **`SliverList`** creates a dynamic list based on the length of `yourItemList`. The **`SliverChildBuilderDelegate`** allows you to build each list item dynamically.

Using SliverGrid for Dynamic Grids:

`SliverGrid` is excellent for displaying items in a grid format. It's particularly useful when you want to show items with varying widths or heights. Here's how to set up a dynamic grid:

```
CustomScrollView(
  slivers: <Widget>[
    SliverAppBar(
      // Your SliverAppBar configuration here
    ),
    SliverGrid(
      gridDelegate: SliverGridDelegateWithFixedCrossAxisCount(
        crossAxisCount: 2, // Number of items in each row
```

```
          childAspectRatio: 1.5, // Width to height ratio of each grid item
        ),
        delegate: SliverChildBuilderDelegate(
          (BuildContext context, int index) {
            // Build your grid item here using the index
            return GridTile(
              child: Card(
                child: Center(
                  child: Text('Item $index'),
                ),
              ),
            );
          },
          childCount: yourItemList.length, // Replace with your actual
          list length
        ),
      ),
    ],
)
```

In this example, **SliverGrid** creates a grid with two items in each row, and the aspect ratio ensures consistent sizing. You can customize `crossAxisCount` and `childAspectRatio` to achieve your desired grid layout.

Remember, both **SliverList** and **SliverGrid** can be customized further with various properties to adjust spacing, scrolling behavior, and more. Experiment with these options to create visually appealing and responsive lists and grids for your Flutter applications!

SliverPadding and SliverToBoxAdapter

SliverPadding and **SliverToBoxAdapter** are essential widgets when you need to add padding to your slivers or integrate non-scrollable widgets within a **CustomScrollView**. Here's how to utilize them effectively:

Using SliverPadding for Padding Inside Slivers:

SliverPadding is instrumental when you need to add space around your slivers. Here's how you can do it:

```
CustomScrollView(
  slivers: <Widget>[
    SliverAppBar(
      // Your SliverAppBar configuration here
    ),
```

```
    SliverPadding(
      padding: EdgeInsets.all(16.0), // Adjust padding as needed
      sliver: SliverList(
        delegate: SliverChildBuilderDelegate(
          (BuildContext context, int index) {
            // Build your sliver item here
            return ListTile(
              title: Text('Item $index'),
            );
          },
          childCount: yourItemList.length, // Replace with your actual
          list length
        ),
      ),
    ),
  ],
)
```

In this example, **SliverPadding** is wrapped around the **SliverList**, adding padding around each list item.

Using SliverToBoxAdapter for Non-Scrollable Widgets:

Sometimes, you might want to insert non-scrollable widgets, like headers or banners, within your scrollable list. `SliverToBoxAdapter` is perfect for this scenario:

```
CustomScrollView(
  slivers: <Widget>[
    SliverAppBar(
      // Your SliverAppBar configuration here
    ),
    SliverToBoxAdapter(
      child: Container(
        padding: EdgeInsets.all(16.0),
        color: Colors.grey[200],
        child: Text(
          'This is a non-scrollable header',
          style: TextStyle(fontSize: 18.0, fontWeight: FontWeight.bold),
        ),
      ),
    ),
    SliverList(
      delegate: SliverChildBuilderDelegate(
        (BuildContext context, int index) {
          // Build your scrollable list items here
```

```
          return ListTile(
            title: Text('Item $index'),
          );
        },
        childCount: yourItemList.length, // Replace with your actual
        list length
      ),
    ),
  ],
)
```

In this example, **SliverToBoxAdapter** allows you to insert a non-scrollable header above the scrollable list.

Custom Slivers

Imagine your screen as a canvas, and each part of it can move independently when you scroll. These moving parts are called **slivers**. Creating your own custom slivers allows you to build unique scrolling elements in Flutter.

To make your custom scrolling section, you need to create a delegate. This delegate manages how your sliver looks and behaves.

Creating Your Custom Sliver:

Let's create a simple custom sliver together:

```
class CustomSliver extends SliverPersistentHeaderDelegate {
  final double minHeight;
  final double maxHeight;
  final Widget child;

  CustomSliver({
    required this.minHeight,
    required this.maxHeight,
    required this.child,
  });

  @override
  double get minExtent => minHeight;

  @override
  double get maxExtent => maxHeight;

  @override
```

```
  Widget build(BuildContext context, double shrinkOffset, bool
  overlapsContent) {
    // Here, you design what your sliver will look like.
    // It will stretch from minHeight to maxHeight as you scroll.
    return SizedBox.expand(child: child);
  }

  @override
  bool shouldRebuild(covariant SliverPersistentHeaderDelegate oldDele-
  gate) {
    // This checks if your sliver needs to be redrawn.
    return true; // You can usually return true here.
  }
}
```

In this code, `CustomSliver` is a special recipe for making your sliver. It has a minimum height (`minHeight`), a maximum height (`maxHeight`), and a child widget that's what your sliver will display.

Implementing Your Custom Sliver:

Now, let's put your custom sliver into action with a list:

```
CustomScrollView(
  slivers: <Widget>[
    SliverAppBar(
      // This is a special app bar that can shrink when you scroll down.
      // You can customize its appearance here.
    ),
    CustomSliver(
      minHeight: 100, // The sliver will start at this height.
      maxHeight: 200, // The sliver will stop growing at this height.
      child: YourCustomWidget(), // Your special widget goes here!
    ),
    SliverList(
      delegate: SliverChildBuilderDelegate(
        (BuildContext context, int index) {
          // This builds your list items.
          // You can make a list of things, like messages or photos.
          return ListTile(
            title: Text('Item $index'),
          );
        },
        childCount: yourItemList.length, // Replace this with your
        actual list length.
      ),
```

```
    ),
  ],
)
```

In this part, you're putting your custom sliver (CustomSliver) alongside a regular list (SliverList). The CustomSliver is like a special box on your screen that can change its height as you scroll. You can put any widget inside it, making it perfect for unique design elements.

Challenge: Create a Clothing E-commerce UI using Slivers

In this challenge, you'll be creating a simple clothing e-commerce user interface utilizing slivers for a smooth scrolling experience. Follow the steps given here to complete the challenge:

Step 1: Setup the Project Structure

Create a new Flutter project. Inside your `lib` folder, create three Dart files: **`main.dart`**, **`clothing.dart`**, and **`clothing_item.dart`**.

Step 2: Design Clothing Items

In **`clothing_item.dart`**, create a model class for clothing items:

```
class ClothingItem {
  final String name;
  final String imageUrl;
  final double price;

  ClothingItem({required this.name, required this.imageUrl, required
  this.price});
}
```

Step 3: Design the Clothing Page

In **`clothing.dart`**, design your clothing page using slivers:

```
import 'package:flutter/material.dart';
import 'clothing_item.dart';

class ClothingPage extends StatelessWidget {
  final List<ClothingItem> items;

  const ClothingPage({Key? key, required this.items}) : super(key: key);
```

```
  @override
  Widget build(BuildContext context) {
    return Scaffold(
      body: CustomScrollView(
        slivers: <Widget>[
          SliverAppBar(
            expandedHeight: 200.0,
            flexibleSpace: FlexibleSpaceBar(
              title: const Text('Clothing Store'),
              background: Image.network(
                'https://example.com/store_banner.jpg', // Replace with
your store banner image URL
                fit: BoxFit.cover,
              ),
            ),
          ),
          SliverList(
            delegate: SliverChildBuilderDelegate(
              (BuildContext context, int index) {
                var item = items[index];
                return ListTile(
                  leading: CircleAvatar(
                    backgroundImage: NetworkImage(item.imageUrl),
                  ),
                  title: Text(item.name),
                  subtitle: Text('\$${item.price.toStringAsFixed(2)}'),
                  onTap: () {
                    // Implement item click action
                  },
                );
              },
              childCount: items.length,
            ),
          ),
        ],
      ),
    );
  }
}
```

Step 4: Implement the Main App

In `main.dart`, implement the main app structure and populate it with some sample clothing items:

```
import 'package:flutter/material.dart';
import 'clothing.dart';
import 'clothing_item.dart';

void main() => runApp(MyApp());

class MyApp extends StatelessWidget {
  @override
  Widget build(BuildContext context) {
    return MaterialApp(
      title: 'Clothing Store',
      home: ClothingPage(
        items: [
          ClothingItem(name: 'T-Shirt', imageUrl: 'https://example.com/
tshirt.jpg', price: 19.99),
          ClothingItem(name: 'Jeans', imageUrl: 'https://example.com/
jeans.jpg', price: 39.99),
          // Add more clothing items as needed
        ],
      ),
    );
  }
}
```

Step 5: Test Your App

Run your app on an emulator or a physical device to see your clothing e-commerce UI in action.

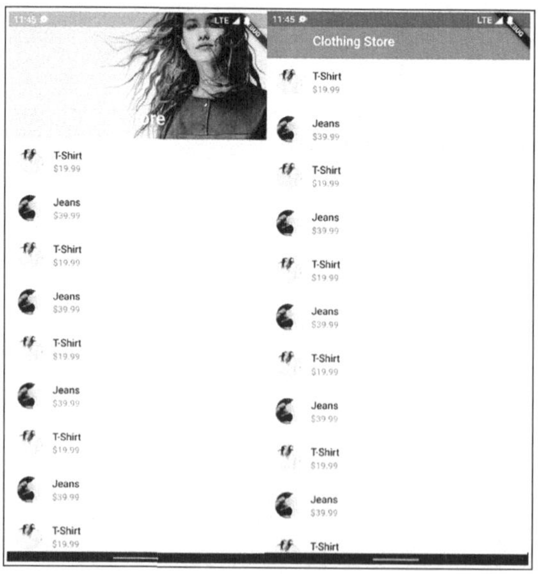

Figure 6.1: *Clothing Store Screen*

You've successfully created a clothing e-commerce user interface using slivers in Flutter. Feel free to customize the UI further and add more features to enhance the user experience!

Implementing complex UI layouts

Designing layouts for applications involves more than just arranging widgets on the screen. It requires understanding various components, incorporating responsive designs, and ensuring a seamless flow of information. In this section, we'll demystify the process, guiding you through the creation of complex UIs step-by-step.

Stack and Positioned Widgets

Think of a `Stack` as a pile of sheets of paper. You can place one sheet (widget) on top of another, creating layers of content. This flexibility opens the door to innovative designs, enabling widgets to overlap, float, or stack in creative ways.

The Stack widget is perfect for scenarios where you want to overlay elements, like text on an image, badges on an avatar, or complex user interfaces with multiple overlapping components.

Let's see how to use the Stack widget to implement complex UI layouts one step at a time. Don't worry; we'll start with the basics and gradually move into more advanced techniques, making sure you grasp the concepts every step of the way. So, let's get started!

Step 1: Implementing a Basic Stack:

To create a basic `Stack`, wrap your widgets with it:

```
Stack(
  children: <Widget>[
    Positioned(
      top: 50,
      left: 20,
      child: Text('Widget 1'), // Positioned widget at top left
    ),
    Positioned(
      bottom: 20,
      right: 40,
      child: Text('Widget 2'), // Positioned widget at bottom right
    ),
    // Add more Positioned widgets as needed
  ],
)
```

Step 2: Utilizing Positioned Widget:

The **`Positioned`** widget is vital within a **`Stack`** because it determines where a child should be placed concerning the top, right, bottom, or left edges of the stack.

Let's say you want to add images precisely positioned on top of each other:

```
Stack(
  children: <Widget>[
    Positioned(
      top: 50,
      left: 20,
      child: Image.asset('assets/image1.png'), // Positioned image at
      top left
    ),
    Positioned(
      top: 80,
      left: 40,
      child: Image.asset('assets/image2.png'), // Positioned image
      slightly below and right
    ),
    // Add more Positioned widgets for other images
  ],
)
```

Step 3: Handling Overlapping Elements:

You can use **`Stack`** to overlap text and buttons creatively:

```
Stack(
  children: <Widget>[
    Positioned(
      top: 20,
      left: 20,
      child: Text('Title', style: TextStyle(fontSize: 24)),
    ),
    Positioned(
      bottom: 20,
      right: 20,
      child: ElevatedButton(
        onPressed: () {
          // Button press logic
        },
        child: Text('Click Me'),
      ),
```

```
    ),
  ],
)
```

Understanding Advanced UI Techniques: `Hero Animations` and `ClipRRect`

In this section, we're going to explore some advanced techniques in Flutter that elevate your user interface from ordinary to extraordinary. Flutter offers a variety of tools and widgets to create smooth and stunning user experiences. Two of these advanced techniques are **`Hero Animations`** and **`ClipRRect`**.

Hero Animations: Elevating Transitions

These are a visually appealing way to transition elements between different screens. Think of it as magically transforming one widget into another while transitioning from one page to another. For instance, you can smoothly transition an image from a thumbnail on one screen to a full-sized image on another, creating an elegant and immersive user experience.

Step 1: Marking Widgets as Heroes:

First, designate the widgets you want to animate as heroes. Typically, this is done with images, but it can be applied to various widgets.

```
// Screen 1
Hero(
  tag: 'hero-tag', // A unique tag for the hero animation
  child: Image.asset('assets/image.png'), // Widget to be animated
)

// Screen 2
Hero(
  tag: 'hero-tag', // Same unique tag as Screen 1
  child: Image.asset('assets/image.png'), // Widget to be animated
)
```

Step 2: The Magic:

Flutter automatically handles the animation when transitioning between the screens. The widget marked as a hero smoothly animates from its position in the first screen to its position in the second.

Step 3: Customizing Hero Animations:

You can customize the animation by specifying additional properties in the Hero widget. For instance, you can adjust the curve for a more dynamic effect:

```
Hero(
  tag: 'hero-tag',
  flightShuttleBuilder: (
    BuildContext flightContext,
    Animation<double> animation,
    HeroFlightDirection flightDirection,
    BuildContext fromHeroContext,
    BuildContext toHeroContext,
  ) {
    return Material( // Customize the animation with Material widget
      child: toHeroContext.widget,
    );
  },
  child: Image.asset('assets/image.png'),
)
```

`ClipRRect`: Crafting Rounded Corners and Clipping

This is a widget that allows you to clip any child widget with rounded corners. This technique is widely used for shaping images, containers, or any other UI element. By rounding the corners, you can add a touch of elegance and modernity to your app's interface. Additionally, **`ClipRRect`** can also be used to clip widgets into various shapes, making your UI design more versatile and visually appealing.

Let's explore how to implement **`ClipRRect`** step-by-step:

Step 1: Implementing ClipRRect:

Wrap the widget you want to round the corners of with the **`ClipRRect`** widget. Specify the **`borderRadius`** property to determine the roundness of the corners.

```
ClipRRect(
  borderRadius: BorderRadius.circular(20), // Specifies the roundness of
  corners
  child: Image.asset('assets/image.png'), // Widget to be clipped
)
```

In this example, the corners of the child widget (an image in this case) are rounded with a circular radius of 20.

Step 2: Customizing ClipRRect:

You can customize the clip further by specifying different radii for each corner. For example, to clip only the top-left and top-right corners:

```
ClipRRect(
  borderRadius: BorderRadius.only(
    topLeft: Radius.circular(20), // Top-left corner radius
    topRight: Radius.circular(20), // Top-right corner radius
  ),
  child: Image.asset('assets/image.png'),
)
```

In this modified example, only the top corners of the child widget are rounded.

Both **`Hero`** and **`ClipRRect`**, when used strategically, can significantly enhance the visual appeal of your applications. Let's look at how this can be done.

Step 1: Preparing the Source and Destination Widgets:

On the source screen, wrap the widget you want to animate with a Hero widget and give it a unique tag:

```
Hero(
  tag: 'imageTag',
  child: Image.asset('assets/source_image.png'),
)
```

On the destination screen, use another Hero widget with the same tag:

```
Hero(
  tag: 'imageTag',
  child: Image.asset('assets/destination_image.png'),
)
```

Flutter automatically animates the transition between these two widgets when navigating from the source screen to the destination screen.

Step 2: Implementing Rounded Image:

Wrap your image with `ClipRRect` and define the `borderRadius` property:

```
ClipRRect(
  borderRadius: BorderRadius.circular(20),
  child: Image.asset('assets/rounded_image.png'),
)
```

The **borderRadius** parameter determines the amount of rounding applied to the corners.

Step 3: Creating a Hero with Rounded Image Transition:

You can combine Hero animations and ClipRRect to smoothly transition rounded images between screens:

```
Hero(
  tag: 'roundedImageTag',
  child: ClipRRect(
    borderRadius: BorderRadius.circular(20),
    child: Image.asset('assets/rounded_image.png'),
  ),
)
```

On the destination screen, use the same Hero widget with the matching tag.

Optimizing Performance in UI Design

As we conclude this chapter, it's important to recognize that creating exceptional UI designs isn't solely about aesthetics; it's also about optimization. Imagine having a beautifully designed app that stutters, lags, or consumes excessive resources; this can lead to a frustrating user experience. To ensure your Flutter app stands out on the app store, it's essential to optimize your design for performance and responsiveness.

Why Optimization Matters:

Optimizing your UI design is all about striking the right balance between visual appeal and efficiency. Here's why it matters:

- **User Experience:**

  Optimized UIs guarantee a seamless user experience. When your app responds promptly and runs smoothly, users are more likely to engage with it regularly.

- **Resource Efficiency:**

  Efficiently designed interfaces consume fewer resources like memory and CPU cycles. This translates to better battery life and a more responsive app.

- **Device Compatibility:**

  Optimized designs adapt seamlessly to various devices and screen sizes. They look and perform well on both high-end flagship phones and budget-friendly devices.

Flutter provides several techniques to achieve this, ensuring your app feels snappy and delightful to use.

Step 1: Efficiently Loading Images:

Load images efficiently, especially large ones, to prevent lags. Utilize packages like **`cached_network_image`** for network images and **`image`** for local assets. These packages offer advanced caching mechanisms, reducing unnecessary network requests and enhancing image loading speed.

```
CachedNetworkImage(
  imageUrl: 'https://example.com/image.jpg',
  placeholder: (context, url) => CircularProgressIndicator(),
  errorWidget: (context, url, error) => Icon(Icons.error),
)
```

Step 2: Minimize Widget Rebuilds:

Avoid unnecessary widget rebuilds, which can slow down your app. Use *const* constructors for widgets that don't change, preventing them from rebuilding when the parent widget rebuilds.

```
class MyWidget extends StatelessWidget {
  const MyWidget({Key? key}) : super(key: key);

  @override
  Widget build(BuildContext context) {
    return const Text('Static Text'); // This widget won't rebuild
    unnecessarily
  }
}
```

Step 3: Implement Lazy Loading:

Implement lazy loading for lists. Use widgets like **`ListView.builder`** and **`GridView.builder`** to load items dynamically as the user scrolls. This prevents loading all items at once, ensuring a smooth scrolling experience, even with a large dataset.

```
ListView.builder(
  itemCount: items.length,
  itemBuilder: (context, index) {
    return ListTile(title: Text(items[index]));
  },
)
```

Step 4: Analyze and Optimize Rebuilds:

Utilize Flutter's built-in tools like the **Performance Overlay** to identify slow frames and optimize rebuilds. Tools like **Dart DevTools** and Flutter **Performance Profiling** provide deep insights into your app's performance, helping you pinpoint bottlenecks.

Conclusion

You've navigated the paths of typography, explored the beauty of Slivers, and delved into advanced UI techniques. As we wrap up this chapter, it's not just the technical skills you've gained that matter; it's the potential you've unlocked.

The ability to craft visually appealing and functionally seamless user interfaces is invaluable. With each line of code, you've written and with every Sliver you've customized, you've honed your craft. You've embraced the richness of typography to communicate not just words but emotions, style, and character. You've conquered the complexities of responsive design, ensuring your apps look stunning on screens of all shapes and sizes. You've mastered advanced UI techniques, making your creations not just interactive but engaging experiences.

But remember, it's not just about the widgets or layouts; it's about the stories your apps will tell. Every pixel you place and every animation you design are the building blocks of user experiences. The speed at which your app loads, the smoothness of its transitions, the elegance of its typography—these are the details that users may not notice consciously, but they deeply influence how they feel about your app.

As you move forward, envision the apps you dream of creating. Picture the impact they will have on users' lives. With the knowledge you've gained in this chapter, those dreams are within your grasp. Your Flutter journey isn't just about learning; it's about innovation, creativity, and making a difference.

So, take a moment to celebrate your achievements, but don't linger too long. Flutter is ever-evolving, with endless possibilities waiting for your touch.

Embrace the challenges ahead with the confidence that you have the skills, the knowledge, and the creativity to overcome them.

In the next chapter, *Building Adaptive UIs for Different Platforms*, we will delve deep into building adaptive UIs for different platforms.

Get ready to embark on another exciting chapter of your Flutter journey!

Points to Remember

- Typography isn't just about fonts; it's a powerful tool to convey emotions and brand identity within your app.
- Slivers are your key to creating dynamic, responsive, and engaging scrollable interfaces, adapting beautifully across different devices.
- Advanced UI techniques like Hero animations and ClipRRect bring life to your designs, making user interactions smooth and visually pleasing.
- Customizing your UI elements using Stack, Positioned, and other techniques provides the flexibility needed to craft unique and tailored user interfaces.
- Optimize not just for visuals but also for speed and efficiency. Users love apps that load fast and run smoothly.
- Proper spacing and line height enhance readability, making your content more accessible and visually appealing.
- Incorporating media like audio and video enriches user experiences, making your app more engaging and entertaining.
- Custom fonts add personality to your app. Choose fonts wisely, ensuring they align with the app's theme and purpose.
- Design with various screen sizes in mind. Slivers are your allies in creating responsive layouts that adapt seamlessly across devices.
- Flutter's vast widget catalog is ever-expanding. Stay curious and keep exploring new widgets and techniques to stay ahead in your Flutter journey.

Assessment

Create a fashion store app with Flutter implementing the advanced UI techniques learned in this chapter.

Objective:

Design a responsive and visually appealing fashion store app that incorporates custom typography, sliver-based scrolling, hero animations, and other advanced UI elements. Ensure the app is optimized for performance and provides an engaging user experience.

Tasks:

1. **Typography and Custom Fonts (15 points):**

   Implement custom fonts for various text elements in your app. Use different font styles and sizes for headings, subheadings, and body text. Ensure the text is readable and aesthetically pleasing.

2. **SliverAppBar (15 points):**

   Create a SliverAppBar that smoothly collapses as the user scrolls, revealing a Hero animation of the store logo. Ensure the app bar provides necessary navigation options and looks visually appealing.

3. **SliverList and SliverGrid (20 points):**

   Implement a SliverList displaying a list of fashion items with accompanying images and details. Implement a SliverGrid displaying categories of items. Ensure both are responsive and provide a smooth scrolling experience.

4. **Hero Animations (15 points):**

   Implement Hero animations for transitioning between the list of items and the detailed view. When the user taps on an item, it should smoothly expand into a detailed view with more information.

5. **Performance Optimization (15 points):**

   Optimize the performance of your app. Use techniques like lazy loading for images, minimize unnecessary rebuilds, and ensure smooth animations. Test the app's performance on various devices and screen sizes.

6. **Custom UI Elements (20 points):**

   Implement at least one custom UI element using Stack, Positioned, or other advanced techniques. This could be a creative way to display item details, such as a popup or an interactive element.

Bonus Task (10 points):

Implement a theme switcher in the app that allows users to toggle between light and dark modes. Ensure that the switch is smooth and visually appealing.

Note: The assessment is designed to test your understanding and application of advanced UI techniques. Focus on both functionality and aesthetics to create an engaging and visually pleasing fashion store app.

Key terms

- **Typography:** The art and technique of arranging type to make written language legible, readable, and visually appealing.
- **Slivers:** Specialized scrollable areas that allow you to create dynamic and customizable scrolling interfaces.
- **Hero Animations:** A Flutter feature that enables smooth and visually pleasing transitions between UI elements when navigating between screens.
- **ClipRRect:** A widget that clips its child using a rounded rectangle, creating visually appealing rounded corners.
- **Custom Fonts:** Fonts that are not part of the default Flutter package, allowing you to add a unique and personalized touch to your app's typography.
- **Responsive Design:** Designing user interfaces that adapt and look great on various screen sizes and orientations.
- **Media Integration:** The process of including audio and video elements within your Flutter app for enhanced user engagement.
- **Performance Optimization:** Techniques and practices for ensuring your app runs smoothly and efficiently, even with complex UI designs.
- **Line Height:** The vertical space between lines of text, crucial for readability and aesthetics in typography.
- **Stack and Positioned:** Widgets used to layer and position UI elements precisely within your app, enabling complex layouts and designs.

Section 3

Creating Cross-Platform UIs

CHAPTER 7

Building Adaptive UIs for Different Platforms

In the world of technology, where innovations unfold at a rapidly fast pace, the landscape of devices we interact with has undergone a revolutionary shift. Enter the era of foldable phones, where screens seamlessly bend, offering a new dimension of interaction. This trend is gradually becoming quite popular amongst many smartphone users around the world. It has fundamentally altered the way we perceive and engage with our devices.

In the early days of mobile app development, the focus was predominantly on specific form factors, occasionally expanding to tablets and desktops. However, with the advent of foldable devices, the concept of adaptive UIs has become more pertinent than ever before. These devices challenge traditional notions of screen sizes and orientations, demanding a level of adaptability and responsiveness previously unexplored.

Figure 7.1: *Photo by 2H Media on Unsplash*

In this chapter, we dive into the nitty-gritty of building adaptive UIs for different platforms. We will observe the core principles that make an interface not just functional but delightful across an array of devices. As technology blurs the lines between smartphones, tablets, and foldable screens, the need for adaptive design is no longer a choice but a necessity.

Structure

In this chapter, we will cover the following topics:

- Understanding the Importance of Adaptive UI Design
- Building Responsive UI Layouts for Various Screen Sizes
- Adapting UI Elements for Different Platforms (iOS, Android)
- Using ScreenUtil Package for Responsive UI

Understanding the Importance of Adaptive UI Design

When it comes to mobile app development, the goal is not just to create visually appealing user interfaces but to craft designs that adapt to the diversity of devices and screens. Why is this adaptive approach so fundamental in today's development scene? Let's explore the few reasons behind its significance.

Reach Across Devices

One of the most exciting challenges is ensuring your app is accessible to users across an array of devices. Gone are the days when a single smartphone screen size was the norm. With the surge in technological innovations, from tablets to foldable phones, users now expect seamless experiences tailored to their specific devices.

Imagine a user seamlessly transitioning from your app on their trusty smartphone during their commute to work, then effortlessly continuing their journey on a tablet at home, and later unfolding their classy foldable phone. Each device presents a unique canvas for your app. Embracing this diversity ensures your users feel at home, regardless of the gadget they're using.

Adaptive UI design is the core that lets you tailor your user interfaces to fit every screen or scenario. Whether it's the compact screen of a smartphone, the expansive canvas of a tablet, or the revolutionary foldable screens, your app should adapt like a chameleon changing its colors. Buttons, images, and text should align well, making interactions intuitive and lovely.

Consistency is the heartbeat of a successful app. A user who switches from a smartphone to a tablet shouldn't feel like they've entered a different universe. Adaptive UI design ensures consistent visual language and interaction patterns, preserving your app's identity across devices. This uniformity fosters a sense of familiarity and trust, which are crucial for user retention.

The global market is full of devices. While one region might favor smartphones, another could lean towards tablets, and yet another may embrace the latest foldable technology. Creating an adaptable UI automatically caters to this varied landscape; you're not just accommodating diverse user preferences but also capturing market niches that might have otherwise remained unexplored.

Ultimately, it all boils down to a user-centric approach. Your app isn't just a piece of software; it's an experience. As you endeavor to ensure that your app reaches across devices seamlessly, you're telling your users, "*We understand you. We've designed this app to fit into your life, no matter what device you prefer.*" This empathy forms the foundation of enduring user relationships.

Changing Screen Orientations

User experiences are greatly influenced by how an app responds to different screen orientations. A smartphone might be held vertically while reading an article or email, but flip it horizontally, and suddenly, it transforms into a widescreen canvas for Netflix movies or a Call of Duty game.

Let's say a user is reclining on their couch, engaging with your app in landscape mode, enjoying beautiful images and expansive content. The very next moment, they switch to portrait mode while on the move, expecting your app to smoothly adjust. Adapting to these changes offers users the flexibility to interact with your app in the way that suits their current context best, enhancing overall usability.

***Figure 7.2**: Photo by Plann on Unsplash*

Different orientations encourage distinct gestures. For instance, in portrait mode, users may prefer vertical scrolling, while in landscape mode, horizontal swiping could be more intuitive. Adapting your UI to these gestures ensures that users don't have to fight against the natural flow of their device, creating a seamless and ergonomic interaction experience.

Changing screen orientations often means different amounts of screen real estate for your content to flex its muscles. Text might need to be reflowed, images could be resized, and menus might be rearranged. Ensuring your content remains relevant and accessible, regardless of the orientation, is pivotal. Users shouldn't feel like they're missing out on vital information just because they switched the way they're holding their device.

In today's multitasking age, users frequently switch between apps. A smooth orientation change experience ensures that when users return to your app, it instantly adjusts to the current screen orientation. This seamless transition makes users more likely to switch back and forth between your app and others, enhancing their overall digital multitasking experience.

Both Android and iOS have specific guidelines regarding UI behavior during orientation changes. Adhering to these platform-specific recommendations not only ensures a consistent experience across all apps on a device but also demonstrates your app's professionalism and attention to detail, earning user trust.

Adapting to changing screen orientations is not merely about rotating elements on the screen; it's about crafting an experience that feels intuitive, natural, and effortless to the users.

Future-Proofing

Where new devices and screen sizes seem to emerge overnight, it's not just enough to make your app compatible with current trends; it's essential to future-proof it. Future-proofing ensures that your app doesn't just survive but thrives amidst the advancements in the tech industry.

Foldable phones and devices with flexible screens have started to reshape the smartphone landscape. By adapting your UI to foldable screens, you tap into a bigger and wider market. Imagine users transitioning from a compact mode to an extended, tablet-like interface. Being ahead of this curve not only attracts early adopters but also demonstrates your app's readiness for future device technologies.

Every new device that hits the market might introduce a unique screen size or aspect ratio. Future-proofing your app involves designing your UI components in a scalable manner. A UI that can adapt to various screen sizes guarantees your app's usability on upcoming devices without requiring major overhauls or redesigns.

Adaptive layouts are the backbone of future-proofing. They enable your app to intuitively adjust its interface based on the available screen space. Whether it's a small smartwatch screen, a standard smartphone display, or a large tablet canvas, adaptive layouts ensure your app delivers an optimal user experience without compromise.

User preferences can be wild, and they never stop changing. Some users might prefer dark mode for its reduced eye strain, while others prefer light mode for its clarity. Accommodating such preferences within your app helps you not only provide a personalized experience but also prepare your app for updates that might introduce new interface styles and themes.

Overall, future-proofing includes being conscious of accessibility standards and guidelines. Designing your app with accessibility in mind ensures that it remains usable for everyone, regardless of their abilities. Additionally, as these standards evolve, your app should be prepared to align with the latest accessibility features and improvements, ensuring inclusivity.

Competitive Advantage

Where users have a plethora of choices at their fingertips, gaining a competitive advantage is not just desirable; it's imperative. As a developer, your goal extends beyond creating a functional app; you aim to offer an unparalleled user experience that keeps users coming back.

An app that seamlessly adapts to various devices and screen sizes offers users a consistent experience, regardless of the platform they use. This consistency builds trust and loyalty. Users are more likely to engage with an app that understands and caters to their device preferences, ensuring they remain active and enthusiastic about using your services.

More than this, user satisfaction directly translates into positive reviews and high ratings. When users find your app easy to use, visually appealing, and functional across different devices, they are more inclined to share their positive experiences. Positive feedback not only boosts your app's reputation but also attracts new users who trust the opinions of their peers.

As earlier discussed, an adaptive UI design allows your app to tap into diverse markets and user demographics. By accommodating various devices and platforms, you break barriers and reach users who might have otherwise been inaccessible. This expansion of your user base not only increases your app's visibility but also enhances your revenue potential.

Technology evolves rapidly, and market trends can shift overnight. An adaptive UI equips your app with the agility to respond to these changes effortlessly. Whether it's a new device form factor or an emerging user behavior pattern, your app can adjust without undergoing serious overhauls. This flexibility ensures you stay ahead of the curve and maintain relevance in the market.

Building UI Layouts for Various Screen Sizes

Creating a visually appealing and user-friendly app is not just about functionality–it's also about how your app adapts to different devices and screen sizes. As the technology landscape expands with a plethora of smartphones, tablets, laptops, and now even foldable devices, ensuring your app looks great and functions seamlessly on each screen is crucial.

Adaptive versus Responsive App

A common question that frequently emerges in the world of Flutter development is understanding the distinction between an adaptive app and a responsive app. It's a fundamental query that can have a profound impact on your app's user experience. Once you grasp this difference, you'll be better equipped to make informed decisions about how to design your app for various devices.

Responsive App

A responsive app is one that seamlessly adjusts its layout and content to fit various screen sizes. It's like having a shape-shifting UI that can comfortably transform itself to look and function optimally on different devices. Responsive apps primarily rely on relative units like percentages for sizing elements, and they adapt to changing screen sizes dynamically. If you've ever encountered a website that seamlessly rearranges its content as you resize the browser window, you've witnessed the concept of responsiveness in action.

Imagine you're building an online shopping app, and you want users to have a seamless shopping experience across devices. In a responsive app:

- **Scenario:** Esther, a user, starts browsing your online store on her smartphone while commuting to work. The product listings, images, and buttons are perfectly scaled and arranged for her small screen. Later, at home, Sarah switches to her tablet. The app recognizes the larger screen and adjusts the layout proportionally. Now, product images are larger, and navigation feels comfortable. Finally, when Sarah accesses the same app on her desktop, the layout expands further, allowing her to see multiple products side by side, making comparison shopping effortless.

Key Characteristics of a Responsive App:

- **Fluid Layout:** Responsive apps use fluid layouts that flexibly adapt to different screen sizes. Elements expand or contract to make the most of the available space, ensuring content remains readable and engaging.
- **Relative Sizing:** Elements are sized proportionally, often using percentages. This relative sizing approach helps maintain the app's visual coherence across a range of devices.
- **Media Queries:** Responsive design often employs media queries in CSS, which allow you to apply specific styles or layouts based on criteria like screen width, height, and orientation.

Adaptive App

On the other hand, an adaptive app is one that is specifically designed and customized for different platforms or devices. Instead of dynamically adjusting to any screen size, an adaptive app offers tailored layouts and experiences for predefined device categories. This approach ensures that the app looks and functions optimally on each type of device. In essence, adaptive design is like having multiple specialized versions of your app, each fine-tuned for a particular class of devices, such as smartphones, tablets, or desktops.

Consider that you're developing a news app where content presentation varies based on the device type. In an adaptive app:

Scenario: Temidayo, a news enthusiast, first opens the app on his smartphone. The layout is streamlined, emphasizing one news story at a time, ensuring optimal readability on a smaller screen. Later, he switches to his tablet. The app detects the change and presents news in a grid layout, allowing Michael to scan multiple headlines simultaneously. When he accesses the app on his desktop, the layout transforms into a newspaper-style format, with multiple columns and additional detailed information alongside headlines, providing a rich reading experience.

Key Characteristics of an Adaptive App:

- **Predefined Layouts:** Adaptive apps feature predefined layouts optimized for specific devices or screen sizes. Each layout is carefully crafted to make the best use of the available screen space.
- **Custom Styling:** Design elements may be customized differently for various device categories. Fonts, images, and other UI components may be tailored to ensure a consistent and polished appearance.
- **Device Detection:** Adaptive apps often employ device detection techniques to identify the user's device and serve the appropriate version or layout. Device-specific code or configurations may be used to enhance performance and usability.

Which is right for you?

The decision between building an adaptive or responsive app depends on your project's goals, target audience, and development resources. Adaptive apps are suitable when you have distinct user experiences in mind for various devices, while responsive apps are more flexible and can be a cost-effective choice for broader compatibility.

Having a clear understanding of the difference between these two approaches empowers you to make the right choice for your app, ensuring that it not only functions impeccably but also delivers a fantastic user experience, regardless of the device in hand. It's a fundamental step toward creating apps that stand out in a diverse digital landscape.

Adapting UI Elements for Different Platforms

Flutter offers a seamless way to ensure your app looks stunning on devices of all shapes and sizes. As users switch between smartphones, tablets, and even desktops, your app can dynamically adjust, providing an intuitive experience. Let's explore the basics of adapting UI elements using Flutter's responsive design principles.

Flutter's responsive design revolves around two key approaches: `LayoutBuilder` and `MediaQuery`. These methods empower you to create UIs that effortlessly adapt to various screen dimensions and orientations.

LayoutBuilder Approach

When constructing Flutter widgets, determining their size can be a puzzle - they might occupy all available space, take a specific portion, or adhere to a fixed size. That's precisely where **LayoutBuilder** steps in to unravel the mystery.

LayoutBuilder not only adapts to dynamic screen size changes but also exhibits real-time responsiveness. For instance, running your app on a web platform like Chrome allows you to witness the immediate adjustments made by **LayoutBuilder**. If you resize the browser window, **LayoutBuilder** dynamically rebuilds its layout, seamlessly adapting to the new constraints imposed by the changing window size. This distinctive behavior sets it apart as a "**builder**" widget, showcasing its ability to construct layouts dynamically in response to varying dimensions.

The Builder Function

In the **LayoutBuilder** widget, you define a **builder** function. This function receives a **BuildContext** and a **BoxConstraints** object. The **BuildContext** provides information about the location of this widget in the widget tree, while the **BoxConstraints** object holds valuable details about the space allocated to your widget.

```
LayoutBuilder(
  builder: (BuildContext context, BoxConstraints constraints) {
    // Your UI building logic goes here
  },
)
```

Using Constraints

The **BoxConstraints** object contains properties like **maxWidth**, **maxHeight**, **minWidth**, and **minHeight**. These properties define the maximum and minimum dimensions your widget can occupy within the parent widget.

```
if (constraints.maxWidth > 600) {
  // Return a layout for larger screens
  return DesktopLayout();
} else {
  // Return a layout for smaller screens
  return MobileLayout();
}
```

Dynamic Adaptation

You use these constraints to dynamically adapt your UI. For instance, you might decide to show a sidebar on wider screens but switch to a bottom navigation bar on narrower screens.

Automatic Rebuilding

The beauty of **LayoutBuilder** lies in its automatic response to changes. If the parent widget's constraints change (due to device rotation or other user interactions), the **builder** function is triggered again. This ensures your UI components adjust instantly, creating a seamless experience for the user.

Building a Responsive AppBar

Let's consider a scenario where you want your app's AppBar to transform based on the screen width. On larger screens, you want to display the title and actions in a row. On smaller screens, you prefer a column layout.

```
LayoutBuilder(
  builder: (BuildContext context, BoxConstraints constraints) {
    if (constraints.maxWidth > 600) {
      // For larger screens
      return AppBar(
        title: Text('My App'),
        actions: <Widget>[
          IconButton(
            icon: Icon(Icons.search),
            onPressed: () {
              // Handle search action
            },
          ),
          IconButton(
            icon: Icon(Icons.settings),
            onPressed: () {
              // Handle settings action
            },
          ),
        ],
      );
    } else {
      // For smaller screens
      return AppBar(
        title: Text('My App'),
```

```
      );
    }
  },
)
```

In this example, the **`LayoutBuilder`** widget dynamically chooses the appropriate layout for the AppBar based on the screen width. This way, your app's AppBar adapts to different devices, ensuring an optimal user experience.

Project: Flutter Music App

Figure 7.3 shows the music app on mobile and tablet screens:

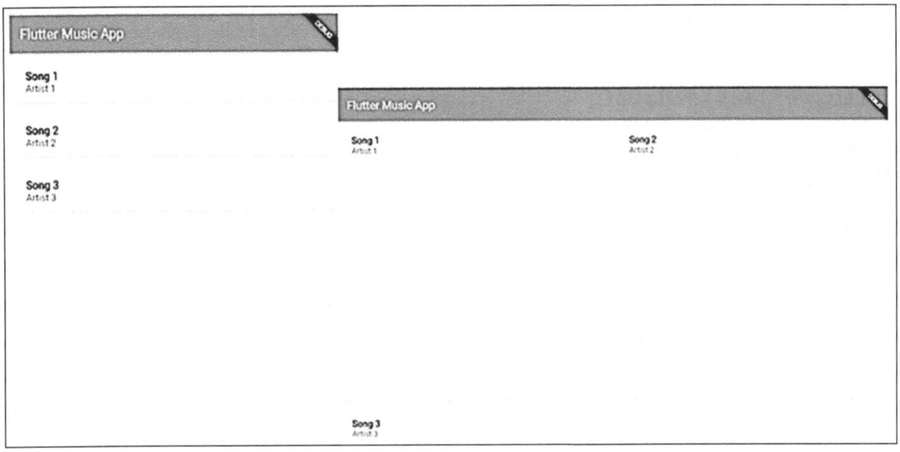

Figure 7.3: *Music App on Mobile and Tablet screens*

Step 1: Setting Up the Project

First, make sure you have Flutter installed. Create a new Flutter project using the following command in your terminal or command prompt:

```
flutter create music_app
```

Step 2: Project Structure

Inside the *lib* folder, create two files: **music.dart** for the data model and **main.dart** for the app's entry point.

Step 3: Implementing the Data Model (music.dart)

```
class Music {
  final String title;
  final String artist;
```

```
  Music(this.title, this.artist);
}

List<Music> musicData = [
  Music('Song 1', 'Artist 1'),
  Music('Song 2', 'Artist 2'),
  Music('Song 3', 'Artist 3'),
  // Add more music data as needed
];
```

Step 4: Building the Responsive UI (main.dart)

1. **Import Statements:**

```
import 'package:flutter/material.dart';
import 'music.dart';
```

First, we're importing necessary packages. **`material.dart`** for Flutter's Material Design components and **`music.dart`** for our custom **`Music`** data model.

2. **`MyApp` Class:**

```
void main() => runApp(MyApp());

class MyApp extends StatelessWidget {
  @override
  Widget build(BuildContext context) {
    return MaterialApp(
      home: Scaffold(
        appBar: AppBar(
          title: Text('Flutter Music App'),
        ),
        body: MusicList(),
      ),
    );
  }
}
```

In the **`MyApp`** class, we define our main application. **`MyApp`** is a **`StatelessWidget`** that returns a **`MaterialApp`**, which provides the basic structure for our app. It has a **`Scaffold`** with an **`AppBar`** and the body containing a **`MusicList`** widget.

3. **`MusicList` Class:**

```
class MusicList extends StatelessWidget {
  @override
  Widget build(BuildContext context) {
    return LayoutBuilder(
      builder: (BuildContext context, BoxConstraints constraints) {
        if (constraints.maxWidth > 600) {
          // Use a grid layout for larger screens
          return GridView.builder(
            gridDelegate:
                SliverGridDelegateWithFixedCrossAxisCount(cros-
                sAxisCount: 2),
            itemCount: musicData.length,
            itemBuilder: (BuildContext context, int index) {
              return MusicCard(music: musicData[index]);
            },
          );
        } else {
          // Use a list layout for smaller screens
          return ListView.builder(
            itemCount: musicData.length,
            itemBuilder: (BuildContext context, int index) {
              return MusicCard(music: musicData[index]);
            },
          );
        }
      },
    );
  }
}
```

`MusicList` is a **`StatelessWidget`** responsible for displaying the list of music items. It uses a **`LayoutBuilder`** to decide between a grid layout (**`GridView`**) and a list layout (**`ListView`**) based on the screen width.

- **`LayoutBuilder`**: It takes a callback function that provides `` `BuildContext` `` and `` `BoxConstraints` ``. `` `BoxConstraints` `` holds information about the maximum and minimum height and width constraints of the parent widget.
- **`GridView.builder`**: If the screen width is greater than 600 (which could be considered a breakpoint for larger screens), it displays a grid of music items with two items in each row. The `` `MusicCard` `` widget is used for each item in the grid.

- **`ListView.builder`:** If the screen width is smaller, it displays a scrollable list of music items using a vertical `ListView`. Again, each item is represented by the `MusicCard` widget.

4. **`MusicCard` Class:**

```
class MusicCard extends StatelessWidget {
  final Music music;

  MusicCard({required this.music});

  @override
  Widget build(BuildContext context) {
    return Card(
      margin: EdgeInsets.all(8.0),
      child: ListTile(
        title: Text(music.title),
        subtitle: Text(music.artist),
        onTap: () {
          // Handle music item click
        },
      ),
    );
  }
}
```

`MusicCard` is a **`StatelessWidget`** that represents an individual music item. It takes a **`Music`** object as a parameter and displays its title and artist within a **`Card`** and **`ListTile`**.

Full main.dart Source code

```
import 'package:flutter/material.dart';
import 'music.dart';

void main() => runApp(MyApp());

class MyApp extends StatelessWidget {
  @override
  Widget build(BuildContext context) {
    return MaterialApp(
      home: Scaffold(
        appBar: AppBar(
          title: Text('Flutter Music App'),
        ),
        body: MusicList(),
```

```
      ),
    );
  }
}

class MusicList extends StatelessWidget {
  @override
  Widget build(BuildContext context) {
    return LayoutBuilder(
      builder: (BuildContext context, BoxConstraints constraints) {
        if (constraints.maxWidth > 600) {
          // Use a grid layout for larger screens
          return GridView.builder(
            gridDelegate:
                SliverGridDelegateWithFixedCrossAxisCount
                (crossAxisCount: 2),
            itemCount: musicData.length,
            itemBuilder: (BuildContext context, int index) {
              return MusicCard(music: musicData[index]);
            },
          );
        } else {
          // Use a list layout for smaller screens
          return ListView.builder(
            itemCount: musicData.length,
            itemBuilder: (BuildContext context, int index) {
              return MusicCard(music: musicData[index]);
            },
          );
        }
      },
    );
  }
}

class MusicCard extends StatelessWidget {
  final Music music;

  MusicCard({required this.music});

  @override
  Widget build(BuildContext context) {
    return Card(
      margin: EdgeInsets.all(8.0),
      child: ListTile(
        title: Text(music.title),
```

```
        subtitle: Text(music.artist),
        onTap: () {
          // Handle music item click
        },
      ),
    );
  }
}
```

Make sure to run your app using `flutter run` to see the responsive layout in action.

MediaQuery Approach

Think of **MediaQuery** as your app's personal information assistant. It provides you with crucial details about the current device and screen, empowering your app to make informed layout decisions.

Flutter allows you to create apps that are truly aware of their environment. The **MediaQuery** class is your window to understanding the device's characteristics and constraints. By tapping into this wellspring of information, you can craft layouts that adapt seamlessly to different screen sizes and orientations.

The MediaQuery Class

The **MediaQuery** class is a fundamental Flutter widget that offers a treasure trove of information about the app's environment. To use it, you typically retrieve the **MediaQueryData** object from your app's **BuildContext**.

```
MediaQueryData mediaQuery = MediaQuery.of(context);
```

The **MediaQueryData** object exposes various properties that are invaluable for building responsive designs, including:

- **size**: Provides the device's screen size as a `Size` object.
- **orientation**: Tells you if the device is in portrait or landscape mode.
- **padding**: Gives you the system padding, which accounts for notches, status bars, and so on.
- **platformBrightness**: Informs you about the device's brightness (light or dark).
- **devicePixelRatio**: Reveals the device's pixel ratio.
- And more.

These properties are the building blocks for creating responsive UIs.

With these device characteristics, you can make decisions about your app's layout.

For instance, you could choose to show a different layout when the device is in landscape mode:

```
if (mediaQuery.orientation == Orientation.landscape) {
  // Display a landscape-specific layout
  return LandscapeLayout();
} else {
  // Display a portrait-specific layout
  return PortraitLayout();
}
```

What's truly amazing is that **`MediaQuery`** automatically updates your UI when device properties change. For instance, if the user rotates the device, the **`mediaQuery`** object will be updated, and your UI can adjust accordingly. No manual intervention is needed.

Here's a practical example. Let's say you want your app's text to be larger on devices with high pixel density (retina screens). You can use **`MediaQuery`** to check the **`devicePixelRatio`** and make your text more legible on such devices.

```
Text(
  'Welcome to My App',
  style: TextStyle(
    fontSize: mediaQuery.devicePixelRatio > 2 ? 24.0 : 18.0,
  ),
)
```

In this case, the text's font size is set dynamically based on the device's pixel density.

Project: Flutter Music App

Let's consider a step-by-step implementation of a simple music app project using the **`MediaQuery`** approach. This approach adapts the UI based on the device's screen size.

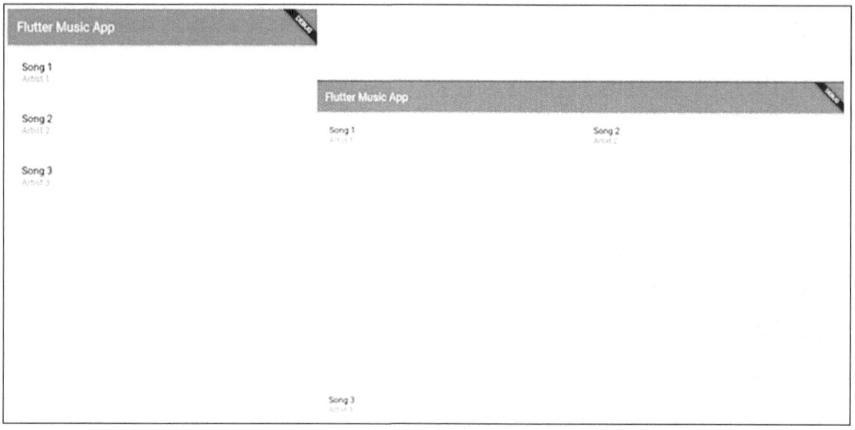

Figure 7.4: *Music app on mobile and tablet screens*

Step 1: Create a Flutter Project

You can create a new Flutter project using your preferred IDE or command line.

Step 2: Define the Data Model

Create a file named **`music.dart`** to define the data model for the music items.

```
class Music {
  final String title;
  final String artist;

  Music({required this.title, required this.artist});
}

// Sample music data
List<Music> musicData = [
  Music(title: 'Song 1', artist: 'Artist 1'),
  Music(title: 'Song 2', artist: 'Artist 2'),
  // Add more music items
];
```

Step 3: Create the Music Card Widget

In a new file named **`music_card.dart`**, create a widget for displaying individual music items.

```
import 'package:flutter/material.dart';
import 'music.dart';

class MusicCard extends StatelessWidget {
```

```
  final Music music;

  MusicCard({required this.music});

  @override
  Widget build(BuildContext context) {
    return Card(
      margin: EdgeInsets.all(8.0),
      child: ListTile(
        title: Text(music.title),
        subtitle: Text(music.artist),
        onTap: () {
          // Handle music item click
        },
      ),
    );
  }
}
```

Step 4: Create the Music List Widget

Create a file named **`music_list.dart`** for the widget responsible for displaying the list of music items.

```
import 'package:flutter/material.dart';
import 'music.dart';
import 'music_card.dart';

class MusicList extends StatelessWidget {
  @override
  Widget build(BuildContext context) {
    return MediaQuery.of(context).size.width > 600
        ? _buildGridList()
        : _buildList();
  }

  Widget _buildList() {
    return ListView.builder(
      itemCount: musicData.length,
      itemBuilder: (BuildContext context, int index) {
        return MusicCard(music: musicData[index]);
      },
    );
  }

  Widget _buildGridList() {
```

```
    return GridView.builder(
      gridDelegate:
          SliverGridDelegateWithFixedCrossAxisCount(crossAxisCount: 2),
      itemCount: musicData.length,
      itemBuilder: (BuildContext context, int index) {
        return MusicCard(music: musicData[index]);
      },
    );
  }
}
```

In this step, we've created the `**MusicList**` widget, which uses `**MediaQuery**` to determine the screen width. If the width is greater than 600 (considered a breakpoint for larger screens), it displays a grid of music items using `**_buildGridList()**`. Otherwise, it displays a list of music items using `**_buildList()**`.

Step 5: Create the Main App

Now, let's put it all together in the main app.

```
import 'package:flutter/material.dart';
import 'music_list.dart';

void main() => runApp(MyApp());

class MyApp extends StatelessWidget {
  @override
  Widget build(BuildContext context) {
    return MaterialApp(
      home: Scaffold(
        appBar: AppBar(
          title: Text('Flutter Music App'),
        ),
        body: MusicList(),
      ),
    );
  }
}
```

This code sets up the main application. It creates an instance of `**MyApp**`, which is a `**MaterialApp**` that contains a `**Scaffold**` with an `**AppBar**` and the body, which is the `**MusicList**` widget.

Step 6: Run the App

You can now run the app on different devices or emulators to see how it adapts to the UI based on the screen size. The `**MediaQuery**` approach ensures a responsive layout for various screen sizes.

This project allows you to display a list of music items with different layouts based on the device's screen width, providing an adaptive user experience.

AspectRatio

The **AspectRatio** is another useful widget for creating an adapting UI element. It is used to enforce a specific aspect ratio on its child. An aspect ratio is the ratio of the width to the height of a widget. It's often used to maintain the proper proportions of UI elements, ensuring they look good on different devices.

Let's consider a scenario where you want to display images in a square aspect ratio, maintaining a 1:1 ratio for width and height. Here's how you can implement it step-by-step:

Figure 7.5: *Square Images Screen*

Step 1: Create a List of Images

First, create a list of image URLs or assets that you want to display. For simplicity, let's assume you have a list of image URLs.

```
//Replace urls with links to your preferred  images
List<String> imageUrls = [
  'https://example.com/image1.jpg',
  'https://example.com/image2.jpg',
```

```
  // Add more image URLs
];
```

Step 2: Create a Widget to Display Images with AspectRatio

Create a new widget named SquareImage that displays images with a square aspect ratio.

```
import 'package:flutter/material.dart';

class SquareImage extends StatelessWidget {
  final String imageUrl;

  SquareImage({required this.imageUrl});

  @override
  Widget build(BuildContext context) {
    return AspectRatio(
      aspectRatio: 1, // 1:1 aspect ratio (square)
      child: Image.network(
        imageUrl,
        fit: BoxFit.cover, // Cover the square area with the image
      ),
    );
  }
}
```

In this widget, the **`AspectRatio`** enforces a 1:1 aspect ratio on its child, which is an **`Image`** widget loaded from the specified URL. The *fit: BoxFit.cover* property ensures that the image covers the entire square area.

Step 3: Create a Widget to Display Image List

Create another widget named **`ImageList`** that uses the **`SquareImage`** widget to display a list of images.

```
class ImageList extends StatelessWidget {
  final List<String> imageUrls;

  ImageList({required this.imageUrls});

  @override
  Widget build(BuildContext context) {
    return ListView.builder(
      itemCount: imageUrls.length,
```

```
      itemBuilder: (BuildContext context, int index) {
        return SquareImage(imageUrl: imageUrls[index]);
      },
    );
  }
}
```

In this widget, the **ListView.builder** displays a list of **SquareImage** widgets, each with a 1:1 aspect ratio.

Step 4: Implement the Main App

Finally, implement the main app, where you can use the **ImageList** widget to display the square images.

```
void main() => runApp(MyApp());
class MyApp extends StatelessWidget {
  @override
  Widget build(BuildContext context) {
    return MaterialApp(
      home: Scaffold(
        appBar: AppBar(
          title: Text('Square Images'),
        ),
        body: ImageList(imageUrls: imageUrls),
      ),
    );
  }
}
```

Now, when you run the app, it will display a list of square images, maintaining a 1:1 aspect ratio for each image.

Try and change the aspect ratio to 2 to see the impact that has on your image.

Figure 7.6: *Square images screen with aspect ratio 2*

This approach ensures that your images maintain a consistent and appealing look, regardless of the device's screen size, providing a better user experience.

OrientationBuilder

The **`OrientationBuilder`** widget stands out as a robust tool for crafting responsive layouts that seamlessly adjust to both portrait and landscape orientations. Unlike screen size changes, it is exclusively tailored to handle orientation shifts, making it adept at delivering a consistent user experience across diverse devices.

This widget springs into action when the device switches between portrait and landscape modes. As the orientation changes, the `OrientationBuilder` widget promptly triggers a rebuild of its builder function. This dynamic behavior empowers you to effortlessly update the UI in real-time, ensuring that your app gracefully adapts to the evolving device orientation.

Let's consider a scenario where you want to display different UI components based on whether the device is in portrait or landscape mode. Here's how you can implement it step-by-step:

Step 1: Create Widgets for Portrait and Landscape Modes

First, create two separate widgets: one for portrait mode (`` `PortraitScreen` ``) and another for landscape mode (`` `LandscapeScreen` ``).

```
import 'package:flutter/material.dart';

class PortraitScreen extends StatelessWidget {
  @override
  Widget build(BuildContext context) {
    return Scaffold(
      appBar: AppBar(
        title: Text('Portrait Mode'),
      ),
      body: Center(
        child: Text('This is the portrait mode UI.'),
      ),
    );
  }
}

class LandscapeScreen extends StatelessWidget {
  @override
  Widget build(BuildContext context) {
    return Scaffold(
```

```
      appBar: AppBar(
        title: Text('Landscape Mode'),
      ),
      body: Center(
        child: Text('This is the landscape mode UI.'),
      ),
    );
  }
}
```

Step 2: Implement OrientationBuilder

Wrap the **OrientationBuilder** around the widgets that you want to adapt based on the device's orientation. In this case, wrap it around the **Scaffold** widgets of both **PortraitScreen** and **LandscapeScreen**.

```
class ResponsiveLayout extends StatelessWidget {
  @override
  Widget build(BuildContext context) {
    return OrientationBuilder(
      builder: (context, orientation) {
        if (orientation == Orientation.portrait) {
          return PortraitScreen();
        } else {
          return LandscapeScreen();
        }
      },
    );
  }
}
```

In the **OrientationBuilder**, the **builder** function is called every time the device's orientation changes. Depending on the orientation, it returns the appropriate screen.

Step 3: Implement the Main App

Finally, implement the main app, where you use the **ResponsiveLayout** widget.

```
void main() => runApp(MyApp());

class MyApp extends StatelessWidget {
  @override
  Widget build(BuildContext context) {
    return MaterialApp(
      home: Scaffold(
```

```
        appBar: AppBar(
          title: Text('Responsive Layout'),
        ),
        body: ResponsiveLayout(),
      ),
    );
  }
}
```

Now, when you run the app, it will display different UIs for portrait and landscape orientations. This approach ensures your app's components are optimally arranged for both orientations, enhancing the user experience.

Using `ScreenUtil` Package for Responsive UI

Building mobile applications that seamlessly adapt to various screen sizes and devices is an essential skill for every Flutter developer. While Flutter provides powerful tools for responsive design, integrating external packages can further enhance your capabilities. One such package that simplifies responsive UI development is the **`ScreenUtil`** package.

In this section, we'll explore how to leverage the **`ScreenUtil`** package to create adaptive and responsive user interfaces. Whether you're targeting smartphones, tablets, or even larger screens, understanding and implementing responsive design principles with **`ScreenUtil`** will empower you to deliver a consistent user experience across a wide range of devices.

The **`ScreenUtil`** package simplifies the process of adapting your UI components to different screen sizes and resolutions. It provides a straightforward solution to handle text scaling, padding, margin, and other dimensions without manual calculations. With **`ScreenUtil`**, you can focus on designing intuitive interfaces while the package takes care of the details of screen responsiveness.

Installation and Setup of `ScreenUtil` Package

Before we get started with creating responsive UIs using the **`ScreenUtil`** package, we need to ensure it's properly installed and set up in our Flutter project.

Flutter `ScreenUtil` Package Usage

Let's explore how to use the Flutter Screen Util package features to make your Flutter app's UI responsive and adaptable to various devices. The Screen Util package provides several methods and properties that make it easier to scale dimensions, fonts, and layouts based on different screen sizes and orientations.

Adapting Width and Height

- `ScreenUtil().setWidth(540)` (or `540.w` if your Dart SDK is 2.6 or newer): This method adapts to the screen width. It's useful for setting widget widths.
- `ScreenUtil().setHeight(200)` (or `200.h` if your Dart SDK is 2.6 or newer): This method adapts to the screen height. In most cases, the height still uses x.w.
- `ScreenUtil().radius(200)` (or `200.r` if your Dart SDK is 2.6 or newer): This method adapts according to the smaller of width or height.
- `ScreenUtil().setSp(24)` (or `24.sp` if your Dart SDK is 2.6 or newer): This is used for adapting font sizes. It's excellent for making your text responsive.
- `12.sm`: Returns the minimum of 12 and `12.sp`.

Screen Properties

- `ScreenUtil().pixelRatio`: Provides the device's pixel density.
- `ScreenUtil().screenWidth` (or `1.sw` if your Dart SDK is 2.6 or newer): Gives the device's width in logical pixels.
- `ScreenUtil().screenHeight` (or `1.sh` if your Dart SDK is 2.6 or newer): Provides the device's height in logical pixels.
- `ScreenUtil().bottomBarHeight`: Offers the bottom safe zone distance, suitable for buttons or elements near the screen's bottom.
- `ScreenUtil().statusBarHeight:` Gives the status bar height. If the device has a notch, the height will be higher.
- `ScreenUtil().textScaleFactor`: Represents the system font scaling factor.

Scale Ratios

- `ScreenUtil().scaleWidth:` Calculates the ratio of the actual width to the UI design. This is useful for scaling various elements.
- `ScreenUtil().scaleHeight`: Similar to `scaleWidth`, but calculates the ratio for the height.

Screen Orientation

- `ScreenUtil().orientation`: Returns the screen orientation (portrait or Landscape).

Here's a step-by-step guide to help you get started:

Step 1: Add ScreenUtil to pubspec.yaml

Firstly, you need to add the **`ScreenUtil`** package to your **`pubspec.yaml`** file. Open the file and add the following line under your `**dependencies**`:

```
dependencies:
  flutter:
    sdk: flutter
  flutter_screenutil: ^latest_version
```

Replace **`latest_version`** with the current version number of the **`ScreenUtil`** package. You can always check the [pub.dev page](https://pub.dev/packages/flutter_screenutil) for the latest version.

Alternatively, you can also use the "**`flutter pub get`**" command and it will automatically add the latest one.

Step 2: Run `flutter pub get`

After adding the dependency, save the **pubspec.yaml** file. Open a terminal or command prompt in your project directory and run the following command to fetch the package:

```
flutter pub get
```

This command will download and install the **`ScreenUtil`** package into your Flutter project.

Step 3: Import ScreenUtil in Your Dart File

Now that the package is installed, you can import it into your Dart files where you intend to use it. In the Dart file where you want to implement responsive design, import `**package:screen_util/screen_util.dart**` at the beginning of the file:

```
import 'package:flutter/material.dart';
import 'package:flutter_screenutil/flutter_screenutil.dart';
```

Step 4: Initialize ScreenUtil in Your `main()` Function

It's essential to initialize `**ScreenUtil**` to set up the design parameters. Typically, this is done in the **`main()`** function of your main.dart file. Add the following lines to your **`main()`** function:

```
void main() => runApp(MyApp());

class MyApp extends StatelessWidget {
  const MyApp({Key? key}) : super(key: key);

  @override
  Widget build(BuildContext context) {
    //Set the fit size (Find your UI design (Figma etc), look at the
dimensions of the device screen and fill it in,unit in dp)
    return ScreenUtilInit(
      designSize: const Size(360, 690),
      minTextAdapt: true,
      splitScreenMode: true,
      // As a note, use builder only if you need to use library outside
of the //ScreenUtilInit context
      builder: (_ , child) {
        return MaterialApp(
          debugShowCheckedModeBanner: false,
          title: Hello World,
          // Feel free to use the library anywhere in the app even in theme
          theme: ThemeData(
            primarySwatch: Colors.blue,
            textTheme: Typography.englishLike2018.apply(fontSizeFactor:
            3.sp),
          ),
          home: child,
        );
      },
      child: const HomePage(title: 'Hello World'),
    );
  }
}
```

In the **ScreenUtilInit()** method, you can specify the design width and height that you want to use as your base. Here, we set the width to 360 and the height to 690 as an example. **minTextAdapt** allows you to specify whether you want ScreenUtil to adapt the text according to the minimum width and height.

Building a Responsive Music Playlist Screen

Now that you have a good grasp of how this package works, it's time to put it to work. We'll follow a step-by-step process for creating a simple music playlist screen using the Flutter Screen Util package. We'll leverage the Screen Util methods to ensure that our UI adapts to various screen sizes.

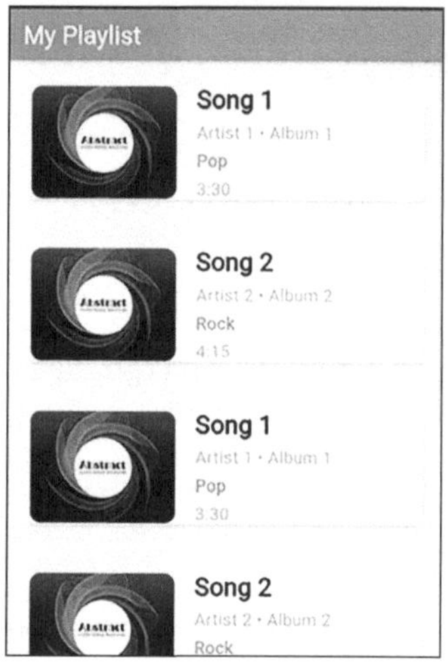

Figure 7.7: *Music playlist screen*

Step 1: Install the Screen Util Package

Add the Screen Util package to your **pubspec.yaml** file and run `flutter pub get`:

```
dependencies:
  # add flutter_screenutil
  flutter_screenutil: ^{latest version}
```

Step 2: Import Necessary Packages

Import the required packages in your Dart file:

```
import ‘package:flutter/material.dart’;
import ‘package:flutter_screenutil/flutter_screenutil.dart’;
```

Step 3: Initialize Screen Util

Initialize Screen Util in the `**main()**` function:

```
void main() => runApp(MyApp());

class MyApp extends StatelessWidget {
  const MyApp({Key? key}) : super(key: key);

  @override
  Widget build(BuildContext context) {
    //Set the fit size (Find your UI design, look at the dimensions of
the device screen and fill it in,unit in dp)
```

```
    return ScreenUtilInit(
      designSize: const Size(360, 690),
      minTextAdapt: true,
      splitScreenMode: true,
      // Use builder only if you need to use library outside
      ScreenUtilInit context
      builder: (_ , child) {
        return MaterialApp(
          debugShowCheckedModeBanner: false,
          title: 'First Method',
          // You can use the library anywhere in the app even in theme
          theme: ThemeData(
            primarySwatch: Colors.blue,
            textTheme: Typography.englishLike2018.apply(fontSizeFactor:
            1.sp),
          ),
          home: MyPlaylistScreen(),
        );
      },

    );
  }
}
```

Step 4: Create a Data Model

Create a more detailed data model to represent a music track:

```
class MusicTrack {
  final String title;
  final String artist;
  final String album;
  final String genre;
  final String duration;
  final String imageUrl;

  MusicTrack({
    required this.title,
    required this.artist,
    required this.album,
    required this.genre,
    required this.duration,
    required this.imageUrl,
  });
}
```

Step 5: Create a Mock Playlist

Generate a list of more detailed mock music tracks for testing:

```
List<MusicTrack> mockPlaylist = [
  MusicTrack(
    title: 'Song 1',
    artist: 'Artist 1',
    album: 'Album 1',
    genre: 'Pop',
    duration: '3:30',
    imageUrl: 'url1',
  ),
  MusicTrack(
    title: 'Song 2',
    artist: 'Artist 2',
    album: 'Album 2',
    genre: 'Rock',
    duration: '4:15',
    imageUrl: 'url2',
  ),
  // ... add more tracks
];
```

Step 6: Build the Playlist Screen

Create a responsive and visually appealing music playlist screen using **`ScreenUtil`** methods:

```
class MyPlaylistScreen extends StatelessWidget {
  @override
  Widget build(BuildContext context) {
    return Scaffold(
      appBar: AppBar(
        title: Text('My Playlist'),
      ),
      body: ListView.builder(
        itemCount: mockPlaylist.length,
        itemBuilder: (context, index) {
          return buildTrackCard(context, mockPlaylist[index]);
        },
      ),
    );
  }
```

```
Widget buildTrackCard(BuildContext context, MusicTrack track) {
  return Padding(
    padding: EdgeInsets.all(16.w),
    child: Card(
      elevation: 4,
      child: Row(
        children: [
          // Left side: Album cover
          Container(
            height: 120.h, // Set a fixed height for the album cover
            width: 120.w, // Set a fixed width for the album cover
            decoration: BoxDecoration(
              borderRadius: BorderRadius.circular(12.r),
              image: DecorationImage(
                image: NetworkImage(track.imageUrl),
                fit: BoxFit.cover,
              ),
            ),
          ),
          // Right side: Track details
          Expanded(
            child: Padding(
              padding: EdgeInsets.symmetric(horizontal: 16.w),
              child: Column(
                crossAxisAlignment: CrossAxisAlignment.start,
                children: [
                  Text(
                    track.title,
                    style: TextStyle(
                      fontSize: 20.sp,
                      fontWeight: FontWeight.bold,
                    ),
                  ),
                  SizedBox(height: 8.h),
                  Text(
                    '${track.artist} • ${track.album}',
                    style: TextStyle(color: Colors.grey),
                  ),
                  SizedBox(height: 8.h),
                  Text(
                    track.genre,
                    style: TextStyle(
                      color: Colors.blue,
                      fontWeight: FontWeight.bold,
                    ),
                  ),
                  SizedBox(height: 8.h),
```

```
                        Text(
                          track.duration,
                          style: TextStyle(color: Colors.grey),
                        ),
                      ],
                    ),
                  ),
                ),
              ],
            ),
          ),
        );
  }
}
```

Step 7: Run Your App

Run your app with `flutter run` and witness the beauty of your responsive and detailed music playlist screen. The UI components will adapt seamlessly to different screen sizes thanks to the `ScreenUtil` package.

Feel free to customize the design further based on your preferences.

Conclusion

In this chapter, we explored building adaptive UIs for different platforms, a crucial skill for any modern developer.

As technology evolves, so do user expectations. The advent of foldable phones and an ever-expanding array of devices makes adaptive UIs more relevant than ever. In this chapter, we delved into the importance of creating UIs that seamlessly adapt to diverse screen sizes, orientations, and devices.

Remember, your app is your digital ambassador. It's not just lines of code; it's an experience. By mastering adaptive UI design, you're not only meeting user expectations but exceeding them. Your users will love the flexibility and responsiveness your app provides, ensuring a stunning experience across various platforms. In the next chapter, we will explore the core of handling navigation and routing for Flutter project.

Points to Remember

- **Adapt or Lag Behind:** The digital landscape is diverse, and users engage with apps on various devices. Building adaptive UIs is not just a skill; it's a necessity to stay relevant.

- **Screen Size Matters:** Consider the real estate your app occupies. Be mindful of screen sizes and resolutions to ensure a consistent and visually appealing user experience.
- **Orientation Awareness:** Users switch between portrait and landscape modes. Design your UI to adapt seamlessly, providing an intuitive experience in both orientations.
- **Future-Proof Your App:** Technology evolves rapidly. Build your app with an eye on the future, ensuring it remains relevant and functional as new devices and screen sizes emerge.
- **Competitive Edge:** An app that works flawlessly on different platforms gains a competitive advantage. Users appreciate consistency and are more likely to stick around.
- **`LayoutBuilder`:** Master the art of using `` `LayoutBuilder` `` for responsive UIs. This widget empowers you to make informed decisions based on the available screen space.
- **`MediaQuery` Mastery:** Understand the power of `` `MediaQuery` `` for making decisions based on the overall app context. It's a versatile tool for creating responsive and adaptive designs.
- **`AspectRatio` Wisdom:** When dealing with images and media, consider the `` `AspectRatio` `` widget. It maintains a desired aspect ratio, ensuring your visuals look great across screens.
- **`ScreenUtil` for Precision:** Leverage the `ScreenUtil` package for precise control over UI elements. It provides a comprehensive set of tools to adapt sizes, spacing, and more.
- **Stay User-Centric:** Throughout your adaptive UI journey, keep the user at the center. An adaptive UI is not just about technical implementation; it's about delivering an exceptional user experience.

Assessment

Objective: Your task is to create a responsive UI that mimics the Google Gmail App Inbox Screen. You can use either the ScreenUtil package for responsiveness or any other Flutter responsiveness widget of your choice.

Instructions:

1. **Setup Project:**
   - Create a new Flutter project using your preferred IDE or text editor.
   - Set up the necessary project structure and dependencies.

2. **Design the App Bar:**
    - Implement the Gmail App Bar with the Gmail logo on the left and search icon on the right.
    - Include any additional elements you find relevant for the App Bar.
3. **Build the Email List:**
    - Display a list of emails with the sender's name, subject, snippet, and time sent.
    - Make sure the list is scrollable and adapts well to various screen sizes.
4. **Incorporate Responsive Design:**
    - Use the ScreenUtil package or other Flutter responsiveness techniques to ensure your UI adapts well to different screen sizes and orientations.
    - Test your UI on both emulators and physical devices.
5. **Optimize for Tablets and Desktops:**
    - If possible, optimize your design for larger screens, such as tablets or desktops.
    - Ensure that the user experience is smooth and visually appealing on these devices.
6. **Add Interactivity:**
    - Implement any interactive elements you find suitable, such as tapping an email to view details or using gestures for navigation.
7. **Add Finishing Touches:**
    - Polish your UI with appropriate colors, fonts, and any additional styling to make it resemble the Gmail App closely.
8. **Documentation:**
    - Provide comments in your code to explain complex parts or decisions.

Key Terms

- **Adaptive UI: A** user interface design that seamlessly adjusts to different screen sizes, resolutions, and orientations.
- L**ayoutBuilder:** A Flutter widget that provides constraints to its builder function, allowing dynamic adjustments based on available space.
- M**ediaQuery:** A Flutter class that provides information about the current app's dimensions, orientation, and other context-related details.

- **AspectRatio:** A Flutter widget that maintains a desired aspect ratio, commonly used for images and media elements.
- **Flutter ScreenUtil:** A Flutter package offering utilities for responsive design, including size adaptation, spacing, and font scaling.
- **OrientationBuilder:** A Flutter widget that rebuilds when the screen orientation changes, enabling adaptive layouts.
- **Screen Size:** The physical dimensions of a device's display, typically measured in inches diagonally.
- **Responsive Design: A** design approach that ensures a consistent and optimal user experience across various devices and screen sizes.
- **Pixel Density:** The number of pixels per unit of length on a screen, often expressed as pixels per inch (PPI).
- **Breakpoint:** A specific screen size or resolution at which a responsive design may change its layout or styling.

Chapter 8
Handling Navigation and Routing

Introduction

Imagine a world where every website and app are confined to a single page. No fluid movement from one section to another, no seamless transitions. It sounds dreadful, doesn't it?

Fortunately, we're far from that reality. Thanks to advancements in technology, we now have the power to access a wealth of information in mere seconds. The magic lies in navigation–our ability to glide effortlessly from one page to another, exploring a digital universe without losing track of the location of specific content.

In this chapter, we're exploring the art of navigation and routing in Flutter. Think of it as the GPS for your app's user experience, guiding users through various screens and enhancing their interaction.

Structure

In this chapter, we will cover the following topics:

- Implementing navigation between screens in Flutter
- Understanding named routes and route arguments
- Handling navigation stack and back button behavior
- Deep linking and handling external app links
- Navigation patterns and best practices

Implementing Navigation between Screens in Flutter

Navigation in mobile apps is like a roadmap for users, guiding them through various sections and pages seamlessly. Every tap on a button or link initiates a journey, transitioning the user from one screen to another. It's the digital equivalent of turning pages in a book, revealing new chapters of information. Similar to what you are doing with this book right now.

Consider the X app (formerly Twitter) –a social media giant. As users scroll through their timelines, they encounter a plethora of content. The magic happens when they decide to explore further. Clicking a post not only reveals the full story but often transports them to an entirely different realm–a thread, a user's profile, or an external link.

Figure 8.1: X *(formerly Twitter) Feeds*

Why is this navigation so critical? Imagine a world where every piece of information is crammed onto a single screen, overwhelming the user. It's impractical and counterintuitive. Navigation, therefore, is the key to creating a user-friendly experience, allowing them to move effortlessly between different aspects of your application.

Types of Navigation

Navigation isn't a one-size-fits-all concept. Different scenarios call for different ways of guiding users through your app. Flutter provides several navigation patterns, each catering to specific needs. Let's explore the three fundamental types of navigation in detail:

Understanding Stack Navigation in Flutter

Imagine a stack of cards, each representing a screen in your app. Stack navigation is akin to flipping through these cards. As you move forward, a new card (screen) is added to the top of the stack. When you go back, the top card is removed, revealing the screen beneath. It's a straightforward and intuitive way to navigate, often used for linear user flows.

How Stack Navigation Works

1. **Pushing onto the Stack:**
    - When you navigate to a new screen, you **`push`** it onto the stack. This means the new screen becomes the top card, and it covers the previous one.
    - The **`Navigator.push()`** method is commonly used for this purpose. It takes a **`BuildContext`** and a **`PageRoute`** and adds the new page to the top of the stack.

    ```
    Navigator.push(
      context,
      MaterialPageRoute(builder: (context) => NewScreen()),
    );
    ```

2. **Popping off the Stack**:
    - Going back is achieved by "**`popping`**" a screen off the stack. This removes the top card, revealing the one beneath.
    - The **`Navigator.pop()`** method is used for this. If you're on the root screen, it might close the app, depending on the platform.

    ```
    Navigator.pop(context);
    ```

3. **Named Routes**:
    - In larger apps, using named routes is beneficial. This involves giving each route a unique name, making it easier to navigate between them.

    ```
    // Define the named route in your MaterialApp
    routes: {
      '/': (context) => HomeScreen(),
      '/details': (context) => DetailsScreen(),
    };

    // Navigate using the name
    Navigator.pushNamed(context, '/details');
    ```

4. **Passing Data:**

   - You often need to pass data between screens. This is achieved by passing arguments with the `Navigator`.

```
// On the sending screen
Navigator.push(
  context,
  MaterialPageRoute(
    builder: (context) => SecondScreen(data: 'Hello from
    the first screen!'),
  ),
);

// On the receiving screen
class SecondScreen extends StatelessWidget {
  final String data;
  SecondScreen({required this.data});

  // ... rest of the widget
}
```

5. **Nested Navigators**:

   - For complex UIs with different navigation flows, you might use nested `Navigator` widgets to manage independent stacks of screens.

```
Navigator(
  onGenerateRoute: (settings) {
    // Define routes for this Navigator
  },
)
```

When to Use Stack Navigation

- **Linear User Flows:**

  Stack navigation is perfect for apps where users navigate through a series of screens in a linear fashion. Think of onboarding processes or form submissions.

- **Modal Overlays:**

  Modal screens that temporarily overlay thc main content can be easily implemented using stack navigation.

- **Wizard-Style Flows:**

  If your app guides users through a wizard with step-by-step instructions, stack navigation provides a logical structure.

Music Player Project

Let's create step-by-step instructions for building a detailed UI for a responsive music playlist screen with navigation to a music player page:

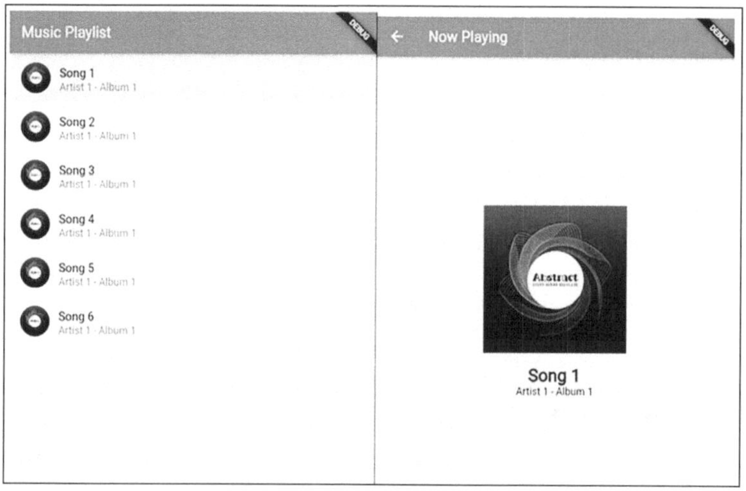

***Figure 8.2**: Music Player project*

Step 1: Set Up the Flutter Project

Assuming you have Flutter installed, create a new Flutter project using:

```
flutter create music_app
cd music_app
```

Step 2: Add Dependencies

In your pubspec.yaml, add the necessary dependencies:

```
dependencies:
  flutter:
    sdk: flutter
  provider: ^6.1.6
  # Add any other dependencies you might need
```

Run flutter pub get to fetch the new dependencies.

Step 3: Create Models

Create a file named **`models.dart`** to define your music model:

```
// models.dart

class Music {
  final String title;
  final String artist;
  final String album;
  final String coverUrl;

  Music({
    required this.title,
    required this.artist,
    required this.album,
    required this.coverUrl,
  });
}
```

Step 4: Create a Mock Data Provider

Create a file named **`data_provider.dart`** to provide mock data:

```
// data_provider.dart
import 'models.dart';

class DataProvider {
  static List<Music> getMusicList() {
    return [
      Music(
        title: 'Song 1',
        artist: 'Artist 1',
        album: 'Album 1',
        coverUrl: 'url_to_image',
      ),
      // Add more mock data
    ];
  }
}
```

Step 5: Create the Playlist Screen

Create a file named **`playlist_screen.dart`** for the playlist screen:

```
// playlist_screen.dart
import 'package:flutter/material.dart';
import 'data_provider.dart';
import 'models.dart';

class PlaylistScreen extends StatelessWidget {
  @override
  Widget build(BuildContext context) {
    List<Music> musicList = DataProvider.getMusicList();

    return Scaffold(
      appBar: AppBar(
        title: Text('Music Playlist'),
      ),
      body: ListView.builder(
        itemCount: musicList.length,
        itemBuilder: (context, index) {
          Music = musicList[index];
          return ListTile(
            title: Text(music.title),
            subtitle: Text('${music.artist} - ${music.album}'),
            leading: CircleAvatar(
              backgroundImage: NetworkImage(music.coverUrl),
            ),
            onTap: () {
              // TODO: Navigate to the music player page
            },
          );
        },
      ),
    );
  }
}
```

Step 6: Create the Music Player Screen

Create a file named **music_player_screen.dart** for the music player screen:

```
// music_player_screen.dart
import 'package:flutter/material.dart';
import 'models.dart';

class MusicPlayerScreen extends StatelessWidget {
  final Music;

  MusicPlayerScreen({required this.music});
```

```
  @override
  Widget build(BuildContext context) {
    return Scaffold(
      appBar: AppBar(
        title: Text('Now Playing'),
      ),
      body: Center(
        child: Column(
          mainAxisAlignment: MainAxisAlignment.center,
          children: [
            Image.network(
              music.coverUrl,
              height: 200,
            ),
            SizedBox(height: 16),
            Text(
              music.title,
              style: TextStyle(fontSize: 24, fontWeight: FontWeight.bold),
            ),
            Text('${music.artist} - ${music.album}'),
            // Add music controls here (play, pause, etc.)
          ],
        ),
      ),
    );
  }
}
```

Step 7: Navigate from Playlist to Music Player

In the `onTap` handler of the **`ListTile`** in **`playlist_screen.dart`**, add the navigation logic to go to the music player screen:

```
onTap: () {
  Navigator.push(
    context,
    MaterialPageRoute(
      builder: (context) => MusicPlayerScreen(music: music),
    ),
  );
},
```

Certainly, let's complete the project by providing the necessary **`main.dart`** file. This file will serve as the entry point for your Flutter application. Follow the steps listed here to set up the `**main.dart**` file:

Step 8: Update `main.dart`

Replace the content of `lib/main.dart` with the following code:

```
// main.dart
import 'package:flutter/material.dart';
import 'playlist_screen.dart';

void main() {
  runApp(MyApp());
}

class MyApp extends StatelessWidget {
  @override
  Widget build(BuildContext context) {
    return MaterialApp(
      title: 'Music App',
      theme: ThemeData(
        primarySwatch: Colors.blue,
      ),
      home: PlaylistScreen(),
    );
  }
}
```

Step 9: Run the App

Run the app using:

```
flutter run
```

You should now have a basic music playlist app with a responsive UI that navigates to a music player screen. Enhance and customize the UI and functionality based on your specific requirements.

Understanding Tab navigation in Flutter

This is a common UI pattern in mobile applications, and Flutter makes it easy to implement. In Flutter, you can use the **`DefaultTabController`** along with **`TabBar`** and **`TabBarView`** widgets to create a tab-based navigation system.

Here's an explanation of how Tab Navigation works in Flutter:

1. **Create Tabs:**

   - Define the tabs you want in your app using the `**Tab**` widget. Each `**Tab**` has a text label that will be displayed in the tab bar.

```
const List<Tab> tabs = <Tab>[
  Tab(text: 'Tab 1'),
  Tab(text: 'Tab 2'),
  // Add more tabs as needed
];
```

2. **Create `TabController`:**

   - Use a `**DefaultTabController**` to manage the state of the tabs. It requires the length of the tabs and a `**child**` widget, which will be the content of the tabs.

```
DefaultTabController(
  length: tabs.length,
  child: Scaffold(
    appBar: AppBar(
      title: Text('Tab Navigation'),
      bottom: TabBar(
        tabs: tabs,
      ),
    ),
    body: TabBarView(
      children: [
        // Content for Tab 1
        Center(child: Text('Tab 1 Content')),

        // Content for Tab 2
        Center(child: Text('Tab 2 Content')),

        // Add more TabBarView children as needed
      ],
    ),
  ),
)
```

3. **Handle Tab Changes:**

   - The **`DefaultTabController`** automatically handles tab changes. When the user taps on a different tab, the corresponding content is displayed in the **`TabBarView`**.

```
DefaultTabController(
  length: tabs.length,
  child: Scaffold(
    appBar: AppBar(
      title: Text('Tab Navigation'),
      bottom: TabBar(
        tabs: tabs,
      ),
    ),
    body: TabBarView(
      children: [
        // Content for Tab 1
        Center(child: Text('Tab 1 Content')),

        // Content for Tab 2
        Center(child: Text('Tab 2 Content')),

        // Add more TabBarView children as needed
      ],
    ),
  ),
)
```

4. **Customization:**
   - You can customize the appearance of tabs by modifying the `**TabBar**` and `**TabBarView**` widgets. For example, you can change the color, style, and more.

```
TabBar(
  tabs: tabs,
  indicatorColor: Colors.red, // Customize indicator color
  labelColor: Colors.blue,     // Customize selected label
  color
),
TabBarView(
  children: [
    // Content for Tab 1
    Center(child: Text('Tab 1 Content')),

    // Content for Tab 2
    Center(child: Text('Tab 2 Content')),

    // Add more TabBarView children as needed
  ],
)
```

When to Use Tab Navigation

Tab navigation is a suitable choice when:

- **Organizing Content:**

  Your app has distinct categories or sections of content that can be logically organized into tabs. For example, a news app might have tabs for "`Top News`," "`Sports`," and "`Entertainment`."

- **Direct Access:**

  Users should have direct access to different sections without the need for a hierarchical structure. Tabs allow for quick and direct navigation between different views.

- **Equal Importance:**

  Each tab represents a section of your app with equal importance. Tabs are often used when different sections don't have a strict hierarchy, and users should have equal visibility into each section.

- **Consistency Across Screens:**

  You want to maintain a consistent navigation pattern across different screens of your app. Tabs provide a familiar interface, especially in applications with multiple top-level views.

- **Limited Screen Space:**

  When screen space is limited, such as on mobile devices, tabs are an efficient way to provide access to multiple views without cluttering the interface.

- **User Expectation:**

  Users are accustomed to tab-based navigation in many mobile apps. Leveraging this familiarity can enhance the user experience and make your app more intuitive.

Let's modify the previous music playlist project to incorporate tab navigation.

Music Playlist Project with Tab Navigation

Step 1: Add Dependencies

In your **pubspec.yaml** file, ensure you have the necessary dependencies:

```
dependencies:
  flutter:
```

```
    sdk: flutter
  cupertino_icons: ^1.0.6
```

Step 2: Create a Tabbed Structure

In your **main.dart**, set up a basic tabbed structure using the **DefaultTabController**:

```
import 'package:flutter/material.dart';
import 'screens/song_list.dart';
import 'screens/liked_songs.dart';

void main() => runApp(MyApp());

class MyApp extends StatelessWidget {
  @override
  Widget build(BuildContext context) {
    return MaterialApp(
      title: 'Music Playlist',
      theme: ThemeData(
        primarySwatch: Colors.blue,
      ),
      home: DefaultTabController(
        length: 2, // Number of tabs
        child: Scaffold(
          appBar: AppBar(
            title: Text('Music Playlist'),
            bottom: TabBar(
              tabs: [
                Tab(icon: Icon(Icons.music_note), text: 'Songs'),
                Tab(icon: Icon(Icons.favorite), text: 'Liked'),
              ],
            ),
          ),
          body: TabBarView(
            children: [
              SongList(), // First tab content
              LikedSongs(), // Second tab content
            ],
          ),
        ),
      ),
    );
  }
}
```

Step 3: Create Tab Content

Now, let's create the content for each tab.

Create a new file **song_list.dart**:

```
import 'package:flutter/material.dart';
import 'package:modern_flutter/music_player_screen.dart';
import 'package:modern_flutter/track.dart';

class SongList extends StatelessWidget {
  @override
  Widget build(BuildContext context) {
    List<Music> musicList = DataProvider.getMusicList();

    return Scaffold(
      body: ListView.builder(
        itemCount: musicList.length,
        itemBuilder: (context, index) {
          Music = musicList[index];
          return ListTile(
            title: Text(music.title),
            subtitle: Text('${music.artist} - ${music.album}'),
            leading: CircleAvatar(
              backgroundImage: NetworkImage(music.coverUrl),
            ),
            onTap: () {
              Navigator.push(
                context,
                MaterialPageRoute(
                  builder: (context) => MusicPlayerScreen(music: music),
                ),
              );
            },
          );
        },
      ),
    );
  }
}
```

Create a new file **liked_songs.dart**:

```
import 'package:flutter/material.dart';

class LikedSongs extends StatelessWidget {
```

```
  @override
  Widget build(BuildContext context) {
    return Center(
      child: Text('Liked Songs'),
    );
  }
}
```

Step 4: Run the App

Run your app, and you should see a tabbed interface with "**Songs**" and "**Liked**" tabs. The content of each tab is displayed in the respective `**SongList**` and `**LikedSongs**` widgets.

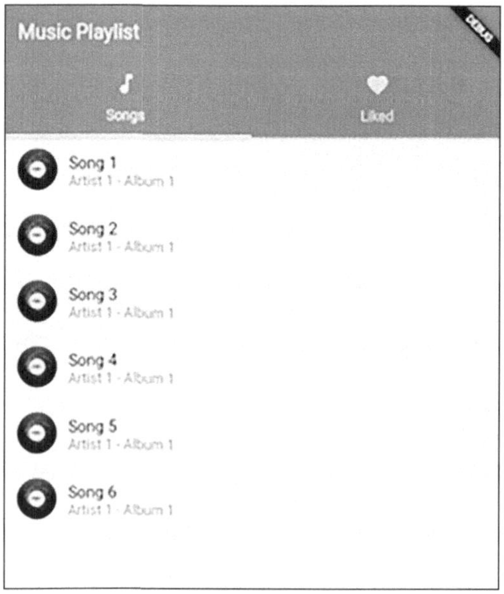

Figure 8.3: *Music Player project with Tab Navigation*

Now, your music playlist app has a more organized structure with tab navigation. Users can easily switch between the list of songs and their liked songs.

Let's explore another way of displaying our tabs. In most scenarios, tabs are rendered below the screen. This approach makes navigation more simplified and accessible by the user.

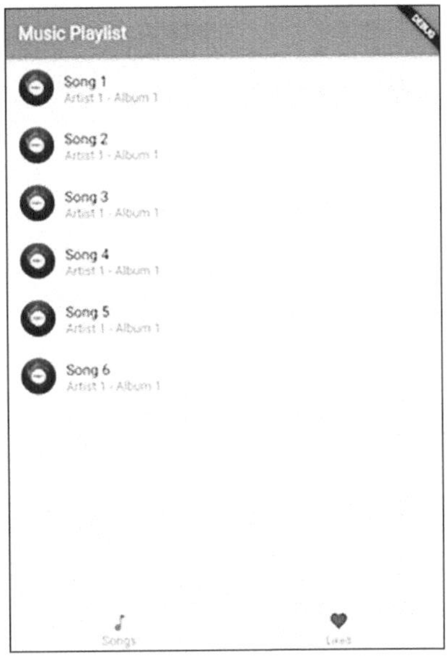

***Figure 8.4**: Music Player project with Bottom Tab Navigation*

Here is a breakdown of how this can be achieved:

Step 1: Add Dependencies

In your pubspec.yaml file, ensure you have the necessary dependencies:

```
dependencies:
  flutter:
    sdk: flutter
  cupertino_icons: ^1.0.6
```

This step includes the Flutter framework itself (`**flutter**`) and the **`cupertino_icons`** package, which provides the Cupertino-style icons used in the bottom navigation bar.

Step 2: Create Bottom Tabbed Structure

In your **`main.dart`**, set up a basic bottom tabbed structure using the **`BottomNavigationBar`**:

```
import 'package:flutter/material.dart';
import 'screens/song_list.dart';
import 'screens/liked_songs.dart';

void main() => runApp(MyApp());
```

```
class MyApp extends StatelessWidget {
  @override
  Widget build(BuildContext context) {
    return MaterialApp(
      title: 'Music Playlist',
      theme: ThemeData(
        primarySwatch: Colors.blue,
      ),
      home: HomeScreen(),
    );
  }
}
```

This part sets up the main app with a `**HomeScreen**` widget, which will contain the bottom navigation bar.

Step 3: Create HomeScreen Widget

```
class HomeScreen extends StatefulWidget {
  @override
  _HomeScreenState createState() => _HomeScreenState();
}
```

```
This creates a stateful widget for the home screen.
```

Step 4: Implement Bottom Tab Navigation

```
class _HomeScreenState extends State<HomeScreen> {
  int _currentIndex = 0;

  final List<Widget> _tabs = [
    SongList(), // First tab content
    LikedSongs(), // Second tab content
  ];

  @override
  Widget build(BuildContext context) {
    return Scaffold(
      appBar: AppBar(
        title: Text('Music Playlist'),
      ),
      body: _tabs[_currentIndex],
      bottomNavigationBar: BottomNavigationBar(
        currentIndex: _currentIndex,
        onTap: (index) {
```

```
          setState(() {
            _currentIndex = index;
          });
        },
        items: [
          BottomNavigationBarItem(
            icon: Icon(Icons.music_note),
            label: 'Songs',
          ),
          BottomNavigationBarItem(
            icon: Icon(Icons.favorite),
            label: 'Liked',
          ),
        ],
      ),
    );
  }
}
```

Here, we create a state for the current index of the selected tab and a list of widgets for each tab content. The **Scaffold** widget contains the AppBar, body, and bottomNavigationBar. The **BottomNavigationBar** includes two items, one for "**Songs**" and the other for "**Liked**," each associated with an icon and a label.

Step 5: Create Tab Content

```
import 'package:flutter/material.dart';
import 'package:modern_flutter/music_player_screen.dart';
import 'package:modern_flutter/track.dart';

class SongList extends StatelessWidget {
  @override
  Widget build(BuildContext context) {
    List<Music> musicList = DataProvider.getMusicList();

    return Scaffold(
      body: ListView.builder(
        itemCount: musicList.length,
        itemBuilder: (context, index) {
          Music music = musicList[index];
          return ListTile(
            title: Text(music.title),
            subtitle: Text('${music.artist} - ${music.album}'),
            leading: CircleAvatar(
              backgroundImage: NetworkImage(music.coverUrl),
            ),
```

```
            onTap: () {
              Navigator.push(
                context,
                MaterialPageRoute(
                  builder: (context) => MusicPlayerScreen(music: music),
                ),
              );
            },
          );
        },
      ),
    );
  }
}

class LikedSongs extends StatelessWidget {
  @override
  Widget build(BuildContext context) {
    return Center(
      child: Text('Liked Songs'),
    );
  }
}
```

These are simple widgets that display text in the center. In a real-world scenario, you would replace this with your actual content.

Step 6: Run the App

Run your app (flutter run), and you should see a bottom tab navigation with "**`Songs`**" and "**`Liked`**" tabs. The content of each tab is displayed in the respective `` `SongList` `` and `` `LikedSongs` `` widgets.

This implementation allows users to switch between the list of songs and their liked songs easily.

Understanding Drawer Navigation in Flutter

A drawer is a slide-in menu that's typically used for navigation. It provides a space to include links to different sections or features of your app. Users can access the drawer by either swiping from the left edge of the screen or by tapping a menu icon, usually placed in the top app bar. It is a power way to organize and present secondary navigation options in your app. It provides a clean and accessible user interface for features that aren't part of the primary content flow.

Navigation drawers include a container, an optional header, optional dividers, objects with inactive text, active text, and an active text overlay, optional subtitles, and an optional scrim.

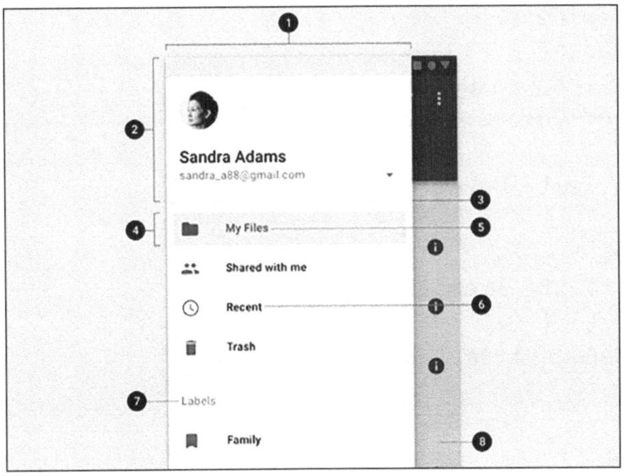

Figure 8.5: *Photo by Material Design*

Here are the key components and steps involved in implementing drawer navigation:

1. Container
2. Header (optional)
3. Divider (optional)
4. Active text overlay
5. Active text
6. Inactive text
7. Subtitle (optional)
8. Scrim (optional)

Adding a Drawer to the Scaffold

In your Scaffold widget, you can include a drawer by using the drawer property. For example:

```
return Scaffold(
  appBar: AppBar(
    title: Text('My App'),
  ),
```

```
  drawer: Drawer(
    // Drawer content goes here
    child: ListView(
      padding: EdgeInsets.zero,
      children: <Widget>[
        DrawerHeader(
          decoration: BoxDecoration(
            color: Colors.blue,
          ),
          child: Text('Drawer Header'),
        ),
        ListTile(
          title: Text('Item 1'),
          onTap: () {
            // Handle item tap
          },
        ),
        ListTile(
          title: Text('Item 2'),
          onTap: () {
            // Handle item tap
          },
        ),
      ],
    ),
  ),
  body: YourMainContent(),
);
```

The content of the Drawer is usually a **ListView** with various **ListTile** widgets. You can customize the appearance, add icons, and handle taps to navigate to different screens.

When a user taps on an item in the Drawer, you would typically navigate to a new screen or update the content of the current screen. This is often done using the Navigator class.

Here's a basic example of navigating to a new screen when an item is tapped:

```
onTap: () {
  Navigator.pop(context); // Close the Drawer
  Navigator.push(
    context,
    MaterialPageRoute(builder: (context) => SecondScreen()),
  );
},
```

In this example, SecondScreen is the screen you want to navigate to.

When to Use Drawer Navigation

Drawer navigation is useful when you have a set of important actions or destinations that are secondary to the main content of the app. It's commonly used for things like settings, account information, or app navigation.

Imagine a news app where the main content is articles. The drawer could contain links to settings, saved articles, and different categories like sports, politics, and technology.

Building a Gmail-like app

Let's create a step-by-step guide to building a Gmail-like app with Navigation Drawers in Flutter.

Step 1: Set Up Flutter Project

Create a new Flutter project using your preferred IDE or the command line.

```
flutter create gmail_app
cd gmail_app
```

Step 2: Design the Drawer

In the **`lib`** folder, create a new file called **`main.dart`**. Replace its content with the following:

```
import 'package:flutter/material.dart';

void main() {
  runApp(MyApp());
}

class MyApp extends StatelessWidget {
  @override
  Widget build(BuildContext context) {
    return MaterialApp(
      title: 'Gmail App',
      theme: ThemeData(
        primarySwatch: Colors.red,
      ),
      home: MyHomePage(),
    );
  }
```

```
}

class MyHomePage extends StatefulWidget {
  @override
  _MyHomePageState createState() => _MyHomePageState();
}

class _MyHomePageState extends State<MyHomePage> {
  @override
  Widget build(BuildContext context) {
    return Scaffold(
      appBar: AppBar(
        title: Text('Gmail'),
      ),
      drawer: Drawer(
        child: ListView(
          padding: EdgeInsets.zero,
          children: <Widget>[
            DrawerHeader(
              decoration: BoxDecoration(
                color: Colors.blue,
              ),
              child: Text('Gmail App'),
            ),
            ListTile(
              title: Text('Primary'),
              onTap: () {
                // Handle primary mail
              },
            ),
            ListTile(
              title: Text('Promotions'),
              onTap: () {
                // Handle promotions mail
              },
            ),
            ListTile(
              title: Text('Sent'),
              onTap: () {
                // Handle sent mail
              },
            ),
            // Add other mail folders
          ],
        ),
      ),
      body: Center(
```

```
        child: Text('Welcome to Gmail'),
      ),
    );
  }
}
```

Step 3: Create Email Model

Create a new file called **email_model.dart** to represent the email model.

```
class Email {
  final String sender;
  final String subject;
  final String body;
  bool isFavorite;

  Email({
    required this.sender,
    required this.subject,
    required this.body,
    this.isFavorite = false,
  });
}
```

Step 4: Design the Inbox Page

Update **main.dart** to include a basic inbox page.

```
import 'package:flutter/material.dart';

class InboxPage extends StatefulWidget {
  @override
  _InboxPageState createState() => _InboxPageState();
}

class _InboxPageState extends State<InboxPage> {
  final List<Email> emails = [
    Email(
      sender: 'John Doe',
      subject: 'Meeting Tomorrow',
      body: 'Hey, let\'s discuss the upcoming meeting...',
    ),
    // Add more mock data
  ];

  @override
  Widget build(BuildContext context) {
```

```
    return Scaffold(
      appBar: AppBar(
        title: Text('Inbox'),
      ),
      body: ListView.builder(
        itemCount: emails.length,
        itemBuilder: (context, index) {
          return ListTile(
            leading: CircleAvatar(
              child: Text(emails[index].subject[0]),
            ),
            title: Text(emails[index].sender),
            subtitle: Text(emails[index].body),
            trailing: IconButton(
              icon: Icon(
                emails[index].isFavorite
                    ? Icons.star
                    : Icons.star_border,
              ),
              onPressed: () {
                // Toggle favorite status
                setState(() {
                  emails[index].isFavorite = !emails[index].isFavorite;
                });
              },
            ),
          );
        },
      ),
    );
  }
}
```

Step 5: Update Drawer Navigation

Integrate the **InboxPage** into the app and update the drawer navigation.

```
// Inside _MyHomePageState class

Widget build(BuildContext context) {
  return Scaffold(
    drawer: Drawer(
      child: ListView(
        padding: EdgeInsets.zero,
        children: <Widget>[
          DrawerHeader(
```

```
          decoration: BoxDecoration(
            color: Colors.blue,
          ),
          child: Text('Gmail App'),
        ),
        ListTile(
          title: Text('Inbox'),
          onTap: () {
            Navigator.pop(context); // Close the Drawer
            Navigator.push(
              context,
              MaterialPageRoute(builder: (context) => InboxPage()),
            );
          },
        ),
        // Add other mail folders
      ],
    ),
  ),
  body:InboxPage(),
 );
}
```

Step 6: Run Your App

Run your app to see the Gmail-like interface with a navigation drawer. Clicking "`Inbox`" in the drawer should navigate to the inbox page.

```
flutter run
```

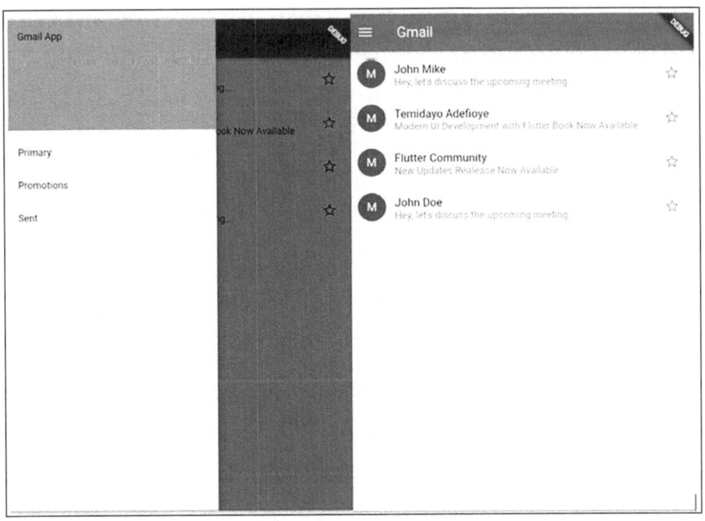

Figure 8.6: *Gmail clone project with Navigation drawer*

Understanding Named Routes and Route Arguments

Flutter provides a robust navigation system, and among its features are named routes and route arguments. Understanding these concepts is crucial for building scalable and maintainable Flutter applications. Named routes and route arguments bring clarity, scalability, and flexibility to your Flutter app's navigation. They make your code more readable, maintainable, and adaptable as your app grows in complexity.

Let's paint a scenario to illustrate the importance of named routes and route arguments. Imagine you're building a social media app with various screens like the login page, user profile, and a feed displaying posts. In traditional navigation, you might do something like this:

```
Navigator.push(
  context,
  MaterialPageRoute(builder: (context) => UserProfileScreen(user)),
);
```

Here, **UserProfileScreen** is pushed onto the navigation stack. It works, but what if you need to pass data to **UserProfileScreen**? You might resort to using a constructor, which works but is not very scalable.

This is where named routes and route arguments come to the rescue.

Named routes provide a clear and structured way to define your app's navigation paths. Instead of hardcoding screen implementations during navigation, you assign names to routes in a central location, typically in the `**MaterialApp**` widget. For our social media app, it could look like this:

```
MaterialApp(
  routes: {
    '/login': (context) => LoginScreen(),
    '/userProfile': (context) => UserProfileScreen(),
    '/feed': (context) => FeedScreen(),
  },
);
```

Now, navigating to the user profile becomes much more readable:

```
Navigator.pushNamed(context, '/userProfile');
```

But what about passing data, like the user's details, to the **UserProfileScreen**? This is where route arguments thrive. Instead of embedding data in constructors, you can pass it directly during navigation:

```
Navigator.pushNamed(
  context,
  '/userProfile',
  arguments: {'userId': '123', 'name': 'John Doe'},
);
```

And in the **UserProfileScreen**, you can access these arguments:

```
final Map<String, String> args = ModalRoute.of(context).settings.arguments;
final userId = args['userId'];
final name = args['name'];
```

Dynamic Routes in Flutter

Dynamic routes add a layer of flexibility to your navigation strategy. Instead of relying on predefined routes for every screen, dynamic routes allow you to generate routes on the fly, often based on runtime data. Let's explore how dynamic routes work and when they can be especially useful.

These routes are defined in the `onGenerateRoute` property of your **MaterialApp**. This function is called whenever the app tries to navigate to a named route that isn't directly defined in the `routes` property.

```
MaterialApp(
  onGenerateRoute: (settings) {
    if (settings.name == '/user') {
      final userId = settings.arguments;
      return MaterialPageRoute(
        builder: (context) => UserProfile(userId),
      );
    }
  },
);
```

In this example, navigating to '/user' with an argument will dynamically generate a route for the **UserProfile** screen.

They become immensely useful when your application's navigation depends on dynamic data. For instance, in a social media app, you might want to generate user profiles based on user IDs.

```
onGenerateRoute: (settings) {
  if (settings.name == '/user') {
    final userId = settings.arguments;
    return MaterialPageRoute(
      builder: (context) => UserProfile(userId),
    );
  }
},
```

This flexibility allows you to maintain a clean and scalable codebase.

When the app tries to navigate to an unknown named route, the **onUnknownRoute** callback is invoked. This is useful for handling situations where the desired screen isn't explicitly defined.

```
onUnknownRoute: (settings) {
  return MaterialPageRoute(
    builder: (context) => NotFoundScreen(),
  );
},
```

These routes are also employed in authentication flows. For instance, if a user attempts to access a protected screen, the app can dynamically generate a login screen and then redirect the user back to the original destination after login.

Dynamic routes also work seamlessly with parameterized routes, allowing you to pass arguments and generate screens accordingly.

```
onGenerateRoute: (settings) {
  if (settings.name == '/article') {
    final articleId = settings.arguments;
    return MaterialPageRoute(
      builder: (context) => ArticleScreen(articleId),
    );
  }
},
```

Flutter Route Arguments

Route arguments allow you to customize your destination screens based on specific data. Let's explore different mechanisms:

Imagine you're developing a **Traveler's Journal** app. Users can document their trips, and each entry is represented by a unique ID. Your app needs to navigate to a detailed view of a journal entry when the user taps on it.

In your route setup, you can use arguments to pass the ID of the selected journal entry.

```
// Navigating to the detailed view
Navigator.pushNamed(
  context,
  '/journal-entry',
  arguments: JournalArguments(entryId: selectedEntry.id),
);
```

On the receiving end, you define your destination screen and extract the arguments.

```
class JournalEntryScreen extends StatelessWidget {
  @override
  Widget build(BuildContext context) {
    // Extracting arguments
    final JournalArguments args = ModalRoute.of(context)!.settings.
arguments as JournalArguments;

    // Using the entry ID to fetch data
    final JournalEntry entry = fetchEntryById(args.entryId);

    return Scaffold(
      appBar: AppBar(
        title: Text('Journal Entry ${entry.id}'),
      ),
      body: Column(
        children: [
          Text('Date: ${entry.date}'),
          Text('Location: ${entry.location}'),
          // Other entry details...
        ],
      ),
    );
  }
}
```

For clarity and type safety, you can define a class to hold your arguments. Type safety ensures that the types of values are checked at compile time. In our context, it means that the argument entryId is guaranteed to be an integer, and the compiler catches any potential mistakes before the app runs.

```
class JournalArguments {
  final int entryId;

  JournalArguments({required this.entryId});
}
```

Thanks to route arguments, your app becomes more dynamic. The same screen can adapt to various data scenarios, making your navigation system flexible and scalable.

Imagine adding new features like comments or photos to your journal entries. With route arguments, you can extend your `JournalArguments` class to accommodate these changes without rewriting navigation logic.

Handling the Unknown

Navigating through an app is often a well-organized experience, but what happens when a user takes an unexpected turn, navigating to a route that doesn't exist? This is where handling unknown routes becomes critical.

Imagine you're developing a **Tourist Map** app, guiding users through exciting locations. Each location has a unique code, and users can navigate to these places by entering the code manually. However, what if a user enters a code for a non-existent location?

You have a route for displaying the details of a location, and users can enter the location code as a route parameter.

```
'/location-details/:code': (context) => LocationDetailsScreen(),
```

To handle routes that are not defined, you set up an unknown route handler. This function triggers when a user attempts to navigate to an undefined route.

```
onUnknownRoute: (settings) {
  return MaterialPageRoute(
    builder: (context) => UnknownRouteScreen(),
  );
},
```

Create a screen specifically designed for unknown routes. It can offer helpful information or suggest valid routes.

```
class UnknownRouteScreen extends StatelessWidget {
  @override
  Widget build(BuildContext context) {
    return Scaffold(
      appBar: AppBar(
        title: Text('404 - Location Not Found'),
      ),
      body: Center(
        child: Column(
          mainAxisAlignment: MainAxisAlignment.center,
          children: [
            Text(
              'Oops! It seems like this location does not exist.',
              style: TextStyle(fontSize: 18),
            ),
            SizedBox(height: 20),
            ElevatedButton(
              onPressed: () {
                Navigator.pop(context); // Navigate back to the previous
                screen
              },
              child: Text('Go Back'),
            ),
          ],
        ),
      ),
    );
  }
}
```

Handling unknown routes is not just about error management; it's an opportunity to enhance the user experience. By guiding users back on track or offering relevant suggestions, you turn potential frustration into a positive interaction.

Another exciting use case is adding logging or analytics to your unknown route handler to track instances where users attempt to navigate to undefined routes. This data can provide insights into user behavior and help improve your app's navigation flow.

Guiding Users Through Authentication Flows

Navigating through an app becomes particularly crucial when dealing with authentication flows. Imagine you're building a social networking app, and users need to log in to access personalized content and connect with others. Let's explore how you can seamlessly guide users through this journey.

In your **Social Connect** app, users must log in to access their feed, post updates, and interact with friends. The authentication process involves logging in with an email and password.

Set up your initial routes, distinguishing between the home screen for authenticated users and the login screen for those who haven't logged in.

```
'/home': (context) => HomeScreen(),
'/login': (context) => LoginScreen(),
```

Create a function to check whether the user is authenticated. This function can be used at the app's entry point or in a dedicated `**SplashScreen**`.

```
bool isUserAuthenticated() {
  // Check if the user is logged in (use shared preferences, Firebase,
  etc.)
  // Return true if authenticated, false otherwise
  // Example: return FirebaseAuth.instance.currentUser != null;
}
```

In your app's main **MaterialApp**, set the initial route based on the authentication status.

```
initialRoute: isUserAuthenticated() ? '/home' : '/login',
```

When users try to access a screen that requires authentication and aren't logged in, guide them to the login screen.

```
onGenerateRoute: (settings) {
  if (settings.name == '/protected-screen') {
    return MaterialPageRoute(
      builder: (context) => isUserAuthenticated()
          ? ProtectedScreen()
          : LoginScreen(),
```

```
    );
  }
  // Handle other routes...
},
```

On the login screen, users can input their credentials. After successful authentication, navigate them to the home screen.

```
// In the login button's onPressed event
onPressed: () async {
  // Perform authentication (use FirebaseAuth, API call, etc.)
  bool authenticationSuccessful = await authenticateUser();
  if (authenticationSuccessful) {
    Navigator.pushReplacementNamed(context, '/home');
  } else {
    // Show an error message or handle failed login
  }
},
```

The final tip is to consider adding animations or visual cues to guide users through the authentication process. For instance, when transitioning from the login screen to the home screen, use a subtle animation to signify a successful login.

Handling Navigation Stack and Back Button Behavior

Understanding how the navigation stack operates and controlling the behavior of the back button is fundamental.

Imagine you're developing an e-commerce app with a shopping cart feature. Users can browse products, add them to the cart, and proceed to checkout. Navigating this experience smoothly involves having a clear understanding of how the navigation stack works.

The navigation stack is like a deck of cards, where each card represents a screen. When users navigate from one screen to another, a new card is added to the stack. Understanding this stack is pivotal for managing the flow.

As users browse products, each product detail screen is added to the stack. When they tap the "`Add to Cart`" button, the cart screen is pushed onto the stack.

```
// Navigating to product details
Navigator.push(
  context,
  MaterialPageRoute(builder: (context) => ProductDetailsScreen(product)),
);

// Adding to cart
Navigator.push(
  context,
  MaterialPageRoute(builder: (context) => CartScreen()),
);
```

Once users review the cart and proceed to checkout, unnecessary screens like product details might clutter the stack. Pop them off to maintain a clean flow.

```
// Navigate to checkout
Navigator.push(
  context,
  MaterialPageRoute(builder: (context) => CheckoutScreen()),
);

// Clear unnecessary screens from the stack
Navigator.popUntil(context, (route) => route.isFirst);
```

The back button can be your ally or adversary. To control its behavior, define what should happen when users press it.

```
// In the checkout screen, override the back button behavior
WillPopScope(
  onWillPop: () async {
    // Perform custom actions, such as asking for confirmation
    bool confirm = await showExitConfirmationDialog(context);
    return confirm;
  },
  child: CheckoutScreen(),
)
```

The stack isn't static—it adapts. If users revisit the cart from the checkout, Flutter intelligently reuses the existing cart screen instead of adding a new one.

```
// Reusing the cart screen

Navigator.pushReplacement(
```

```
  context,
  MaterialPageRoute(builder: (context) => CartScreen()),
);
```

Deep linking and handling external app links

Setting up deep linking for your Flutter app on both Android and iOS might seem like a daunting task, but fear not! We'll take it step-by-step.

Installation for Android:

1. Open `android/app/src/main/AndroidManifest.xml`:

Add an `<intent-filter>` inside your main `<activity>` tag, which will capture the deep links.

```
<activity
    ...
    <intent-filter>
        <action android:name="android.intent.action.MAIN" />
        <category android:name="android.intent.category.LAUNCHER" />
        <!-- Deep linking intent filter -->
        <action android:name="android.intent.action.VIEW" />
        <category android:name="android.intent.category.DEFAULT" />
        <category android:name="android.intent.category.BROWSABLE" />
        <data
            android:host="your-host-name"
            android:scheme="your-scheme" />
    </intent-filter>
</activity>
```

Replace `"your-host-name"` and `"your-scheme"` with the host name and scheme you've chosen for your app.

2. Open `android/app/build.gradle`:

Add the following dependency for deep linking:

```
dependencies {
    implementation 'com.android.support:support-{LATEST_VERSION}'
}
```

Make sure to sync your project after making changes.

Installation for iOS:

1. Open `ios/Runner/Info.plist`:

Add the following key-value pairs inside the **<dict>** tag:

```
<key>CFBundleURLTypes</key>
<array>
    <dict>
        <key>CFBundleTypeRole</key>
        <string>Editor</string>
        <key>CFBundleURLName</key>
        <string>com.yourname.yourapp</string>
        <key>CFBundleURLSchemes</key>
        <array>
            <string>your-scheme</string>
        </array>
    </dict>
</array>
```

Replace `**”com.yourname.yourapp”**` with your app’s bundle identifier and `**”your-scheme”**` with the scheme you’ve chosen.

Handle Incoming Deep Links in Dart Code

Use the **uni_links** package to handle incoming deep links in your Dart code. Add the following to your `pubspec.yaml` file:

```
dependencies:
  uni_links: ^0.5.1
```

Run **flutter pub get** to install the package.

Import the package in your Dart code:

```
import ‘package:uni_links/uni_links.dart’;
```

Imagine you have a blog, and you want users to be able to click a link in a blog post and be directly taken to a specific page in your Flutter app. This is where deep linking comes into play.

Deep linking is like having a secret map to a specific location within your app. It allows users to transition from the web, an email, or any other external source directly into a particular screen in your Flutter app.

Let's say you have a product page in your app, and you want users to access it via a link. First, you need to define a deep link for your product page:

```
// Define the deep link for the product page
const String productDeepLink = 'myapp://product?id=123';
```

When a user clicks the link, your app needs to know what to do. You can handle this by using a package like **uni_links** to detect and parse incoming deep links.

```
import 'package:uni_links/uni_links.dart';

// Handle incoming links
void handleDeepLink() async {
  String initialLink = await getInitialLink();
  // Parse the link to extract relevant information
  // Navigate to the product page based on the information in the link
}
```

Once you have the link information, you can navigate to the specific product page within your app:

```
void navigateToProductPage(String productId) {
  // Use the parsed productId to fetch the product details
  // Navigate to the product page
  Navigator.push(
    context,
    MaterialPageRoute(builder: (context) => ProductPage(productId)),
  );
}
```

As a note, before deploying your app to the Play Store, it's essential to test your deep links. You can use tools like ADB (Android Debug Bridge) for Android or the Apple Developer tools for iOS to simulate deep linking scenarios.

Navigation Patterns and Best Practices

1. **Stack-based Navigation:**
    - **Usage:** Ideal for simple app flows with a hierarchical structure, like going back and forth between screens.
    - **Best Practice:** Use `Navigator` and `PageRoute` for managing the stack.

2. **Tab-based Navigation:**
    - **Usage:** Suitable for apps with multiple sections or categories that can be accessed independently.
    - **Best Practice:** Implement `BottomNavigationBar` or `CupertinoTabBar` to switch between tabs.
3. **Drawer-based Navigation:**
    - **Usage**: Effective for housing secondary navigation options or settings accessible from any screen.
    - **Best Practice:** Employ `Drawer` to provide easy access to less frequently used destinations.

Best Practices for Navigation in Flutter

- Consistency:
    - Maintain a consistent navigation structure across your app to provide users with a familiar experience.
- Clear Hierarchies:
    - Establish clear navigation hierarchies for stack-based navigation, ensuring users can easily navigate back.
- Intuitive UI Elements:
    - Use recognizable UI elements like icons, labels, and gestures for navigation actions.
- Route Management:
    - Efficiently manage routes using named routes, making navigation more maintainable and understandable.
- State Preservation:
    - Preserve the state of screens intelligently, especially when users navigate back and forth between them.
- Handling Back Navigation:
    - Implement correct back navigation behavior, especially with nested navigators and route stacks.
- Error Handling:
    - Gracefully handle navigation errors, such as invalid routes or unexpected behavior, to avoid crashing the app.
- Testing Navigation Flows:
    - Thoroughly test your app's navigation flows to ensure seamless transitions and a bug-free experience.

Conclusion

As we conclude this chapter, you've explored the core of navigation in Flutter, learning about various patterns and best practices. Navigating through an app is akin to guiding users on a journey, and employing the right patterns can significantly enhance their experience.

Remember, consistency is the key. Users appreciate a predictable navigation structure, and by adopting the navigation, routing, and best practices outlined here, you're well on your way to creating a seamless and enjoyable user experience.

Now that you are familiar with navigation, it's time to explore the device features and APIs in the next chapter. We'll uncover how Flutter allows you to tap into the full potential of the device, opening avenues for creating more immersive and feature-rich applications.

Points to Remember

- **Navigation is the Backbone:** Navigation is not just about moving between screens; it's the backbone of user experience. Thoughtful navigation contributes significantly to how users perceive and interact with your app.
- **Types of Navigation:** Understand the various types of navigation, such as stack, tab, and drawer navigation. Each type serves different purposes and is suitable for specific app architectures.
- **Stack Navigation Fundamentals:** Stack navigation follows the Last In, First Out (LIFO) principle. Mastering the fundamentals of stack navigation is crucial for managing the flow of screens in your app.
- **Tab Navigation for Structured UIs:** Tab navigation is ideal for organizing your app into sections. It offers a clear and structured user interface, making it easy for users to access different parts of your app.
- **Drawer Navigation for Seamless Access:** Drawer navigation provides a hidden menu for additional app options. It's perfect for giving users seamless access to various functionalities without cluttering the main screen.
- **Named Routes for Clarity:** Implementing named routes enhances code readability and provides a clear structure for navigation. It comes in handy for larger applications with complex navigation needs.
- **Route Arguments for Data Passing:** Master the art of passing data between screens using route arguments. This is fundamental for creating dynamic and data-driven applications.

- **Handling Unknown Routes:** Prepare your app to handle unknown routes. This ensures a smooth user experience even when unexpected navigation scenarios arise.
- **Authentication Flows:** Learn to navigate users through authentication flows seamlessly. Whether it's a login, registration, or password recovery, the navigation should guide users intuitively.
- **Optimizing Navigation Stack:** Understand how to optimize the navigation stack and manage back button behavior. This is important for ensuring that users can navigate your app effortlessly and intuitively.

Assessment

Gmail Clone Project Assessment

Objective: Replicate the Gmail app UI.

Project Requirements:

1. **Navigation Drawer:**
    a. Implement a navigation drawer with the key sections like Primary, Promotions, Sent, and so on, similar to the Gmail app.
    b. Ensure that the inbox is the default page when the app is launched.
2. **Email List:**
    a. Display a list of emails on the inbox page.
    b. Each item in the list should include:
    c. A thumbnail of the first letter in the email subject.
    d. The sender's name.
    e. A sneak peek description of the email body.
    f. A star icon to mark the email as a favorite.
3. **Favorite Emails:**
    a. Implement the functionality to mark an email as a favorite using the star icon.
    b. Ensure that the star icon toggles between filled and unfilled states based on the favorite status.

4. **Mock Data:**
   a. Use at least 15 mock data entries to simulate real emails.
   b. Each entry should have a different sender, subject, and body.
5. **Tips: Design and Theming:**
   a. Apply an appealing and user-friendly design.
   b. Use a suitable font to enhance readability.
   c. Apply a theme that is consistent with the Gmail app.
6. **Responsiveness:**
   a. Ensure that the app is responsive and looks good on different screen sizes.

Key Terms

- **Navigation Stack:** A collection of screens or routes arranged in a stack data structure, following the Last In, First Out (LIFO) principle, where new screens are pushed onto the stack and removed when navigated back.
- **Tab Navigation:** A type of navigation that organizes an app's content into tabs, allowing users to switch between different sections or categories of the app.
- **Drawer Navigation:** Utilizes a hidden side menu or drawer to provide access to various app functionalities or navigation options.
- **Named Routes:** A technique in Flutter where routes are assigned names for clarity and ease of navigation, making the code more readable and maintainable.
- **Route Arguments:** Parameters or data passed between different screens or routes while navigating an application.
- **Authentication Flows**: The series of screens or steps guiding users through authentication processes, such as login, registration, or password reset, ensuring secure access to an application.
- **Deep Linking:** A method of linking to specific content or pages within an app, allowing users to access particular sections directly from external links.
- **Route Generation:** The process of creating or generating routes dynamically based on various conditions or user interactions within the app.

CHAPTER 9

Utilizing Device Features and APIs

Not too long ago, our digital lives were shackled by passwords – long strings of characters we were destined to forget, leading to countless resets. Fast forward to today, where a touch of our fingertip or a glance at our face grants us access to our devices and applications seamlessly. It's more than convenience; it's a leap in user experience.

Have you ever marveled at how apps effortlessly recognize your face or fingerprint, providing a secure and efficient gateway? All thanks to device APIs – gateways to the core features and sensors of our devices. From cameras capturing moments to face detection, fingerprint authentication, Bluetooth connections, and navigating the realm of Wi-Fi, these APIs empower developers to harness the full potential of modern technology.

You may already be wondering what API stands for. It represents the Application Programming Interface. Think of it as a bridge between different software and hardware systems. It defines the rules and tools that enable one piece of software to interact with another.

Imagine a waiter taking orders in a restaurant. Customers don't go to the kitchen to give their orders; instead, they tell the waiter, who then communicates that information to the kitchen. Similarly, an API is like that waiter – it's the intermediary that allows different software applications and hardware to talk to each other without needing to know the details of how they work internally.

For instance, consider a banking app. It needs to give login access to a user through a fingerprint. The smartphone device operating system provides an API that the app can use. This API allows the app to request access to the user's fingerprint information from the device's database without needing access to the database itself.

In simpler terms, an API is a set of rules that allows different software applications to communicate and share information. It specifies how software components should interact, making it easier for developers to integrate different systems and build new functionalities in their apps without starting from scratch.

Structure

In this chapter, we will cover the following topics:

- Utilizing Device Permissions and User Authentication
- Accessing Device Hardware and Sensors
- Working with Platform-Specific Plugins

Utilizing Device Permissions and User Authentication

Have you ever been asked by an app for permission to access your camera, location, or contacts? It's like standing at a door where you need to show your ID before entering. That's exactly what device permissions are – an app's way of politely asking for access to certain parts of your phone.

Now, think of user authentication as a secret handshake before entering a secured facility. Your fingerprint, face scan, or a specific code might be required to ensure that it's truly you trying to access your app's super-secret stash of information.

Permissions for Photo Upload

Let's imagine that your users are thrilled to capture and share their favorite moments through your newly built social media app. But before they can begin to enjoy this experience, your app needs to politely ask for permission to access the device's camera and gallery.

The `permission_handler` package is your trusty sidekick for managing permissions. To kick things off, let's add this package to your **pubspec.yaml**:

Please note that if you already have the app installed on your device or emulator, and you're integrating the `permission_handler` package, it's recommended to uninstall the app first and then reinstall it for the changes to take effect.

```
dependencies:
  permission_handler: ^11.1.0 #use latest version on pub.dev
```

Now, let's create a function that requests camera and storage permissions when users attempt to upload a photo:

```
import 'package:permission_handler/permission_handler.dart';

// ...
void requestPermissions() async {
  Map<Permission, PermissionStatus> status = await [
    Permission.camera,
    Permission.storage,
  ].request();

  if (status[Permission.camera] == PermissionStatus.granted &&
      status[Permission.storage] == PermissionStatus.granted) {
    // Permissions granted! Proceed with the photo upload.
  } else {
    // Handle denied permissions.
  }
}
```

In this illustration, you're developing an application that prioritizes user privacy. By explicitly seeking permissions only when necessary, you're creating a user-centric environment.

Let's delve into the code breakdown:

1. **Permission Requests:** The `request` method triggers the solicitation of camera and storage permissions.
2. **`PermissionStatus` Check:** The resulting status map captures the permission status for each requested permission.
3. **Decision Time:** If both camera and storage permissions are granted, you're ready to proceed with the photo upload. However, if any permission is denied, you can handle it gracefully to provide meaningful feedback to the user.

This approach ensures a user-friendly experience, mitigating potential frustrations and building trust between your app and its users.

Secure User Authentication Using Fingerprint or Face

Let's say your social media app is evolving, and you want to offer users a more seamless and secure way to access their accounts. Leveraging fingerprint or face recognition could be the game-changer that makes signing in seamless while ensuring top-notch security.

You can integrate biometric authentication using the **`local_auth`** package. Let's dive into adding this package to your **pubspec.yaml**:

```
dependencies:
  local_auth: ^2.1.7 #use latest pub.dev version
```

Before diving into authentication methods, let's ensure the device is ready. The **`canCheckBiometrics`** function verifies whether the device supports biometric authentication. If you also need to confirm general device-level authentication, **`isDeviceSupported()`** can come in handy:

```
import 'package:local_auth/local_auth.dart';

// ...

final LocalAuthentication auth = LocalAuthentication();

final bool canAuthenticateWithBiometrics = await auth.canCheckBiometrics;
final bool canAuthenticate = canAuthenticateWithBiometrics || await auth.
isDeviceSupported();
```

The available biometric types include face, fingerprint, weak, and strong. To fetch the enrolled biometrics, use **`getAvailableBiometrics()`**.

Currently, the following biometric types are implemented:

```
BiometricType.face
BiometricType.fingerprint
BiometricType.weak
BiometricType.strong
final List<BiometricType> availableBiometrics = await auth.
getAvailableBiometrics();
```

```
if (availableBiometrics.isNotEmpty) {
  // Some biometrics are enrolled.
}
```

Now, let's dive into the actual authentication process. The `authenticate` method is your gateway to seamless and secure user authentication:

```
try {
  final bool didAuthenticate = await auth.authenticate(
      localizedReason: 'Please authenticate to display private photos);
  // Handle successful authentication...
} on PlatformException {
  // Handle authentication errors...
}
```

To enforce biometric authentication only, pass `**AuthenticationOptions**` with `**biometricOnly**` set to true:

```
final bool didAuthenticate = await auth.authenticate(
    localizedReason: 'Please authenticate to  display private photo',
    options: const AuthenticationOptions(biometricOnly: true));
```

As a note, **`biometricOnly`** is not supported on Windows due to limitations in the underlying API.

`local_auth` provides default dialogs for cases such as passcode/PIN/pattern not set or biometrics not enrolled. If you prefer to customize or disable these dialogs, use the **`useErrorDialogs`** option:

```
import 'package:local_auth/error_codes.dart' as auth_error;

// ...

try {
  final bool didAuthenticate = await auth.authenticate(
      localizedReason: 'Please authenticate to show account balance',
      options: const AuthenticationOptions(useErrorDialogs: false));
  // Handle authentication...
} on PlatformException catch (e) {
  if (e.code == auth_error.notAvailable) {
    // Handle no hardware...
  } else if (e.code == auth_error.notEnrolled) {
    // Handle not enrolled...
  } else {
```

```
    // Handle other errors...
  }
}
```

For a personalized touch, customize dialog messages using **AuthMessages**:

```
import 'package:local_auth_android/local_auth_android.dart';
import 'package:local_auth_ios/local_auth_ios.dart';

// ...

final bool didAuthenticate = await auth.authenticate(
    localizedReason: 'Please authenticate to show account balance',
    authMessages: const <AuthMessages>[
      AndroidAuthMessages(
        signInTitle: 'Oops! Biometric authentication required!',
        cancelButton: 'No thanks',
      ),
      IOSAuthMessages(
        cancelButton: 'No thanks',
      ),
    ]);
```

For robust error handling, **local_auth** throws **PlatformException** in various error cases. Check **error_codes.dart** for known error codes and handle them accordingly.

On iOS, note that the plugin works seamlessly with both Touch ID and Face ID. Remember to include **NSFaceIDUsageDescription** in your **Info.plist** for Face ID:

```
<key>NSFaceIDUsageDescription</key>
<string>Why is my app authenticating using face id?</string>
```

When it comes to Android permissions, ensure your **AndroidManifest.xml** includes the **USE_BIOMETRIC** permission:

```
<manifest xmlns:android="http://schemas.android.com/apk/res/android"
          package="com.example.app">

    <!-- Other manifest declarations go here -->

    <uses-permission android:name="android.permission.USE_BIOMETRIC"/>

    <application>
```

```
        <!-- Other application-related configurations go here -->

    </application>
</manifest>
```

To maintain compatibility, update your project's **AndroidManifest.xml** to use **`FlutterFragmentActivity`**.

To keep your experience seamless, you can enable **`stickyAuth`** to retry authentication when the app resumes, preventing authentication failures when the app is put to the background.

Now, let's explore how you can enable users to sign in with biometric authentication:

1. Import Dependencies:

```
import 'package:flutter/material.dart';
import 'package:local_auth/local_auth.dart';
```

We are importing necessary packages: `**flutter/material.dart**` for Flutter widgets and `**local_auth.dart**` for local authentication (biometrics).

2. Define the Main App:

```
void main() {
  runApp(MyApp());
}
```

This is the entry point of our app, where we run the `**MyApp**` widget.

3. Create the App Widget:

```
class MyApp extends StatelessWidget {
  @override
  Widget build(BuildContext context) {
    return MaterialApp(
      home: BiometricAuthenticationScreen(),
    );
  }
}
```

`**MyApp**` is a Flutter widget that extends `**StatelessWidget**`. It creates a `**MaterialApp**` with a home screen represented by the `**BiometricAuthenticationScreen()**`.

4. Create the Biometric Authentication Screen:

```
   class BiometricAuthenticationScreen extends StatefulWidget {
     @override
     _BiometricAuthenticationScreenState createState() =>
_BiometricAuthenticationScreenState();
   }
```

We define a stateful widget (`BiometricAuthenticationScreen`) to manage the state of our app during the biometric authentication process.

5. Implement State for Biometric Authentication Screen:

```
   class _BiometricAuthenticationScreenState extends
State<BiometricAuthenticationScreen> {
     final LocalAuthentication localAuth = LocalAuthentication();
     String authenticationResult = '';
```

We create the state for our screen, including an instance of `LocalAuthentication` for handling biometric authentication and a variable to store the authentication result.

6. Build the UI:

```
   @override
   Widget build(BuildContext context) {
     return Scaffold(
       appBar: AppBar(
         title: Text('Biometric Authentication Demo'),
       ),
       body: Center(
         child: Column(
           mainAxisAlignment: MainAxisAlignment.center,
           children: [
             ElevatedButton(
               onPressed: () async {
                 await authenticateWithBiometrics();
               },
               child: Text('Authenticate with Biometrics'),
             ),
             SizedBox(height: 20),
             Text(
               authenticationResult,
               style: TextStyle(fontSize: 16),
             ),
```

```
          ],
        ),
      ),
    );
  }
```

We build the user interface using a `**Scaffold**` with an `**AppBar**` and a centered column.

The column contains an elevated button triggering biometric authentication and a text widget to display the authentication result.

7. Implement Biometric Authentication Function:

```
  Future<void> authenticateWithBiometrics() async {
    bool canCheckBiometrics = await localAuth.canCheckBiometrics;
    List<BiometricType> availableBiometrics = await
localAuth.getAvailableBiometrics();

    if (canCheckBiometrics && availableBiometrics.isNotEmpty) {
      bool authenticated = await localAuth.authenticate(
        localizedReason: 'Authenticate to access your account',
        biometricOnly: true,
      );

      setState(() {
        if (authenticated) {
          authenticationResult = 'Biometric authentication
          successful!';
        } else {
          authenticationResult = 'Biometric authentication failed or was
          canceled.';
        }
      });
    } else {
      setState(() {
        authenticationResult = 'Biometrics not available or supported
        on this device.';
      });
    }
  }
```

We define a function (`**authenticateWithBiometrics**`) to handle the biometric authentication process.

It checks if the device supports biometrics, then attempts authentication and updates the result accordingly.

8. Run the App:

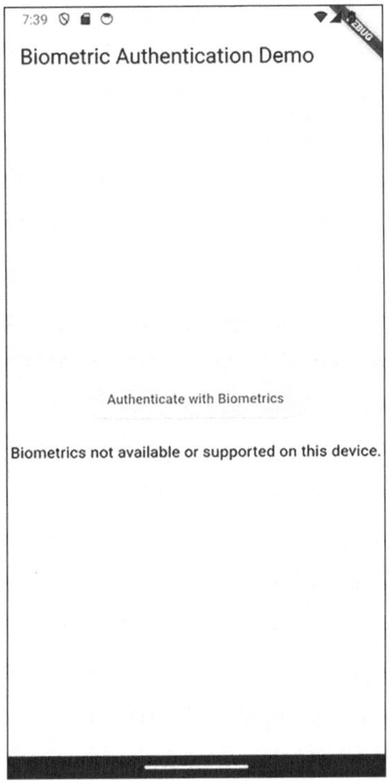

Figure 9.1: *Biometric Authentication Demo*

If the device running the app doesn't support this feature, the message shown in the preceding figure (see *Figure* 9.1) will be displayed. This message will also appear if you are using an emulator for this project.

When it comes to Android permissions, ensure your **AndroidManifest.xml** includes the **`USE_BIOMETRIC`** permission:

```
<manifest xmlns:android="http://schemas.android.com/apk/res/android"
         package="com.example.app">

    <!-- Other manifest declarations go here -->

    <uses-permission android:name="android.permission.USE_BIOMETRIC"/>

    <application>
        <!-- Other application-related configurations go here -->
```

```
    </application>
</manifest>
```

Run the app, and you'll see a button. When pressed, it will trigger biometric authentication, and the result will be displayed here.

Exploring Phone Contacts

Let's say we are building a messaging app where users can interact with their phone contacts. Let's explore how this could be implemented in Flutter.

Before attempting to access users' contacts, you must ensure your app has the necessary permissions. Let's utilize the **permission_handler** package to manage permissions, just like we did for the camera and storage:

```
import 'package:permission_handler/permission_handler.dart';

// ...

void requestContactPermission() async {
  Map<Permission, PermissionStatus> status = await [Permission.
  contacts].request();

  if (status[Permission.contacts] == PermissionStatus.granted) {
    // Contacts permission granted! Proceed with accessing phone
    contacts.
  } else {
    // Handle denied permission.
  }
}
```

To access phone contacts, Flutter provides the **contacts_service** package. Begin by adding it to your **pubspec.yaml**:

```
dependencies:
  contacts_service: ^0.6.3
```

Now, let's retrieve the contacts:

```
import 'package:contacts_service/contacts_service.dart';

// ...

void getPhoneContacts() async {
```

```
  Iterable<Contact> contacts = await ContactsService.getContacts();

  // Loop through contacts and handle them as needed.
  for (Contact contact in contacts) {
    print(‘Name: ${contact.displayName}, Phone: ${contact.phones}’);
  }
}
```

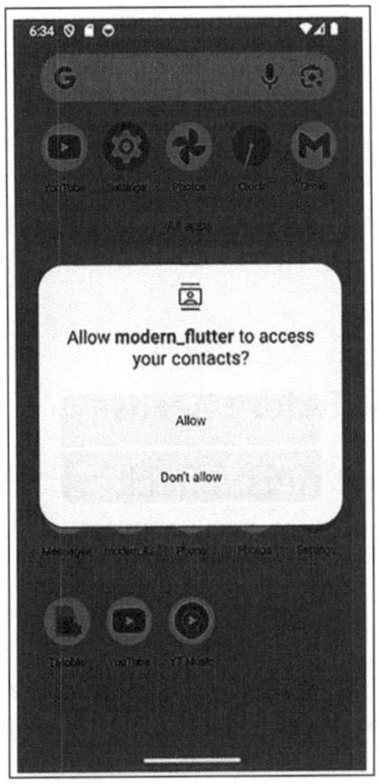

Figure 9.2: *Contact Permission Request on Android*

Navigating Permissions and Device API Access Best Practices

Handling permissions and accessing device APIs are critical aspects that shape user experience and app functionality. Let's explore some general best practices to ensure your app is user-friendly, secure, and respectful of privacy:

1. **Clear Permission Explanations**

   When requesting permissions, provide concise and clear explanations to users about why your app needs specific access. Transparency builds trust, and users are more likely to grant permissions when they understand the purpose.

```
void requestPermission() async {
  Map<Permission, PermissionStatus> status = await [Permission.
  location].request();
  if (status[Permission.location] == PermissionStatus.granted) {
```

```
  // Location permission granted! Proceed with location-based features.
} else {
  // Handle denied permission.
```

2. **Handle Denied Permissions**

   If a user denies permission, guide them on how to enable it through device settings. Avoid aggressive or persistent prompts, as this can lead to a negative user experience.

```
void handleDeniedPermission() {
  // Display a user-friendly message guiding them to enable the
  necessary permission.
}
```

3. **Check for Permissions Before Access**

   Before accessing device APIs, check whether the required permissions are granted. This helps prevent unexpected crashes or errors in your app.

```
void checkPermissionsBeforeAccess() async {
  bool isPermissionGranted = await checkLocationPermission();

  if (isPermissionGranted) {
    // Proceed with accessing location API.
  } else {
    // Prompt the user to grant location permission.
  }
}
```

4. **Prioritize User Privacy**

   Respect user privacy by only accessing the information or features necessary for your app's functionality. Minimize the data collected and processed, and communicate your app's privacy policy to users.

```
void prioritizePrivacy() {
  // Only access and process data essential for the app's core
  functionality.
}
```

5. **Provide Opt-Out Options**

   For features that require sensitive permissions, consider providing users with the ability to opt-out or disable specific functionalities. This gives users more control over their experience.

```
void provideOptOutOption() {
  // Allow users to disable certain features that require sensi-
  tive permissions.
}
```

6. **Handle API Access Asynchronously**

   When accessing device APIs, especially those requiring user permission, handle the process asynchronously. This prevents freezing the UI and ensures a smooth user experience.

```
void handleApiAccessAsynchronously() async {
  // Access device API asynchronously to avoid UI freezing.
}
```

7. **Stay Informed about Platform Changes**

   Stay updated with the latest changes in Flutter and the underlying platforms (iOS, Android). Updates may introduce new permissions or alter existing APIs, and adapting early ensures your app remains compatible.

```
void stayInformedAboutPlatformChanges() {
  // Regularly check for Flutter and platform updates to stay
  informed about changes.
}
```

8. **Test on Multiple Devices and OS Versions**

   Test your app on various devices and operating system versions to ensure consistent behavior. This helps identify and address any device-specific issues or discrepancies.

```
void testOnMultipleDevicesAndOSVersions() {
  // Conduct thorough testing on different devices and OS versions.
}
```

Accessing Device Hardware and Sensors

Flutter allows you to interact with various hardware components of your device, such as the camera, microphone, and more. These features can add a whole new dimension to your app. Let's see how we can make the most of them!

Have you ever wanted to capture moments directly within your app? Flutter makes it a lot easier! You can use the **camera** package to integrate the camera functionality seamlessly. Start by adding the package to your **pubspec.yaml** file:

```
dependencies:
  camera: ^0.10.5+5
```

Once you've added the package, you can initialize the camera, display a live camera preview, and even take pictures. The **camera** package provides simple and effective ways to incorporate this feature into your app:

```
import 'package:camera/camera.dart';

// Get a list of available cameras.
List<CameraDescription> cameras = await availableCameras();

// Initialize the first camera.
CameraController controller = CameraController(
  cameras[0],
  ResolutionPreset.medium,
);

// Initialize the camera and display the preview.
await controller.initialize();
```

You've just added camera functionality to your Flutter app.

Using the Image Picker Plugin in Flutter

The `**image_picker**` plugin is a powerful tool that enables your Flutter app to access and pick images or videos from device storage, capture new ones using the device camera, and more. Here's a step-by-step guide to get started:

Installation

1. Adding the Dependency

Run the following flutter command in your IDE terminal to add the necessary dependency to **pubspec**:

```
flutter pub add image_picker
```

2. iOS Setup

Update your iOS project's `**Info.plist**` file:

- `NSPhotoLibraryUsageDescription`: Describe why your app needs permission to access the photo library.
- `NSCameraUsageDescription`: Explain why your app needs camera access.
- `NSMicrophoneUsageDescription`: If recording videos, describe microphone access.

Picking Images or Videos

1. Picking from the Gallery

Use the `pickImage` method to choose an image from the gallery:

```
 final picker = ImagePicker();
final XFile? image = await picker.pickImage(source: ImageSource.gal-
lery);
```

2. Capturing a Photo

Utilize the `pickImage` method with `ImageSource.camera` to take a new photo:

```
final XFile? photo = await picker.pickImage(source: ImageSource.camera);
```

3. Picking Videos

Similarly, use `pickVideo` to select videos:

```
final XFile? galleryVideo = await picker.pickVideo(source:
ImageSource.gallery);
final XFile? cameraVideo = await picker.pickVideo(source: ImageSource.
camera);
```

4. Multiple Selection

You can choose multiple images or videos using the appropriate method:

```
final List<XFile> images = await picker.pickMultiImage();
final List<XFile> medias = await picker.pickMultipleMedia();
```

Following is a step-by-step example of a Flutter project using the `**image_picker**` plugin. This example demonstrates how to create a simple app that allows users to pick an image from the gallery and capture a new photo using the camera.

Step 1: Create a New Flutter Project

Open your terminal and run the following commands:

```
flutter create image_picker_example
cd image_picker_example
```

Step 2: Add Dependency

Run the following flutter command in your IDE terminal to add the necessary dependency to pubspec:

```
flutter pub add image_picker
```

Step 3: Import Required Packages

In your `**main.dart**` file, import the necessary packages:

```
import 'dart:io';

import 'package:flutter/material.dart';
import 'package:image_picker/image_picker.dart';
```

Step 4: Create a Stateful Widget

Create a stateful widget that will be the main component of your app:

```
import 'dart:io';

import 'package:flutter/material.dart';
import 'package:image_picker/image_picker.dart';

void main() {
```

```
  runApp(MyApp());
}

class MyApp extends StatelessWidget {
  @override
  Widget build(BuildContext context) {
    return MaterialApp(
      home: MyHomePage(),
    );
  }
}

class MyHomePage extends StatefulWidget {
  @override
  _MyHomePageState createState() => _MyHomePageState();
}

class _MyHomePageState extends State<MyHomePage> {
  XFile? _pickedImage;

  @override
  Widget build(BuildContext context) {
    return Scaffold(
      appBar: AppBar(
        title: Text('Image Picker Example'),
      ),
      body: Center(
        child: Column(
          mainAxisAlignment: MainAxisAlignment.center,
          children: [
            _pickcdImage != null
                ? Image.file(
                    File(_pickedImage!.path),
                    height: 200.0,
                  )
                : Container(),
            ElevatedButton(
              onPressed: () async {
                final picker = ImagePicker();
                final XFile? image =
                    await picker.pickImage(source: ImageSource.gallery);

                setState(() {
                  _pickedImage - image;
                });

                if (_pickedImage != null) {
```

```
                  // Do something with the picked image
                  print('Picked Image Path: ${_pickedImage!.path}');
                }
              },
              child: Text('Pick Image from Gallery'),
            ),
            SizedBox(height: 16.0),
            ElevatedButton(
              onPressed: () async {
                final picker = ImagePicker();
                final XFile? photo =
                    await picker.pickImage(source: ImageSource.camera);

                setState(() {
                  _pickedImage = photo;
                });

                if (_pickedImage != null) {
                  // Do something with the captured photo
                  print('Captured Photo Path: ${_pickedImage!.path}');
                }
              },
              child: Text('Capture Photo'),
            ),
          ],
        ),
      ),
    );
  }
}
```

Step 5: Run the App

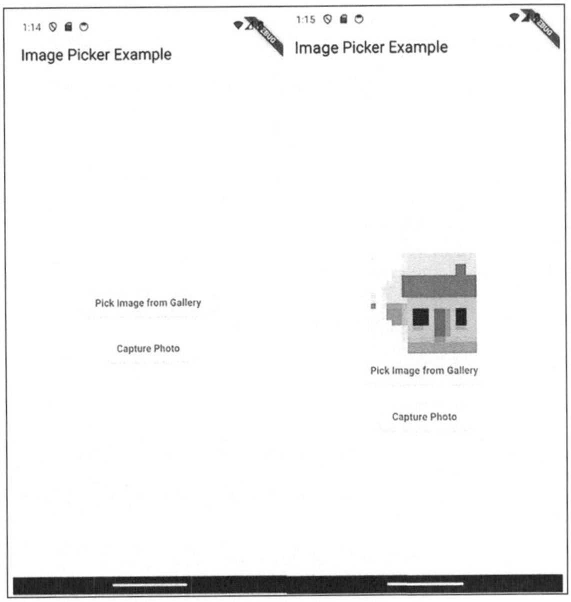

Figure 9.3: *Image Picker Demo*

Save your changes and run the app using the following command:

```
flutter run
```

Flutter also allows you to tap into your device's sensors, opening up more possibilities. Do you want to make your app respond to device orientation changes? The **`sensors`** package has got you covered!

To use the sensors package, add it to your **pubspec.yaml** file:

```
dependencies:
  sensors_plus ^3.1.0
```

First up, let's tap into the accelerometer to detect changes in device acceleration. The **`accelerometerEvents`** stream is your gateway. Take a look at the following code snippet:

```
accelerometerEvents.listen(
  (AccelerometerEvent event) {
    print(event);
  },
  onError: (error) {
    // Handle error logic, especially for Android if the sensor is not
    available
```

```
  },
  cancelOnError: true,
);
// [AccelerometerEvent (x: 0.0, y: 9.8, z: 0.0)]
```

Now your Flutter app can respond dynamically to changes in device acceleration.

Next is the **userAccelerometerEvents** stream, which provides information about the user's acceleration excluding gravity. Take a look at the following code snippet:

```
userAccelerometerEvents.listen(
  (UserAccelerometerEvent event) {
    print(event);
  },
  onError: (error) {
    // Handle error logic, especially for Android if the sensor is not
    available
  },
  cancelOnError: true,
);
// [UserAccelerometerEvent (x: 0.0, y: 0.0, z: 0.0)]
```

Now your Flutter app can sense more precise movements, making it even more interactive and engaging.

The **gyroscopeEvents** stream is your ticket to detecting rotational changes in the device. Take a look at the following code snippet:

```
gyroscopeEvents.listen(
  (GyroscopeEvent event) {
    print(event);
  },
  onError: (error) {
    // Handle error logic, especially for Android if the sensor is not
    available
  },
  cancelOnError: true,
);
// [GyroscopeEvent (x: 0.0, y: 0.0, z: 0.0)]
```

Now your Flutter app can respond to the rotations of the device. It's time to add some spin to your app!

Last but not least, let's consider the **magnetometerEvents** stream, which provides data about the Earth's magnetic field as sensed by the device. Take a look at the following code snippet:

```
magnetometerEvents.listen(
  (MagnetometerEvent event) {
    print(event);
  },
  onError: (error) {
    // Handle error logic, especially for Android if the sensor is not
    available
  },
  cancelOnError: true,
);
// [MagnetometerEvent (x: -23.6, y: 6.2, z: -34.9)]
```

With this, your Flutter app gains the ability to sense the magnetic forces around, opening up possibilities for creative and innovative features.

Step-by-Step Guide to Using `sensor_plus` in a Flutter App

Ready to add some sensor magic to your Flutter app? Let's break it down into simple steps. In this example, we'll focus on using the accelerometer sensor.

Step 1: Add Dependencies

Start by adding the **sensors_plus** package to your **pubspec.yaml** file:

```
dependencies:
  sensors_plus: ^3.1.0
```

Run `flutter pub get` in your terminal to fetch the package.

Step 2: Import the Package

Import the necessary package in your Dart file:

```
import 'package:sensors_plus/sensors_plus.dart';
```

Step 3: Set Up the Flutter App

Create a Flutter app structure with the **MyApp** and **AccelerometerDemo** classes. The class will handle the accelerometer sensor:

```
void main() {
  runApp(MyApp());
}

class MyApp extends StatelessWidget {
  @override
  Widget build(BuildContext context) {
    return MaterialApp(
      theme: ThemeData(
        primarySwatch: Colors.green,
      ),
      debugShowCheckedModeBanner: false,
      home: AccelerometerDemo(),
    );
  }
}
```

Step 4: Implement the AccelerometerDemo Widget

Create the **AccelerometerDemo** widget. This widget will display accelerometer data in your app:

```
class AccelerometerDemo extends StatefulWidget {

  const AccelerometerDemo({super.key});
  @override

  State<AccelerometerDemo> createState() => _AccelerometerDemoState();
}
```

Step 5: Initialize and Subscribe to Accelerometer Events

In the **_AccelerometerDemoState** class, initialize the **accelerometer** subscription in the `initState` method and listen for accelerometer events:

```
class _AccelerometerDemoState extends State<AccelerometerDemo> {
  // List to store accelerometer data
  List<AccelerometerEvent> _accelerometerValues = [];

  // StreamSubscription for accelerometer events
  late StreamSubscription<AccelerometerEvent> _accelerometerSubscription;
  @override
  void initState() {
    super.initState();
```

```
    // Subscribe to accelerometer events
    _accelerometerSubscription = accelerometerEvents.listen((event) {
      setState(() {
        // Update the _accelerometerValues list with the latest event
        _accelerometerValues = [event];
      });
    });
  }

  // ... (Other methods)

  @override
  void dispose() {
    // Cancel the accelerometer event subscription to prevent memory leaks
    _accelerometerSubscription.cancel();
    super.dispose();
  }

  // ... (Build method)
}
```

Step 6: Display Accelerometer Data in the UI

Modify the `build` method to display accelerometer data in your app's UI:

```
@override
Widget build(BuildContext context) {
  return Scaffold(
    appBar: AppBar(
      title: Text('Accelerometer Demo),
    ),
    body: Center(
      child: Column(
        mainAxisAlignment: MainAxisAlignment.center,
        children: <Widget>[
          Text(
            'Accelerometer Data:',
            style: TextStyle(fontSize: 20),
          ),
          SizedBox(height: 10),
          if (_accelerometerValues.isNotEmpty)
            Text(
              'X: ${_accelerometerValues[0].x.toStringAsFixed(2)}, '
              'Y: ${_accelerometerValues[0].y.toStringAsFixed(2)}, '
              'Z: ${_accelerometerValues[0].z.toStringAsFixed(2)}',
              style: TextStyle(fontSize: 16),
```

```
          )
        else
          Text('No data available', style: TextStyle(fontSize: 16)),
      ],
    ),
  ),
);
}
```

Step 7: Run Your Flutter App

Save your changes and run your Flutter app using the following command:

```
flutter run
```

Now, your app will display accelerometer data in real time. Tilt your device and watch the magic happen!

Working with Platform-Specific Plugins

Flutter is designed to be a cross-platform framework, meaning you can write code once and run it on both iOS and Android. However, there are instances where you need to perform actions or access features that are specific to each platform. Here's where platform-specific plugins come into play.

In simpler terms, a platform-specific plugin acts as a bridge, connecting your Flutter code with the native code of the device it's running on. This allows you to use features that might be unique to iOS or Android, providing a seamless and integrated user experience.

Imagine you want to access a device's camera or GPS functionality. While Flutter provides a consistent way to work with these features, there are cases where the native capabilities of iOS or Android offer more granular control or unique functionalities. Platform-specific plugins allow you to harness these capabilities without sacrificing the cross-platform nature of your app.

The magic behind platform-specific plugins lies in something called platform channels. These channels enable communication between Dart code (the language Flutter is built with) and native code (Swift/Java/Kotlin) running on the device.

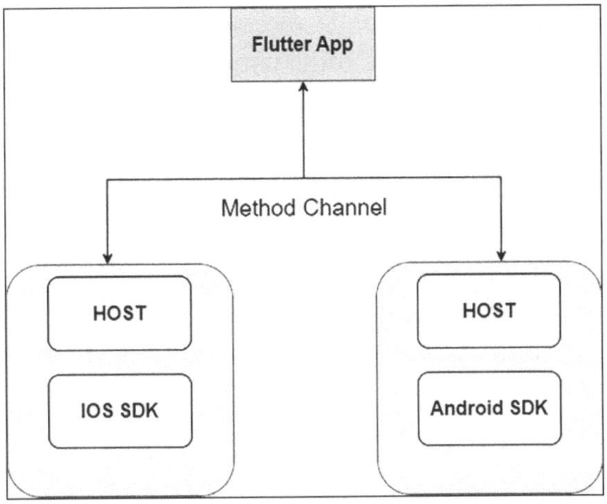

***Figure 9.4**: Flutter Method Channel*

Conclusion

Throughout this chapter, we delved into the exciting realm of utilizing device features and APIs in Flutter, allowing your applications to interact with various native components and access device functionalities. We covered accessing sensors, working with contacts, and understanding platform-specific plugins to create versatile and feature-rich Flutter apps.

In the next chapter, we'll explore the critical aspect of ensuring the robustness and reliability of your Flutter applications through unit testing. Specifically, we'll focus on testing UI components, which is crucial for maintaining a stable and crror-free user experience.

Points to Remember

- **Accessing Device Sensors:** Utilize packages like `sensors_plus` to access various sensors like accelerometer and gyroscope. Leverage these sensors to create dynamic and responsive applications that react to device movements.
- **Working with Contacts:** Utilize the `contacts_service` package to retrieve contact information from the user's device. Ensure proper permission handling and user-friendly presentation of contact details in your app.
- **Platform-Specific Plugins:** Understand the concept of platform channels to establish communication between Dart code and native code. This enables the utilization of platform-specific functionalities while maintaining cross-platform compatibility.

- **Permission Handling:** Always request necessary permissions when accessing device features. Guide users through the permission request process to ensure smooth app functionality.
- **Error Handling:** Implement robust error handling mechanisms when working with device APIs. Use try-catch blocks or error-specific handling to manage errors and exceptions that might occur during API calls.
- **Testing and Debugging:** While implementing device API functionalities, thoroughly test and debug your code on different devices and platforms. Ensure the reliability and stability of your app by addressing device-specific behaviors.

Assessment

In this assessment project, you'll create a Flutter app that displays the contacts on your phone. We'll use the `contacts_service` package to retrieve contact information and then build a simple interface to display them.

Prerequisites

- Ensure you have Flutter installed on your machine.
- Set up your preferred Flutter IDE (for example, VS Code, Android Studio).
- Basic understanding of Flutter widgets and the Dart programming language.

Step 1: Create a New Flutter Project

1. Open your terminal or command prompt.
2. Run the command `flutter create contact_list_app` to create a new Flutter project.
3. Move into the project directory with `cd contact_list_app`.

Step 2: Add Dependencies

1. Open the **pubspec.yaml** file in your project.
2. Add the following dependencies under the `dependencies` section:

```
dependencies:
  flutter:
    sdk: flutter
  contacts_service: ^0.6.3
```

3. Save the file.
4. Run `flutter pub get` in the terminal to fetch the new dependencies.

Step 3: Request Permission

1. Open the **main.dart** file in the **lib** folder.
2. Replace the existing code in **main.dart** with the provided code for requesting permission and displaying contacts.
3. When it comes to Android permissions, ensure your **AndroidManifest.xml** includes the `READ_CONTACTS` permission:

```
<manifest xmlns:android="http://schemas.android.com/apk/res/an-
droid"
          package="com.example.app">

    <!-- Other manifest declarations go here -->

   <uses-permission android:name="android.permission.READ_CON-
TACTS" />

    <application>
        <!-- Other application-related configurations go here -->

    </application>
</manifest>
```

Step 4: Run the App

1. Ensure your device is connected or an emulator is running.
2. Run the app using `flutter run` in the terminal.

Now, check if your Flutter app successfully displays a list of contacts. If you encounter any issues or have questions, feel free to check the solution!

Solution

Step 1: Create a New Flutter Project

Create a new Flutter project using the following command in your terminal or command prompt:

```
flutter create contact_list_app
cd contact_list_app
```

Step 2: Add Dependencies

Open the **pubspec.yaml** file in your project and add the following dependencies:

```
dependencies:
  flutter:
    sdk: flutter
  contacts_service: ^0.6.3
```

Save the file and run the following command:

```
flutter pub get
```

Step 3: Retrieve Contacts

In your **main.dart** file, request permission to access contacts. Replace the existing code with the following:

```
import 'package:flutter/material.dart';
import 'package:contacts_service/contacts_service.dart';
import 'package:permission_handler/permission_handler.dart';

void main() {
  runApp(MyApp());
}
class MyApp extends StatelessWidget {
  @override
  Widget build(BuildContext context) {
    return MaterialApp(
      home: ContactListScreen(),
    );
  }
}

class ContactListScreen extends StatefulWidget {
  @override
  _ContactListScreenState createState() => _ContactListScreenState();
}

class _ContactListScreenState extends State<ContactListScreen> {
```

```
List<Contact> contacts = [];

@override
void initState() {
  super.initState();
  _requestPermissions();
}

Future<void> _requestPermissions() async {
  if (await Permission.contacts.request().isGranted) {
    await getContacts();
  } else {
    // Permission denied, handle accordingly
  }
}

@override
Widget build(BuildContext context) {
  return Scaffold(
    appBar: AppBar(
      title: Text('Contact List App'),
    ),
    body: FutureBuilder(
      future: getContacts(),
      builder: (context, snapshot) {
        if (snapshot.connectionState == ConnectionState.waiting) {
          return CircularProgressIndicator();
        } else {
          return ListView.builder(
            itemCount: contacts.length,
            itemBuilder: (context, index) {
              return ContactCard(contact: contacts[index]);
            },
          );
        }
      },
    ),
  );
}

Future<void> getContacts() async {
  Iterable<Contact> contactsIterable = await ContactsService.
  getContacts();
  setState(() {
    contacts = contactsIterable.toList();
  });
}
```

```
}

class ContactCard extends StatelessWidget {
  final Contact contact;

  ContactCard({required this.contact});

  @override
  Widget build(BuildContext context) {
    return Card(
      margin: EdgeInsets.all(8.0),
      child: ListTile(
        title: Text(contact.displayName ?? ''),
        subtitle: Text(contact.phones?.isNotEmpty == true
            ? contact.phones!.first.value!
            : ''),
      ),
    );
  }
}
```

This code defines a simple Flutter app with a **ContactListScreen** that retrieves contacts and displays them using a `**ListView**` and `**ContactCard**` widgets.

Step 4: Run the App

Connect your device or use an emulator, and run the app:

```
flutter run
```

You should see a basic app displaying a list of contacts from your device.

Key Terms

- **Sensors:** Physical components in devices that measure various types of data such as motion, orientation, or environmental conditions. In Flutter, accessing sensors allows applications to respond to real-world interactions.
- **Accelerometer:** A sensor that measures the acceleration force applied to a device, including the force of gravity. It detects movements, tilts, and gestures.
- **Gyroscope:** A sensor that measures the rate of rotation around a device's three axes. It provides information about the device's orientation and angular velocity.

- **`contacts_service`:** A Flutter package that provides functionality to access and manage contacts stored on a device. It allows reading, creating, updating, and deleting contacts.
- **Platform Channels:** A communication mechanism that enables interaction between Dart code in Flutter and platform-specific code (Java, Kotlin, Swift, and Objective-C). It facilitates invoking platform-specific functionalities.
- **Permission Handling:** The process of requesting and managing permissions from the user to access sensitive device features. It involves handling permission requests gracefully and ensuring proper user consent.
- **Native Code Integration:** The incorporation of platform-specific (Android/iOS) code into a Flutter project. This integration is achieved using platform channels to leverage native functionalities.

SECTION 4

Testing and Debugging Flutter UIs

CHAPTER 10

Widget Testing UI Components

Flutter, with its powerful capabilities for crafting visually appealing and high-performance user interfaces, often captures developers' attention, drawing them into creating stunning user interfaces. Oftentimes, it's easy to overlook the importance of ensuring that each UI component functions seamlessly.

Throughout this journey, from understanding the fundamentals of widgets to refining the art of styling and rendering, we have built a foundation for creating exceptional user experiences. However, as the complexity of Flutter applications grows, it becomes imperative to safeguard the quality of the UI components and prevent regression issues that may compromise the user interface.

Testing plays a crucial role in ensuring the reliability and functionality of applications. There are three primary types of testing that Flutter developers commonly employ: unit testing, widget testing, and integration testing.

Unit testing focuses on testing individual units or functions of the application in isolation. In the context of Flutter, this involves testing specific methods, classes, or functions to ensure they produce the expected output for various inputs. Unit testing is an essential practice for maintaining code quality and catching errors at an early stage of development.

Widget testing, on the other hand, is concerned with testing Flutter widgets. Widgets are the building blocks of Flutter UI, and widget testing involves verifying their behavior and appearance. This type of testing is particularly valuable for ensuring that UI components, such as buttons, forms, and interactive elements, work as intended and look appropriate in different scenarios.

Integration testing takes a broader perspective by testing the collaboration and interaction between different components of the application. In a Flutter context, integration testing helps ensure that the different parts of the app work seamlessly together, identifying potential issues that may arise when combining various functionalities. Integration testing is crucial for assessing the overall performance and behavior of the application in a more holistic manner.

This chapter will primarily focus on widget testing, a fundamental aspect of Flutter development. Throughout this chapter, we will explore the core principles and practices of widget testing, providing insights into how you can effectively test and validate your Flutter widgets.

Structure

In this chapter, we will cover the following topics:

- Introduction to Widget Testing in Flutter
- Writing Unit Tests for UI Components
- Testing UI Interactions and State Changes
- Using Test-Driven Development (TDD) Approach
- Best Practices for Testing Flutter UI Components

Introduction to Widget Testing in Flutter

Widget testing is akin to the rigorous inspections and tests conducted during the construction of a house. Just as a house requires a strong foundation to withstand the test of time and external forces, your app demands a robust testing strategy to ensure reliability and resilience.

In construction, the foundation serves as the backbone, providing stability and support for the entire structure. Similarly, widget testing forms the architectural groundwork of your Flutter app. It involves systematically testing individual components or units of code to guarantee they function as intended.

Figure 10.1: *Photo by Etienne Girardet on Unsplash*

Just as builders conduct inspections to verify the structural integrity of a house, developers use unit tests to confirm that each module of code performs its designated function without compromising the overall application.

During house inspections, weak points are identified and addressed promptly. Similarly, widget testing reveals vulnerabilities in your code, allowing developers to strengthen these areas and fortify the overall resilience of the application.

The construction of a house involves distinct phases, each requiring meticulous examination. Likewise, Flutter app testing involves breaking down your application into manageable units and scrutinizing them individually to ensure they meet specific criteria.

Imagine discovering a flaw in the foundation of a house during construction – rectifying it early prevents future problems. Widget testing acts as a bug-detection mechanism, allowing developers to identify and rectify issues in their code before they escalate.

Just as investing in high-quality materials pays off in construction, investing time in widget testing ultimately saves resources by reducing the likelihood of costly bug fixes and improvements post-launch.

In essence, rigorous testing in Flutter is your tool for constructing a reliable, resilient, and bug-resistant application.

Writing Unit Tests for UI Components

Now that we've laid the foundation for understanding the importance of widget testing, let's consider the practical component – writing tests for your app's user interface (UI) components. Imagine this phase as the final inspection before unveiling your newly constructed house to your family and friends.

Before we start writing tests, it's essential to set the stage fundamental. In house construction, this would be the moment just before the final walk-through. For our app, this involves preparing our codebase and ensuring that our UI components are ready for scrutiny.

Much like a builder selects the right tools for the job, developers must choose suitable testing frameworks. Flutter provides a user-friendly testing environment, making it accessible for everyone. We'll be using tools like `test` and `flutter_test` to execute our tests effortlessly.

Let's consider writing a test as creating a detailed blueprint for your house's final inspection. In our case, this involves creating a script that defines the expected behavior of your UI components. As we continue in this chapter, we'll guide you through the process with simple, step-by-step examples.

The same as an inspector checks every nook and cranny of a house, our tests will scrutinize each widget and interaction within your app. From buttons to text fields, we'll ensure that every component performs as designed.

What if the house faces an unexpected weather event? Similarly, our tests will explore edge cases, ensuring your app can handle unexpected scenarios seamlessly. We'll cover scenarios like handling invalid input and unexpected user interactions.

The final inspection often involves addressing minor issues. Our tests serve as debugging tools, helping you identify and resolve any glitches in your UI components. It's all about fine-tuning your code to perfection.

Finding Widgets in Flutter

Finding widgets is a crucial aspect of testing and interacting with your application's user interface. The ability to locate and manipulate widgets allows you to validate UI elements, simulate user interactions, and ensure the functionality of your app. There are a few techniques and tools at your disposal for finding widgets in Flutter.

Widget Finder Methods

Flutter provides a set of powerful methods under the `find` function that enables you to locate widgets within your widget tree during testing. Some commonly used finder methods include:

- **`find.byType()`**: Locates widgets by their type.
- **`find.byKey()`**: Finds widgets by their `Key` property.
- **`find.byTooltip()`**: Locates widgets by their tooltip.
- **`find.text()`**: Finds widgets containing specific text.

Flutter Tool Tip

A tooltip in Flutter is a brief, informative message that appears when a user interacts with a widget, typically by hovering over it or tapping and holding. Tooltips are used to provide additional context or details about the purpose or functionality of a particular widget. They are a form of user interface enhancement that contributes to a more user-friendly and informative application.

In the context of Flutter testing, `find.byTooltip()` is a method used to locate widgets based on their associated tooltips. This can be particularly useful when writing widget tests to interact with or verify the presence of specific widgets that have tooltips. Using `find.byTooltip()`, testers can locate widgets by the content of their tooltips, facilitating the identification and interaction with widgets in a test environment.

Step-by-Step Example: Using Widget Finder Methods in Flutter Testing

Let's walk through a step-by-step example of how to use various widget finder methods in Flutter testing. For this scenario, imagine you have a simple Flutter project with a screen containing a list of items. Each item is a **ListTile** widget with specific keys, tooltips, and text content.

1. Create a Flutter Project:

Begin by creating a new Flutter project. Open your terminal and run the following commands:

```
flutter create widget_finder_example
cd widget_finder_example
```

2. Define the ListItem Widget:

In the **lib/main.dart** file, define a **ListItem** widget. Each **ListItem** contains a **ListTile** with a specific key, tooltip, and text:

```
import 'package:flutter/material.dart';

class ListItem extends StatelessWidget {
  final Key;
  final String tooltip;
  final String text;

  ListItem({
    required this.key,
    required this.tooltip,
    required this.text,
  });

  @override
  Widget build(BuildContext context) {
    return ListTile(
```

```
      key: key,
      title: Text(text),
      subtitle: Text(tooltip),
    );
  }
}
```

3. Create a List Screen:

Create a simple screen that displays a list of **ListItem** widgets:

```
import 'package:flutter/material.dart';

void main() {
  runApp(MyApp());
}

class MyApp extends StatelessWidget {
  @override
  Widget build(BuildContext context) {
    return MaterialApp(
      home: ListScreen(),
    );
  }
}

class ListScreen extends StatelessWidget {
  @override
  Widget build(BuildContext context) {
    return Scaffold(
      appBar: AppBar(
        title: Text('Widget Finder Example'),
      ),
      body: ListView(
        children: [
          ListItem(
            key: Key('item_1'),
            tooltip: 'Item 1 Tooltip',
            text: 'Item 1 Text',
          ),
          ListItem(
            key: Key('item_2'),
            tooltip: 'Item 2 Tooltip',
            text: 'Item 2 Text',
          ),
          // Add more ListItems as needed
        ],
```

```
      ),
    );
  }
}
```

4. Write Widget Tests:

Now, let's write widget tests to find widgets using various finder methods. Create a **test/widget_finder_test.dart** file with the following content:

```
import 'package:flutter_test/flutter_test.dart';
import 'package:widget_finder_example/main.dart';

void main() {
  testWidgets('Find Widgets using Finder Methods', (tester) async {
    await tester.pumpWidget(MyApp());

    // Find widgets by type
    expect(find.byType(ListItem), findsNWidgets(2));

    // Find widgets by key
    expect(find.byKey(Key('item_1')), findsOneWidget);
    expect(find.byKey(Key('item_2')), findsOneWidget);

    // Find widgets by tooltip
    expect(find.byTooltip('Item 1 Tooltip'), findsOneWidget);
    expect(find.byTooltip('Item 2 Tooltip'), findsOneWidget);

    // Find widgets by text
    expect(find.text('Item 1 Text'), findsOneWidget);
    expect(find.text('Item 2 Text'), findsOneWidget);
  });
}
```

5. Run the Tests:

Execute the tests using the following command:

```
flutter test
```

Keys and Accessibility

Assigning keys to widgets is crucial for identifying them uniquely, especially in testing scenarios. Use the **Key** class to give your widgets a specific identifier, making it easier to locate them programmatically. Keys are particularly useful when dealing with dynamically generated lists or when widget positions may change.

Ensure your app is accessible by utilizing **Semantics** and **`AutomatedAccessibilityTestWidgets`**. These tools not only make your app more inclusive but also provide additional methods for widget discovery.

Step-by-Step Example: Using Keys and Accessibility in Flutter Testing

In this example, let's use keys to enhance accessibility in Flutter widget testing. We'll continue with the Flutter project created earlier.

1. Assign Keys to Widgets:

Update the **`ListItem`** widget to include keys for better identification in tests:

```
class ListItem extends StatelessWidget {
  final Key key;
  final String tooltip;
  final String text;

  ListItem({
    required this.key,
    required this.tooltip,
    required this.text,
  }) : super(key: key);

  @override
  Widget build(BuildContext context) {
    return ListTile(
      key: key,
      title: Text(text),
      subtitle: Text(tooltip),
    );
  }
}
```

2. Enhance Accessibility with Semantics:

Improve accessibility by adding **Semantics** widgets to the `**ListItem**`:

```
class ListItem extends StatelessWidget {
  final Key key;
  final String tooltip;
  final String text;
```

```
  ListItem({
    required this.key,
    required this.tooltip,
    required this.text,
  }) : super(key: key);

  @override
  Widget build(BuildContext context) {
    return Semantics(
      label: text, // Provide a label for screen readers
      child: ListTile(
        key: key,
        title: Text(text),
        subtitle: Text(tooltip),
      ),
    );
  }
}
```

3. Update Tests with Keys and Semantics:

Modify the widget tests to include assertions based on keys and semantics:

```
testWidgets('Use Keys and Accessibility in Tests', (tester) async {
  await tester.pumpWidget(MyApp());

  // Find widgets by key
  expect(find.byKey(Key('item_1')), findsOneWidget);
  expect(find.byKey(Key('item_2')), findsOneWidget);

  // Find widgets by tooltip
  expect(find.byTooltip('Item 1 Tooltip'), findsOneWidget);
  expect(find.byTooltip('Item 2 Tooltip'), findsOneWidget);

  // Find widgets by text
  expect(find.text('Item 1 Text'), findsOneWidget);
  expect(find.text('Item 2 Text'), findsOneWidget);

  // Verify accessibility with Semantics
  expect(tester.getSemantics(find.text('Item 1 Text')), matchesSemantics(
    label: 'Item 1 Text',
  ));
  expect(tester.getSemantics(find.text('Item 2 Text')), matchesSemantics(
    label: 'Item 2 Text',
  ));
});
```

4. Run the Tests:

Execute the tests using the following command:

```
flutter test
```

The tests should pass, demonstrating how keys and accessibility features are utilized in widget testing.

Testing with `WidgetTester`

When writing widget tests in Flutter, you'll frequently use **`WidgetTester`** to interact with your widgets and verify their behavior. The **tester** provides methods like **`pumpWidget()`** to build and attach widgets for testing, **`tap()`** to simulate taps on widgets, and **`pump()`** to trigger widget rebuilds.

Step-by-Step Example: Testing with `WidgetTester` in Flutter

In this example, we'll explore the process of testing widgets using **`WidgetTester`** in Flutter. We'll continue working with the existing Flutter project.

1. Update the ListItem Widget:

Ensure that the **`ListItem`** widget is testable by adding a **`key`**:

```
class ListItem extends StatelessWidget {
  final Key key;
  final String tooltip;
  final String text;

  ListItem({
    required this.key,
    required this.tooltip,
    required this.text,
  }) : super(key: key);

  @override
  Widget build(BuildContext context) {
    return Semantics(
      label: text,
      child: ListTile(
        key: key,
        title: Text(text),
        subtitle: Text(tooltip),
```

```
      ),
    );
  }
}
```

2. Write a Test Using WidgetTester:

Create a widget test that uses **`WidgetTester`** to interact with the widgets:

```
import 'package:flutter_test/flutter_test.dart';
import 'package:your_project/main.dart'; // Replace with the actual
import

void main() {
  testWidgets('WidgetTester Test', (WidgetTester tester) async {
    // Build the widget tree
    await tester.pumpWidget(MyApp());

    // Find a widget by key and perform an action
    await tester.tap(find.byKey(Key('item_1')));

    // Allow time for animations to complete
    await tester.pumpAndSettle();

    // Verify the expected changes in the widget tree
    expect(find.text('Item 1 Text'), findsNothing);
    expect(find.text('Item 2 Text'), findsOneWidget);
  });
}
```

3. Run the Test:

Execute the test using the following command:

```
flutter test
```

Testing UI Interactions and State Changes

In this section, we'll create a simple Heart Monitoring App UI screen with Flutter. We'll then explore the process of testing UI interactions and state changes within this app.

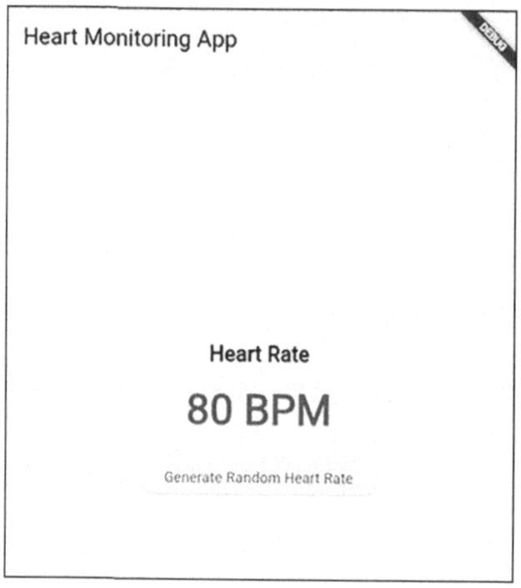

***Figure 10.2**: Heart Monitoring App UI screen*

1. Design the Heart Monitoring App UI:

```
import 'package:flutter/material.dart';

class HeartMonitoringApp extends StatefulWidget {
  const HeartMonitoringApp({super.key});

  @override
  _HeartMonitoringAppState createState() => _HeartMonitoringAppState();
}

class _HeartMonitoringAppState extends State<HeartMonitoringApp> {
  int heartRate = 75;

  @override
  Widget build(BuildContext context) {
    return MaterialApp(
      home: Scaffold(
        appBar: AppBar(
          title: Text('Heart Monitoring App'),
        ),
        body: Center(
          child: Column(
            mainAxisAlignment: MainAxisAlignment.center,
            children: [
              const Text(
                'Heart Rate',
               style: TextStyle(fontSize: 20, fontWeight: FontWeight.bold),
              ),
              SizedBox(height: 10),
```

```
                Text(
                  '$heartRate BPM',
                  key: const Key('heartRateText'),
                  style: const TextStyle(
                      fontSize: 40,
                      fontWeight: FontWeight.bold,
                      color: Colors.red),
                ),
                const SizedBox(height: 20),
                ElevatedButton(
                  onPressed: () {
                    setState(() {
                      heartRate = _generateRandomHeartRate();
                    });
                  },
                  child: Text('Generate Random Heart Rate'),
                ),
              ],
            ),
          ),
        ),
      );
  }

  int _generateRandomHeartRate() {
    // Simulate a random heart rate between 60 and 100 BPM
    return 60 + (DateTime.now().millisecondsSinceEpoch % 40);
  }
}
```

2. Writing UI Interaction Test:

Now, let's write a test to simulate a user interaction with the app:

```
import 'package:flutter/material.dart';
import 'package:flutter_test/flutter_test.dart';
import 'package:modern_flutter/heart_rate.dart';

void main() {
  testWidgets('Heart Rate Button Tap Test', (WidgetTester tester) async {
    // Build our app and trigger a frame.
    await tester.pumpWidget(HeartMonitoringApp());

    // Tap the button.
    await tester.tap(find.byType(ElevatedButton));
```

```
    // Wait for all animations and microtasks to complete.
    await tester.pumpAndSettle(Duration(seconds: 1));

    // Now check for the widget using the key.
    expect(find.byKey(Key('heartRateText')), findsOneWidget);
  });
}
```

3. Run the Test:

Execute the test using the following command:

```
flutter test
```

Using Test-Driven Development (TDD) Approach

This is a software development approach that emphasizes writing tests before writing the actual code. The fundamental principle behind TDD is to iteratively create tests, implement the corresponding code to make those tests pass, and then refactor the code as needed. This cyclic process ensures that the codebase remains reliable, maintainable, and scalable throughout the development lifecycle.

Imagine you're tasked with building a Flutter application that features a button triggering a counter increment. In Test-Driven Development (TDD), you'd start by outlining the desired behavior through a set of tests.

In this scenario, you'd write a test to ensure that the initial state of the counter is zero. This test would look something like this:

```
testWidgets('Counter starts at 0', (WidgetTester tester) async {
  await tester.pumpWidget(MyApp()); // Assuming MyApp is your
  application widget

  expect(find.text('0'), findsOneWidget); // Ensure '0' is present on the
  screen
});
```

Naturally, this test would fail initially, as the counter display would likely start with a different value. The next step would be to implement the minimal code needed to make this test pass. In this case, you'd set the initial value of the counter to zero:

```
class MyApp extends StatelessWidget {
  @override
  Widget build(BuildContext context) {
    return MaterialApp(
      home: Scaffold(
        body: Center(
          child: Text('0'), // Initial counter value
        ),
      ),
    );
  }
}
```

With this change, your initial test will now pass. However, you wouldn't stop there. You'd continue this cycle, adding more tests and corresponding code to handle different aspects of your application's functionality.

For instance, the next test might focus on checking if the counter increments when the button is pressed:

```
testWidgets('Increment button increases the counter', (WidgetTester
tester) async {
  await tester.pumpWidget(MyApp());

  await tester.tap(find.byType(ElevatedButton)); // Assuming you have an
ElevatedButton in your app
  await tester.pump();

  expect(find.text('1'), findsOneWidget); // Ensure '1' is present after
tapping the button
});
```

Again, this test would initially fail, prompting you to implement the necessary logic to increment the counter when the button is pressed.

It's interesting to know that one of the primary advantages of TDD is its ability to provide a clear roadmap for development. Developers begin by defining the expected behavior of a specific piece of functionality through a set of unit tests. These tests are initially expected to fail since the corresponding code hasn't been implemented yet. The developer then proceeds to write the minimal amount of code necessary to make these tests pass.

By adopting TDD, developers are compelled to think deeply about the design and architecture of their code. Since the tests are created first, they serve as a blueprint for the actual implementation. This encourages the creation of modular, loosely coupled, and easily maintainable code, reducing the likelihood of bugs and easing the process of future enhancements or modifications.

Beyond a clear roadmap, TDD also promotes a more robust and dependable codebase. As new features or changes are introduced, developers can quickly run the existing suite of tests to ensure that the modifications do not break existing functionality. This automated testing process becomes especially pertinent in larger projects, where manual testing might become cumbersome and error-prone.

Despite its numerous benefits, adopting TDD requires a shift in mindset for developers. It demands discipline and a commitment to writing tests for every piece of functionality. However, the long-term advantages, including reduced debugging time, enhanced code quality, and improved project maintainability, make TDD a valuable practice in modern software development workflows.

Best Practices for Testing Flutter UI Components

Testing UI components is a fundamental part of building robust and reliable applications. As we explore best practices, we'll consider key strategies to enhance the effectiveness and maintainability of your UI tests.

1. **Isolate Tests for Widgets:**
    - **Why it Matters:**

      Isolating tests for individual widgets allows you to focus on specific functionalities and catch potential issues early in the development process.
    - **How to Implement:**

      Create tests that target a single widget or a small group of closely related widgets. This ensures that the behavior of each widget is thoroughly examined.
2. **Use `WidgetTester`:**
    - **Why it Matters:**

      Leveraging the power of `` `WidgetTester` `` enables you to interact with widgets programmatically, simulating user interactions for comprehensive testing.

- **How to Implement:**

  Utilize `WidgetTester` methods like `tap`, `enterText`, and `pump` to mimic user actions and observe how widgets respond.

3. Group Tests Logically:

- **Why it Matters:**

  Logical grouping of tests enhances the organization and readability of your test suite, making it easier to maintain.

- **How to Implement:**

  Group tests based on shared characteristics, such as testing similar widgets or features. This promotes clarity and reduces the cognitive load when navigating through tests.

4. Arrange, Act, Assert (AAA) Pattern:

- **Why it Matters:**

  Following the AAA pattern brings consistency to your tests, making them more readable and facilitating collaboration within your development team.

- **How to Implement:**

  Clearly separate the arrangement of initial conditions, the execution of the test scenario, and the assertion of expected outcomes in your test methods.

5. Use Keys Thoughtfully:

- **Why it Matters:**

  Strategic use of `Key` objects ensures that your tests can uniquely identify and interact with specific widgets, especially in scenarios involving repeated elements.

- **How to Implement:**

  Assign keys to widgets, especially when dealing with lists or dynamically generated widgets. This aids in precise widget identification during testing.

6. Mock External Dependencies:

- **Why it Matters:**

  Mocking external dependencies isolates your tests from external services, allowing you to focus on the widget's behavior without relying on real-world interactions.

- **How to Implement:**

  Use packages like `mockito` to create mock objects that simulate the behavior of external dependencies, such as databases or APIs.

7. **Golden Tests for Visual Regression:**

- **Why it Matters:**

  Golden tests provide a safety net against unintended visual changes, ensuring that the UI remains consistent across updates.

- **How to Implement:**

  Capture golden images of your UI in a known good state, and compare subsequent test runs to these images to detect visual regressions.

8. **Test Across Multiple Screen Sizes:**

- **Why it Matters:**

  Ensuring responsiveness across various screen sizes guarantees a consistent user experience on different devices.

- **How to Implement:**

  Utilize the `WidgetTester` to simulate different screen dimensions, verifying that your UI gracefully adapts to various form factors.

9. **Continuous Integration (CI):**

- **Why it Matters:**

  Integrating UI tests into your CI/CD pipeline automates the testing process, providing rapid feedback on code changes and reducing the likelihood of introducing bugs.

- **How to Implement:**

  Configure CI services (for example, Jenkins, Travis CI, or GitHub Actions) to run your UI tests automatically upon each code push.

10. **Test Error and Loading States:**

- **Why it Matters:**

  Ensuring proper handling of error and loading states enhances the user experience during suboptimal conditions.

- **How to Implement:**

  Create test scenarios that mimic error responses or loading states, and verify that your UI components respond appropriately.

11. Clear Test Naming:

- **Why it Matters:**

  Well-named tests act as documentation, aiding developers in understanding the purpose and expected outcomes of each test.

- **How to Implement:**

  Choose descriptive names that convey the intent of the test, making it easier for team members to grasp the test's purpose.

12. Regularly Review and Update Tests:

- **Why it Matters:**

  As your application evolves, keeping tests up-to-date ensures that they accurately reflect changes in requirements and functionality.

- **How to Implement:**

  Periodically review and update tests to align with the current state of your application. This proactive approach prevents outdated tests from providing misleading information.

Conclusion

The significance of widget testing for UI components cannot be overstated. As we wrap up this chapter, let's reflect on the insights gained and the principles that can guide us in ensuring the resilience and reliability of our user interfaces.

As we transition to the next chapter, we will consider the concluding insights and explore the broader landscape of Flutter development. *Chapter 11*, titled "*Conclusion and Next Steps*," will provide a holistic overview of the journey we've undertaken, offering guidance on how to consolidate your learnings and embark on the next phase of your Flutter journey.

Points to Remember

- **Early Testing, Lasting Impact:** Initiating unit tests early in the development lifecycle significantly impacts the stability and reliability of your app.
- **Building Blocks of Resilience:** Each unit test for UI components serves as a building block that fortifies the overall resilience of your application.
- **Shift-Left Approach:** Adopting a "**shift-left**" mentality by integrating

testing from the start ensures proactive bug identification and smoother development.

- **Continuous Improvement:** Regularly revisiting and refining tests keeps them aligned with evolving app requirements and industry best practices.
- **Balancing Speed and Quality:** Widget testing maintains equilibrium between rapid iteration and delivering high-quality, dependable software.
- **Strategic Automation:** Automated testing, especially when integrated into CI/CD pipelines, safeguards against regressions and ensures consistent performance.
- **User-Centric Assurance:** Robust widget testing directly correlates to a positive user experience by ensuring the expected behavior of UI components.
- **Holistic Validation:** Unit tests cover diverse scenarios and screen sizes, validating the UI's functionality across the application's spectrum.
- **Testing as a Foundation:** Widget testing serves as the bedrock upon which the stability of our applications is built. It empowers developers to catch bugs early, validate the expected behavior of individual components, and ultimately deliver a seamless user experience. Remember, every well-tested widget is a proof of the robustness of your application.
- **Shift-left Mentality:** Embracing a "**shift-left**" mentality, where testing is integrated into the development process from the outset, not only accelerates the feedback loop but also cultivates a culture of quality assurance.
- **Continuous Improvement:** Widget testing is not a one-time endeavor; it's an ongoing commitment to excellence. Regularly revisiting and refining your tests ensures that they remain aligned with the evolving requirements of your application. Be vigilant in identifying opportunities for improvement, and don't shy away from optimizing your testing strategy.
- **Balance Speed and Quality:** While the pace of development is fundamental, it should not come at the expense of quality. Widget testing strikes a balance between rapid iteration and the delivery of reliable software. Through meticulous testing, we find a convergence of speed and quality, crafting applications that stand the test of time.

Assessment

Objective:

Build a Flutter app that displays phone contacts using the Test-Driven Development (TDD) approach. The app should include a list of contacts and a details screen for each contact, allowing users to navigate between them. Additionally, integrate any Google font of your choice.

Steps:

1. **Project Setup:**
   - Create a new Flutter project using your preferred development environment (Visual Studio Code, IntelliJ, Android Studio, and more).
2. **TDD Setup:**
   - Choose a testing framework for Flutter, such as `flutter_test`.
   - Set up your project for TDD by creating test folders and files alongside your source code.
3. **Define Contact Model:**
   - Create a contact model with properties like name, phone number, and any other relevant information.
4. **Implement UI Widgets:**
   - Develop widgets for displaying a list of contacts and a details screen.
   - Use the Google font of your choice for styling.
5. **TDD for UI:**
   - Write tests for the UI components before implementing them.
   - Run the tests to ensure they fail initially.
6. **UI Implementation:**
   - Develop the UI components based on the tests.
   - Ensure the list of contacts and details screen are interactive and visually appealing.
7. **Navigation:**
   - Implement navigation between the list of contacts and the details screen.
8. **Integration of Google Font:**
   - Choose a Google font and integrate it into your app's styling.
9. **Final Testing:**
   - Run all your tests to ensure that both UI and navigation work as expected.

10. **Refactoring:**
    - Refactor your code as needed to improve readability and maintainability.

Once completed, your Flutter app should display a list of phone contacts with a details screen, all implemented using the TDD approach. The integrated Google font should enhance the overall aesthetic.

Key Terms

- **Unit Testing:** The practice of testing individual units or components of a software application to ensure they function as intended.
- **UI Components:** User Interface elements or widgets that users interact with, such as buttons, text fields, and images.
- **TDD (Test-Driven Development):** A software development approach where tests are written before the actual code. It emphasizes a repetitive cycle of writing a test, writing code to pass the test, and then refactoring.
- **Widget Testing:** A form of UI testing in Flutter specifically targeting UI components or widgets to ensure they render and behave correctly.
- **`WidgetTester`:** A utility provided by the Flutter testing framework to interact with and test widgets during the testing process.
- **Test Expectations:** The conditions or outcomes that a test expects to be true. If these conditions are not met, the test fails.
- **Automation:** The use of tools and scripts to automatically execute tests, reducing the need for manual intervention and improving efficiency.
- **CI/CD (Continuous Integration/Continuous Deployment):** A software development practice that involves automatically testing and deploying code changes as they are made, ensuring a consistent and streamlined development process.

CHAPTER 11

Conclusion and the Next Steps

We began our Flutter journey starting with the foundational concepts and gradually delving into more interesting and practical topics. The initial chapters laid the groundwork, introducing Flutter's robust environment and Dart programming language. We not only set up the development environment but also gained insights into Flutter's project structure, widgets, and the process of building a basic app.

Moving forward, our focus shifted to the core of Dart programming, where we explored syntax, variables, control flow, functions, and the effective use of packages and libraries. As we moved on, we transitioned into Flutter widgets and UI elements. Basic layout widgets, text, image, and user input handling, laying the foundation for subsequent chapters.

As we advanced, styling, theming, and interactive UI designs took center stage. We explored Flutter's styling options, learned to customize widget appearances, and mastered the art of creating visually appealing UI designs. Chapters dedicated to images, media, and effects further enriched our understanding, covering everything from loading images to implementing custom painting and shaders.

Chapter 6, Typography, Slivers, and Advanced UI Techniques in Flutter, elevated our UI expertise, covering advanced typography, scrollable UIs with slivers, and intricate layout techniques. With a focus on optimization and performance, we honed our skills in creating high-quality Flutter applications.

The journey into adaptive UIs showcased the importance of designing for various platforms. Responsive layouts for diverse screen sizes, platform-specific UIs, and architectural patterns like BLoC and Provider were all part of the extensive toolkit we acquired.

Our exploration continued with navigation and routing, where we implemented seamless transitions between screens, leveraged named routes, and handled complex navigation scenarios. *Chapter 9, Utilizing Device Features and APIs*, took us into device features and APIs, providing insights into accessing hardware, utilizing sensors, and integrating with platform-specific plugins.

The final chapter, a focal point of this recap, delves into unit testing UI components. We not only learned the fundamentals of unit testing but also embraced a test-driven development (TDD) approach. Best practices for testing Flutter UI components were outlined, emphasizing the importance of robust testing in the development lifecycle.

Structure

This final chapter will discuss on:

- Guidance on Further Learning Resources for Flutter
- Final Thoughts

Guidance on Further Learning Resources for Flutter

As you conclude this book and embark on the next steps of your Flutter journey, it's essential to continue expanding your knowledge and honing your skills. Flutter is a fast-paced framework, and staying updated with the latest developments and best practices is crucial for your growth as a Flutter developer. Here's a guide to further learning resources:

- **Official Flutter Documentation:**

  The Flutter team maintains comprehensive and up-to-date documentation. It covers everything from basic concepts to advanced topics. Regularly check for updates and explore new features introduced by Flutter.

- **Flutter Community:**

  Engage with the vibrant Flutter community. Platforms like the Flutter Dev Google Group (https://groups.google.com/g/flutter-dev) and Stack Overflow (https://stackoverflow.com/questions/tagged/flutter) are excellent for asking questions, sharing knowledge, and staying informed about common challenges and solutions.

- **Flutter YouTube Channel:**

  The official Flutter YouTube channel (https://www.youtube.com/flutterdev) hosts a variety of videos, including tutorials, talks, and updates. Watching videos can provide a different perspective and visual understanding of Flutter concepts.

- **Online Courses:**

  Consider enrolling in more structured online courses. Platforms like Udacity, Coursera, and others offer courses on Flutter, often taught by industry professionals. These courses can provide in-depth insights and hands-on projects.

  If you want to learn about Dart in depth, feel free to check out the two courses on Dart on LinkedIn Learning:

  - Dart Clean Code: Writing High-Efficiency, Maintainable Dart Programs
  - Introduction to Dart

- **Open-Source Projects:**

  Always endeavor to contribute to open-source Flutter projects on platforms like GitHub. This allows you to work on real-world projects, collaborate with other developers, and gain practical experience.

- **Books and Blogs:**

  Consider additional books and blogs on Flutter. Reading different perspectives and experiences can deepen your understanding of Flutter development and provide valuable insights.

- **Flutter Conferences and Events:**

  Attend Flutter conferences and events. These gatherings provide opportunities to connect with other developers, hear about the latest trends, and attend workshops or hands-on sessions

Final Thoughts

As we reach the conclusion of this Flutter journey together, let us take a moment to reflect on the incredible progress you've made. You've explored the core basics of Flutter, from setting up your development environment to crafting beautiful, responsive user interfaces. Your commitment to learning and exploring Flutter has been commendable.

Now, as you stand at the threshold of the next steps in your Flutter adventure, we want to offer a few words of encouragement. As you may already know Flutter is fast-paced and ever-evolving, and your journey doesn't end here – it's a stepping stone to more challenges.

Embrace Challenges as Opportunities:

Challenges are not roadblocks; they are opportunities for growth. As you encounter complex problems or explore advanced Flutter features, remember that overcoming challenges is an integral part of the learning process.

Build, Break, Learn, Repeat:

The most profound learning often happens when you're hands-deep in code. Build projects, break things, and learn from every experience. Each bug fixed and every improvement made contributes to your expertise. It's okay to make mistakes; they're stepping stones to mastery.

Connect with the Flutter Community:

The Flutter community is a huge, welcoming space filled with enthusiastic developers, just like you. Engage in conversations, seek advice, and share your knowledge. The collaborative spirit of the community can provide insights, solutions, and a sense of belonging.

Stay Curious and Keep Exploring:

Technology evolves, and so does Flutter. Stay curious about the latest updates, features, and best practices. The desire to explore and learn is a powerful driver of success in software development.

Celebrate Your Achievements:

Take a moment to celebrate your achievements, no matter how small. Whether you've successfully implemented a complex feature or fixed a seemingly elusive bug, acknowledge your progress. Each step forward is proof of your dedication and commitment.

Contribute and Give Back:

Consider contributing to the Flutter ecosystem. Open-source projects, community initiatives, or sharing your knowledge through tutorials – all contribute to the growth of Flutter. Giving back to the community is not just altruistic; it's a pathway to continuous improvement.

Set Ambitious Goals:

Your Flutter journey doesn't have to plateau. Set ambitious goals for yourself. Whether it's mastering advanced Flutter topics, building novel and intuitive apps, or even mentoring others, challenge yourself to reach new heights.

Take Action Today:

The knowledge gained from this journey is a powerful tool, but its true potential is unlocked when you put it into action. Start a new project, implement that feature you've been contemplating, or contribute to an open-source project. Your actions today shape the world-class developer you become tomorrow.

Finally, this is not the end; it's a commencement. The skills you've acquired and the experiences you've gathered are the foundation for an exciting future in Flutter. Seize the opportunities, stay resilient in the face of challenges, and let your passion for Flutter propel you forward.

Thank you for joining in on this Flutter adventure. May your code be clean, your UIs be beautiful, and your Flutter journey be endlessly fulfilling.

Index

Symbols

A

D

G

H

I

K

L

M

N

T